Raymon

M000234944

McFarland Classics

Raymond Burr

A Film, Radio and Television Biography

by Ona L. Hill

McFarland & Company, Inc., Publishers
Jefferson, North Carolina, and London

To my sister, Edna M. Hill, for her encouragement and belief
in my writing career and for her help in proofreading the manuscript

I also dedicate this book to Al (Skip) Koenig,
who gave me sound advice and encouragement

The present work is a reprint of the library bound edition of
Raymond Burr: A Film, Radio and Television Biography,
first published in 1994. McFarland Classics is an imprint of
McFarland & Company, Inc., Publishers, Jefferson, North
Carolina, who also published the original edition.

Frontispiece: Publicity still of Raymond Burr, age 32

Library of Congress Cataloguing-in-Publication Data

Hill, Ona, 1921–
    Raymond Burr : a film, radio and television biography / by Ona L.
Hill.
    p. cm.
    Includes bibliographical references and index.
    ISBN 0-7864-0833-2 (paperback : 50# alkaline paper) ∞
    1. Burr, Raymond, 1917–1993. 2. Television actors and actresses—
United States—Biography. I. Title.
PN2287.B88H56 1999   791.45'028'092—dc20   [B]   93-39505 CIP

British Library Cataloguing-in-Publication data are available

Manufactured in the United States of America

McFarland & Company, Inc., Publishers
  Box 611, Jefferson, North Carolina 28640
  www.mcfarlandpub.com

Contents

Acknowledgments

There are a great many people I wish to thank for all their help and encouragement during the many years I have worked on this manuscript.

My first special thanks go to Alice J. Murray, the law librarian at the McGeorge School of Law, now retired. Alice allowed me to handle and look at Raymond Burr's copy of the "Perry Mason" scripts, among many other items. I offer a special thanks to Harold M. Kambak, associate dean of professional programs at the McGeorge School of Law, for his kindness and cheerful, encouraging letters through the years. Hal took care of the Minerva Smith Burr Memorial Fund.

Thanks go to Norman Wheeler, of Sydney, Australia, friend and researcher. His help has been immeasurable. Thank you, Bob Robison of Accolades, for sending me valuable information from *Variety* and other sources about Burr's early movies and radio shows.

I am grateful to Paul Myers, former curator of the Theatre Collection at Lincoln Center, New York City, and his reliable staff, who were a great help in ferreting out hard to find material. Thanks also go to others at the Theatre Collection at Lincoln Center. Dorothy Swerdlove and her staff, particularly the photographic department; David Bartholomew, periodicals librarian, and Roderick Bladel, librarian, all were especially helpful.

Many thanks to David Javorsky of Chehalis, Washington, now a librarian in Salt Lake City, Utah. I am indebted to him for giving me the complete list of the "Perry Mason" episodes arranged both alphabetically and by the date each episode was shown on television.

Milton T. Moore, of Dallas, Texas, drove over a hundred miles to a place that had a large batch of "Perry Mason" photos, which he sent me right away and then waited almost a year for me to complete the payments. I am very grateful to Mr. Moore.

I wish to thank the John Oxley Library in Brisbane, Australia. They sent me a great many clippings and photos about Burr's visits to Australia.

Many grateful thanks to Joan (Joss) Halverson, reference librarian at

New Westminster Public Library, British Columbia, Canada. She and her helpful staff were able to supply me with the early history of the Burr family and many clippings of Raymond Burr.

The *Columbian,* in Vancouver, British Columbia, provided many clippings. My appreciation goes to Archie W. Miller, curator of the New Westminster Historic Centre and Museum, for copies of old *New Westminster* and for articles from the 1870s and later. I am grateful to the University of British Columbia, Department of History, for supplying the master's thesis of Margaret Lillooet McDonald (1947), giving the history of the Burr family.

Many thanks go to David B. Mason, chief archivist and director of library programs, Provincial Archives of British Columbia, for the copy of *British Columbia, Earliest Times to the Present,* volumes 3 and 4, for the biographical history of the Burr family.

To Joyce Piney, former librarian of the Pasadena, California, Public Library, and her staff and to Elaine Zorbas, head of the research section, go my thanks for sending me copies of playbills and rare photos of Raymond Burr's acting days at the Pasadena Playhouse.

Many thanks to Marlene Wagner, another Burr fan, for valuable advice and encouragement and for letting me know when Raymond would be on shows *not* listed in *TV Guide.*

Many thanks to Ken Greenwald, member of the Pacific Pioneer Broadcasters Archives. He gave me valuable information on the "Fort Laramie" radio series and gave me tapes of old radio programs from Burr's early radio career.

Thanks to Jim Davidson, president of the National Association for the Advancement of Perry Mason, for his very interesting and informative articles about the Perry Mason era.

Thank you to all the service personnel from Korea and Vietnam who wrote me the letters and sent photographs about their meetings with Burr.

A big thank you to Aviva Radbord of KDKA, Pittsburgh, for her valuable information on both Burr and Barbara Hale.

Thank you to Valerie Sutherland of South Wales for her cheery calls and the tape of her interview with Raymond Burr in Paris while he was filming a "Perry Mason" episode.

To Susan Naulty, librarian of the Rare Book Division at the Huntington Library in San Marino, California, who sent me valuable photos of Burr's Pasadena Playhouse days as well as copies of the playbills, I express my gratitude.

Last but not least, I want to thank Al (Skip) Koenig for all his help, encouragement, cheerful and sometimes funny letters, advice, and most of all his help in finding the right publisher for my manuscript.

There are so many other people I wish to thank for helping and encouraging me to keep writing and researching. I appreciate their help.

I

Growing Up in California

Raymond William Stacy Burr came from a hardworking, long-lived Canadian family. He inherited their talent, thirst for knowledge, and mania for working long hours along with their sense of humor and bad Irish temper. Another trait he inherited was both a curse and a blessing: Weight problems plagued him almost all his life.

This excess girth, along with steel-blue eyes, dark brown hair, a massive chest, and a powerfully built body, was inherited from an ancestor of the 1800s. A photo from the Canadian Archives shows they are almost identical in facial features as well as body type. He wore a Van Dyke beard and looked distinguished as a tycoon of the 1800s. Raymond appeared in a television saga as an 1860s silversmith, dressed in a costume resembling the man in the photo.

Three brothers came to Canada from County Carlow, Ireland, by way of London and Dublin. One brother, Hugh Burr, emigrated to Canada in the early 1800s, settling on the island of Victoria, British Columbia. Later he moved to New Westminster on the mainland, about 35 miles from Vancouver. He taught school for a few years and invested in rich, untapped farm land.

Hugh bought property in Burrard Inlet, developed the first dairy and fruit farm and made a prosperous living selling butter, milk, fruit and vegetables to ships docked in the Fraser River. Raymond inherited Hugh's love of farming and his teaching talents. Raymond also invested in a great deal of real estate later on in life and eventually bought an island. Raymond is a sixth generation of the Burrs of New Westminster.

Raymond's grandfather, Joseph Burr, became a saddlemaker. Later he moved to the town of Yale, British Columbia, and joined the provincial police. He was made a government agent when he moved to Ashcroft. Joseph had a cousin, also named Joseph, who worked in the New Westminster jail. Raymond's great-uncle Benjamin Burr worked in the federal penitentiary. Most of his early relatives had connections with law and order throughout western Canada.

Four generations of the Burr and Smith families. *Top row (from left):* Minerva Hamlin, cousin of Raymond's maternal grandmother; Anna M. Smith, Raymond's maternal grandmother; Minerva Smith Burr, Raymond's mother; *seated (from left):* Nancy Robinson, Raymond's maternal great-grandmother; Anna Smith, Raymond's paternal great-grandmother; young Raymond; and Mary Jane Johnston Burr, Raymond's paternal grandmother. Photo was taken in New Westminster, British Columbia, Canada, on May 21, 1919, Raymond's second birthday.

Joseph W. Burr, Raymond's grandfather, died in 1927, soon after his fiftieth wedding anniversary. He left a wife, Mary Jane Johnston Burr, four daughters, and two sons. She lived to be 102, and her son William Johnston Burr was Raymond's father. William's younger brother, James B. Burr, became the keeper of the first insane asylum in the area, and his son, called Joseph, Jr., became a guard of the New Westminster jail, while his brother Benjamin worked as a guard in the federal penitentiary, situated about a mile or so east of the jail along the Fraser River. Raymond used the techniques he learned from stories about these relatives when he became a lawman on several television shows after he became famous as an actor.

Raymond's father was born in New Westminster, Canada, in 1889. He left school at age 12 to work as a delivery boy for the W. S. Collister Dry Goods Company. When he was 14, William went to work as a clerk in the hardware business for Anderson and Lusby, Wholesalers, and became a

The Burr House before 1897. Photograph no. 759, New Westminster Public Library. Date: C. 1970. Source: Archie Miller, Irving House. Photographer: Archie Miller. This is *not* the house Raymond Burr lived in. This is the house of his grandmother Burr. His parents also lived here at one point. However, Raymond was born in a house on Queens Avenue, which has since been torn down and replaced by an apartment house. The Burr house in this photograph was at Royal Avenue and 7th Street and was built prior to 1897. This was torn down in 1975.

traveling salesman for hardware material at the age of 17. At 22 he became a clerk for the T. J. Trapp Company, then a salesman for the M. Dumond Company. During the 1930s William went to work as a hardware salesman for the McLennan, McFeely and Prior Company, remaining there until he retired at the age of 71.

Raymond's mother, Minerva Smith, was born of Scottish and English ancestry in Chicago in 1893 and was a domineering, strong-willed woman. She was also a very loving, understanding, and wise individual. Minerva lived in Michigan until the age of five, when the family moved to Canada. Her early musical training was obtained in various parts of Canada. Her parents, Anna and William Smith, retained their U.S. citizenship while they lived in Canada, returning to the United States when World War I broke out. Bill Smith enlisted in the Navy and was stationed at Mare Island Naval Shipyards in California. Discharged after the war, he stayed on at the same facility as a civilian employee. Upon his retirement he invested in the purchase of the Empress Hotel in Vallejo, California.

Minerva was 21 years old, still living in Canada, when she met and married William Johnston Burr, age 25, in 1914. They settled in New Westminster, where on May 21, 1917, Raymond William Stacy Burr was born. Minerva told Raymond years later that he had weighed 12 pounds at birth. Daughter Geraldine Mary was born in 1920, followed by James Edmond on July 13, 1921.

For many years, the ancestral home at 624 Royal Avenue, which William inherited, was presumed to be the house Raymond was born in. His parents lived at 718 Queens Avenue, however, and all three children were born in this house.

Raymond expressed fond memories of his grandmother Burr's house at 624 Royal Avenue. He recalled in great detail also the summer home of his grandparents at Botany Bay, where he spent hours collecting barnacles, stones, and shells washed up on the beach. He pursued shell collecting as an adult and had a valuable collection from all over the world. "My grandmother taught me how to swim when I was little," recalled Raymond in an interview. "She also flew a Ford Trimotor airplane!" He also remembered watching wasps being smoked out of the summer home chimney when the family moved in, and winter sleigh rides on the steep hills near his home in New Westminster.

Raymond remembered horses and sleigh rides from New Westminster to visit relatives in Ladner, British Columbia. He had a vague recollection of the small church he attended, which stood at the end of the block, and the kindergarten he was sent to when he was four years old. Raymond fell down quite often and was scolded for tearing his clothes because outfits for a chubby boy were hard to come by.

"My grandparents pulled out the rose garden in order to plant potatoes and all kinds of vegetables. Everyone grew their own food. This was one of the reasons I grew up as a chubby boy, overweight for my age. I also think my grandparents' home was the first to have electricity, since the wires were placed on the *outside* of the house. That's how it was done in the old days." There are memories of his father's hardware store with its smells of oil, kerosene, rubber, and barrel after barrel filled with nuts, bolts, screws, and nails of various sizes.

In 1922 Minerva made a decision that would change all of their lives. She took the three small children down to Vallejo, California, to visit her parents. Raymond was five years old when Minerva separated from her husband. One of her excuses was she wanted her parents to see and get to know their grandchildren.

Raymond probably knew that the happy home life was not all that happy; it was an emotional scene in which Minerva left the house with the children and a few suitcases. Raymond clung to his father, tears rolling down his face. He could not understand why his father was not coming with them, and he sensed he might not see him again.

The journey was a long and tiring one by boat, train, ferry, and street-car to the Empress Hotel in Vallejo, California. Despite the separation, Minerva kept in touch with William and pleaded with him in her letters to join them in California.

William did follow a short time later, when he could obtain an extended leave of absence. He got a job, rented a house, and they were a family once more. William stayed about eight months and was unhappy with the situation. Finally, he told Minerva he wanted to return to his beloved Canada and begged her to come back with him. Minerva refused. She believed California offered a better future for all three children.

Once again, Raymond clung tearfully to his father as he prepared to leave. He knew this time his father would not return. As his father went out the door, Raymond felt as if someone he loved had just died.

Both parents were torn apart by their love for each other and by their strong love of their respective countries. Love for their countries won out; William returned to Canada, and eventually they divorced.

Minerva and the children settled down in the Empress Hotel, operated by her parents. The children were sent to Sunday school at the nearest Presbyterian church, though all three had been baptized in the Episcopalian church of New Westminster. They were taken to every church in the area of Vallejo, however, since Minerva played the organ for any church or organization that would hire her. As a result, the children learned respect for all religions. Minerva gave recitals and played piano to accompany silent movies in order to make a living and to save enough money to go back to college. Raymond recalled, "Mother took good care of us and did a fine job of raising all three of us during the Depression."

To keep Raymond and Edmond out of mischief, Grandpa Smith taught them skills ranging from repairing electric wiring to painting rooms; from replacing locks to reglazing windows; and from mixing cement to working with bricks and mortar. "I'm grateful for all the training," said Raymond. "He trained me so well I have put the knowledge to work many times in my daily life. He was an excellent disciplinarian too, and I idolized him."

Raymond was seven years old when his grandparents Anna and William H. Smith decided to take him with them on a trip to Scotland, touring many ancestral locations in and around Glasgow, Edinburgh, and West Scotland. Later in the year Bill took a diplomatic assignment in the Middle East. He brought Raymond with him, staying at the old Winter Palace Hotel on the east bank of the Nile River in Egypt.

They returned to America in time for Raymond to enter first grade. He wound up atetnding six different schools in the San Francisco Bay area by the time he reached junior high school. In junior high Raymond joined the drama classes and enjoyed acting in all sorts of plays and operettas, including an early version of *Naughty Marietta*, which acquainted him with the music of Victor Herbert.

Minerva was the pipe organist for a church when the minister retired. The new minister's wife had majored in the theater and directed many shows that featured Raymond in a number of roles. He knew then he wanted to be an actor when he grew up.

Grandma Smith realized this fact more quickly than Raymond did as she watched him study the guests of the hotel and listened to the vivid imaginary stories he made up about each guest. If she was busy elsewhere, he would corral anyone who would take the time to listen to his fanciful tales. Raymond would pretend he was on a stage and would play to a captive audience of his mother, grandparents, sister, and brother. Years later Raymond could still recall Grandma Smith saying to him when funds were low, "The only true joy comes from giving, even if the gift is only a hug or a kiss. This is the best happiness of all."

At age 11, Raymond was sent to San Rafael Military Academy and had problems right from the start. The uniforms did not fit his chubby body, and he was deeply hurt when he was denied the right to ride a horse in dress parade. He escaped over the walls every chance he got. To compensate, Raymond excelled at swimming, football, or any other sport he could squeeze into his schedule. However, he hated the regimentation and begged his mother to take him out of this school.

During the summer when Raymond was 12, Minerva decided to take the children up to Canada to visit their father. Raymond spotted an advertisement in the local Vancouver newspaper for a boy actor to replace a young man who had been taken ill. Raymond asked Minerva to please let him try out for the part. Since it would only be for the summer months, she consented. Raymond got the part and toured all over Canada, having the best time of his young life. There was no doubt in his mind now that he wanted to be an actor.

"The summer was over too quickly," said Raymond as he returned to school in the States—but not to the military academy this time. Minerva had decided to go back to college to obtain a master's degree in music and fulfill her dream of becoming a music teacher.

They bid a tearful good-bye to Minerva's parents and the Empress Hotel. Minerva found rooms near the college in Berkeley, California, and thus Mama and the three children began a new life. Minerva worked all day and went to college at night, relying on Raymond to care for his sister and younger brother. While trying to keep a tight rein on them, Raymond cooked, cleaned house, and still attended Willard Junior High School. Sometimes his bossiness caused loud arguments and fistfights.

Raymond excelled on the volleyball team. He also learned to play the cello, but hated it. He despised lugging the awkward instrument to and from school and finally rebelled and refused any more cello lessons. Brother James Edmond Burr became the musician of the family, inheriting Minerva's talent, while Raymond fulfilled his ambition in the area of drama.

The summer he was 13, Minerva sent Raymond to a ranch in Roswell, New Mexico. Although he had grown very tall, he was a typical awkward teenager, all arms and legs.

Raymond loved being outdoors, working hard alongside a ranch hand who patiently taught him about ranch life. Raymond received 25 cents a day plus room and board. When summer was over Minerva, Geraldine, and Edmond hardly recognized him—Raymond came home 80 pounds lighter. Their chubby boy had sunburned to a dark brown and was now a rugged outdoorsman who had almost reached six feet tall. Raymond told them how he had learned to mend fences, milk cows, shear sheep, help with the birth of lambs and calves, and ride for miles in the hot sun, checking to make sure no animals were trapped in the range watering holes.

One day, while on a camping trip in the mountains, Raymond began to experience severe pains in his right side. When he got to a hospital, he was found to have acute appendicitis. Raymond survived this peril only to run into another one. In 1932, when he was 15, Raymond was about to go fishing near Vallejo, California. He opened a compartment door on the boat to step down into the cabin and was bitten on the right foot by a rattlesnake. How the snake got into the compartment is a mystery, but from that day forward Raymond walked with his right foot turned slightly inward.

Since Raymond had had a singing part in *Naughty Marietta* at Willard Junior High School, one of his teachers sent him to sing on Benny Walker's KGO radio show at the Hale Brothers' store in San Francisco. After this first broadcast, he was hired as a host of a nightly "Slumber Hour" on KGW (now radio station KCBS). Raymond's duties included opening the station early in the morning, sweeping floors, and performing every menial chore around the place. He liked what he was doing, though, and the pay was good for that depression year.

Raymond tried to convince Minerva to let him quit school and go to work. Mother wanted Raymond to finish high school but realized her son was an overgrown, restless teenager. Finally giving in to his pleas, Minerva reluctantly signed Raymond's working papers. Minerva told Raymond, "The money will help with the bills."

Raymond followed in his father's footsteps as a salesman and sold tinted photographs door to door. His next job was as a stock clerk for a J. C. Penney department store in San Jose, California. He joined a WPA (Works Progress Administration) project, a program engineered by President Franklin D. Roosevelt to put men and boys to work during the Depression. Raymond dug ditches, worked with road crews, and drove a 50 ton diesel bulldozer cutting roadbeds for bridges and dams. He used all the manual labor knowledge his American grandfather had taught him. After this project was finished, Raymond joined the CCC (Civilian Conservation Corps).

"All of us learned the meaning of hard work, the joy of a job well done, while being paid for it. I was paid 30 dollars per month and 20 dollars went to my family." The old CCC Camp was located at Seiad, California, about an hour's drive from the Oregon border. Some high school girls from the nearby Yreka, California, High School, went down the Klamath River to Happy Camp, where a dance was held on Saturday night for the young men.

A girl named Rowena remembered that a tall, shy youth approached her and bowed courteously, asking her to dance. Later on she thought it was very odd her new CCC friend could only dance backward. Years later she realized her dance partner was Raymond Burr.

Another place Raymond was sent to while still in the CCC was the Mount Shasta–Mount Lassen area on the Klamath River in Northern California. Here he learned to fight fires, as well as to build roads, dams, and bridges. Among other tasks, Raymond planted trees and learned about conservation of the forest. He said in an interview,

> I learned the need to conserve water and keep it pure. I learned a lot about carpentry and construction skills. One winter I was involved in a snow survey, taking samples in order to try to predict whether there would be floods the next year or enough water for the watersheds.
>
> I learned first aid, how to run a weather station, to teach and be a leader. Mostly I learned about this great country of ours. The boys and men were from all walks of life but were united as one group. Our bodies became hardened, healthy, minds free and our self-respect returned.

After leaving the CCC, Raymond took his savings and moved to Pasadena, California, to enroll in the Pasadena Playhouse acting school. Unfortunately he did not have enough for the first year's tuition.

Raymond was 17 in 1934 and out of work. Minerva decided now was a good time to send him up to Canada to visit his father. Even in Canada Raymond was a restless boy, eager for new adventures. He did not stay long with his father before he joined the Berkeley Players in Toronto and toured all over Canada, learning everything about acting and behind the scenes jobs pertaining to show business.

Raymond joined another group that traveled to India and Australia and ended up touring England, performing Shakespeare. Raymond was the youngest Macbeth at the time to act at the famous Stratford-upon-Avon Shakespeare Theatre.

Raymond came back to the States after the tours were over and entered Long Beach, California, Junior College for one semester only. Grandfather Smith needed someone to go to Chungking, China, to liquidate family property and decided Raymond should go, since he was still out of work. In the six months he spent there, Raymond took several courses at the University of Chungking and learned a number of Chinese dialects.

When the job was finished to his grandfather's satisfaction, Raymond came home to enter San Jose Junior College but not as a student—he became a teacher for one semester. At night he worked at radio station KQW as a radio actor and sang with Eva Gruninger Atkinson and did radio shows with Benny Walker. In between, Raymond traveled to the Pasadena Playhouse to pursue his acting career.

Burr formed theatrical groups to put on plays at the YMCA, where he lived at the time. Raymond wrote the scripts and put on a play a week. "Oh, those old scripts I wrote!" Raymond exclaimed to a reporter. "They shouldn't have happened, but when you are a young daring eighteen year old and asked to play Macbeth, you say yes right away, reporting to the theater the following morning! Then when you get older and wiser, you say, 'Yes, but I want to work on it for six or more months!'"

The urge to travel surfaced once more in Toronto. Raymond met Anatole Litvak, a famous film director, at a picnic a mutual friend had invited them to. In the course of their conversation, Litvak said he could help Raymond connect with a repertory group of players.

Raymond joined the repertory company and performed in a series of plays all over England. After four performances in Brighton, the manager absconded with the receipts, leaving the troupe stranded.

Looking for new adventures, Raymond decided in 1938 to tackle Los Angeles and Hollywood. His many attempts to enter film studios for acting jobs in any capacity failed to get him even an interview.

Raymond's lifestyle of not eating properly or getting enough sleep began to take its toll on his health, and he became extremely ill. The doctor's prescription was to get away from Hollywood to a place with clean air, to eat properly, and to get enough sleep. He ordered Raymond to stay outdoors as much as possible.

Pondering about his health problems, Raymond took the bus to downtown Los Angeles, where his mother now had a music store. Minerva had opened a music store during the Depression, but nobody bought pianos or sheet music then. She had lost everything in the stock market crash of 1929 and had to start over. Now she owned and operated several music stores in the area.

Raymond found a solution to his problems before he reached Minerva's store. On the bus he saw advertisements for the Forestry Service. The work sounded interesting and challenging, and most of it would be outdoors. Upon further investigation, Raymond signed up.

The north woods deep in the heart of Oregon were the assignment given to Raymond in 1938. Everything the doctor ordered was here: clean air, outdoor work, peace and quiet.

Raymond's duty was to look out for forest fires. Soon afterward he became a fire warden, snow surveyor, and weatherman. Along with these chores he ran a general store, planted trees, and learned more about flowers, birds, the animals of the forest, ecology, and conservation than any book could ever teach him. All of this knowledge was put to good use later on in his life.

Free time was not wasted either when, via correspondence courses, Raymond kept up his college assignments and wrote articles for national magazines. Much to his amazement, some of his articles were bought.

Almost two years of outdoor living had given Raymond a healthy outlook on life. The day came to make another decision about what to do next. He was 22 years old in 1939 and wanted to continue his acting career.

Two plays established Raymond Burr's career as a professional stage actor. His role as Danny in Emlyn Williams's *Night Must Fall* was his biggest during his tour of Australia and England. The second play was titled *Mandarin*. No playbills of these two plays can be found in Australia or England, since the Williamson Theatre Organization had many groups touring these countries with the same two plays. No reviews of the Burr version have been found.

War was imminent in Europe when Raymond decided to form his own Shakespearean group touring Great Britain. He played Macbeth, Hamlet, Richard III and many other Shakespearean roles that challenged him. Someone from the overseas branch of Paramount Pictures saw Raymond in one of these plays and signed him for a film, but the film was never made. This failure to break into movies did not matter at the moment because Raymond had fallen in love.

Raymond had become smitten with a young ballerina from the Ballet de Monte Carlo and followed her all over Europe, wherever she performed —Hungary, Germany, France—and learned to speak the languages of the various countries along the way. He broke up his Shakespearean troupe because of the infatuation. To earn a living at one point, he got a job singing in a small smoke-filled French nightclub called Le Ruban Bleu. He performed songs six nights a week in the languages he had learned and saved enough for his passage home. Gradually the infatuation faded as the two of them became more and more separated by their careers. They parted by mutual consent.

Before Raymond left France, he met many famous people. One person stood out above the rest. "Bricktop" ran a famous nightclub and was well known all over France. Her real name was Ada Beatrice Queen Victoria Louise Virginia Smith Duconge but everyone called her by her nickname. She became a legendary entertainer and saloon keeper who owned clubs in Paris, Rome, and Mexico City. Raymond often frequented her club in Paris to listen to jazz, and he met many jazz singers of the era.

Raymond decided it was time to come home when Germany began to invade one country after another. As soon as France was invaded, the clubs, along with Raymond's livelihood, disappeared.

Upon his return to the United States, Raymond entered Stanford University and later transferred to the University of California, where he played baseball and swam for the Olympic Club. He finally received a degree in psychology and English literature after six years of campus and correspondence courses.

The *Hollywood Reporter* for February 1940 ran a small item about Burr as a young San Franciscan anxious to break into movies. At the time he was doing little theater work in and around the San Francisco area and was nightclubbing with actress Ona Munson, a family friend.

In Jack Mathis's book titled *Republic Confidential, The Players*, he lists three films for Raymond Burr: *Unmasked, A Man Alone,* and *The Earl of Puddlestone*. This last film was made from June 14 to June 27, 1940, and released August 31, 1940. Raymond Burr played the part of Mrs. Millicent Potter's chauffeur. He was paid $66 on a weekly basis, but as far as can be determined from the script, he was in only one or two scenes: he rings the doorbell, and when the door opens says, "Mrs. Potter's car for the Honorable Elizabeth Higgins." A few scenes later he is seen standing by the car.

If he had only these two scenes, he would likely have been paid only a day player's contract. He might have been in other scenes that ended upon the cutting room floor. He was not billed in the cast list.

The movies did not want him, it seemed. Instead of going back to Europe or Australia, Raymond decided to conquer New York and the Broadway theaters.

II

New York and
Crazy with the Heat

Before Pearl Harbor, the cheapest place to live in New York City was lower Manhattan, around Greenwich Village. Raymond found a furnished room for a reasonable price per week and started making the rounds of the casting offices. After the usual "Don't call us, we'll call you" routine, he found a steady job at Abercrombie and Fitch, an exclusive department store, selling neckties, sportswear, and men's apparel. He also worked for a motion picture company as a proofreader of mysteries and westerns. Twice a week he traveled to the Burnham School for Girls, part of Smith College in Northampton, Massachusetts, where he taught radio acting.

A musical titled *It Goes to Show* was put on at the Barbizon Plaza Hotel. Raymond appeared in this one and performed other small parts in plays, but none lasted very long.

He also found time to be a substitute teacher of drama, for one semester, at Columbia University in 1940, but no record of his teaching activities can be found.

The *Hollywood Reporter* for June 24, 1940, listed Raymond Burr signing for a film titled *Should Wives Work?* He never made it, for a very good reason. Raymond had started rehearsals in Manhattan for a musical comedy to be called *Crazy with the Heat*. The star was the great comedian Willie Howard. Some of the sketches were written by his brother, Eugene Howard. Kurt Kasznar was the director and newspaperman Ed Sullivan was a backer of the show, investing $20,000.

The show opened in Boston on December 26, 1940, and was a flop. A lot of rewriting, revising, and eliminating had to be done before opening day on Broadway, January 1, 1941. A young Milton Berle helped rewrite some of the sketches, and Kurt Kasznar added his talents by writing some new lyrics for one of the songs composed for the show.

Raymond appeared in four sketches, singing and dancing in at least one of them. He portrayed an Active Lion, L'Acrobat, the Groom's Friend, and one of the Ushers and appeared singing and dancing in the finale with the entire company. The show managed to survive four months and was shortened in April to a vaudeville revue. The revue lasted about an hour after the movie playing at the State Theater on Broadway. Before it got to this stage, however, Raymond and most of the cast had already left. Ed Sullivan lost his $20,000 investment in the play and $4,000 more.

One interesting sidelight of this play was the future fortunes of the young cast members. Thomas Mitchell, who later became a beloved dramatic character actor, was in some of the sketches with Raymond. Richard Kollmar, future husband of newspaperwoman Dorothy Kilgallen, sang with Gracie Barrie. He later gained fame as part of the team of "Dorothy and Dick," a radio talk show. Al Kelly, the famous double-talking comedian, had some funny sketches with Willie Howard. Then there was 17-year-old Betty Kean, doing a single act as a tap dancer, without sister Jane. Kean's tap dancing routine brought wild applause and shouts of encore. Max Liebman put the knowledge he had gained acting in this show to good use later in producing many live early television shows.

Gracie Barrie and Luella Gear performed comedy in *Crazy with the Heat* and later became dramatic actresses on stage and in films. Director Kurt Kasznar later became an excellent dramatic actor, comedian, and villain in all fields of show business. He invested $130,000 in the show and lost all of it. He had to stop the show a week after it opened at the Shubert Theatre in Boston because it was so bad and needed so much more work.

Crazy with the Heat opened at the Forty-fourth Street Theatre on Broadway, February 5, 1941, as a revue in two acts and 27 scenes and ran for 12 weeks. Raymond and most of the original cast members had been replaced. The new show opened at Loew's State Theatre on Broadway, running 57 minutes, followed by a movie, *Andy Hardy's Private Secretary*.

Years later in an interview, Raymond told a reporter, "That musical comedy opened the same week as *Lady in the Dark*, which ran for years on Broadway. Some of the material in the sketches of our show, banned in Boston, never was put back in the New York version."

After Raymond left the show he toured the country with British War Relief and appeared in *Charley's Aunt, Jason, Arsenic and Old Lace, Tonight at 8:30, Holiday*, and other plays.

Raymond left New York for California to make a screen test for a role in *Sister Kenny*, a Rosalind Russell film. The role went to Dean Jagger. Raymond tried out for other film roles that wound up canceled before they were filmed, or he was turned down by the powers that be. Disappointed, he continued to act on stage and on radio. There are many radio programs that do not mention Raymond in the cast. Sometimes he would speak only one sentence and rush to another studio to say a few lines as part of the next cast. He might rush through four or five dramatic parts in one day.

III

Pasadena Playhouse

Two members of the Pasadena Playhouse knew Raymond wanted to pursue his stage career. About a week before the play *Quiet Wedding* was to open in November 1942, the producer lost her leading man. The two members suggested Raymond might be suited for the role. The producer asked him to audition, and he got the part.

Quiet Wedding was Raymond's debut for the Pasadena Playhouse and started a strong friendship with Lenore Shanewise, the producer of the play. The reviews for his debut were excellent, calling him "engaging as the young lover," and an "extremely personable fiancé." A few months later, Raymond played the macabre Jonathan Brewster in *Arsenic and Old Lace*.

Lenore Shanewise said in her oral history that Raymond Burr proved to be a loyal, dedicated actor for Gilmor Brown. She remembered the time Raymond was on a ladder outside the Playbox Theater, which had moved from Herkimer Street to North Hudson. He bought the paint and utensils and was painting the exterior. When he finished that job, he recruited several helpers, and they painted the interior of the theater. Raymond did anything he could to help Gilmor.

As a drama teacher, Raymond taught several students who played an interesting part in his later career. One was Isabella Ward, and the other two were John Merivale and Sally Cooper, who were students at the Pasadena Playhouse during the years Raymond was a teacher.

John Merivale is the son of the late Gladys Cooper and Phillip Merivale, who were great British actors of their day and famous on stage, screen, and radio, both in the U. S. and Britain. Sally Cooper is the daughter of Gladys Cooper by a former marriage. Her name was Joan Buckmaster, but she changed it to Sally Cooper. She later married the great British actor Robert Morley and gave up her career to raise a family. Gladys Cooper was on the faculty of the Playhouse as a teacher and adviser.

Raymond continued to act in the plays as well as teach until other interests took over. Long after he became famous he would come back to address the graduating classes and receive honors from the Playhouse.

14

Raymond Burr, the Pasadena Playhouse, 1942.

Gilmor asked Shanewise to become a staff director, and she stayed at the Pasadena Playhouse from 1923 until 1960, when she retired to Treasure Island, California. She died December 22, 1980, at the age of 91 in a San Diego retirement home.

After Gilmor Brown died, the Playhouse began to go downhill. Efforts to keep it going by the staff, friends, and students proved fruitless. The Bank of America took over when the Playhouse was forced into bankruptcy. By 1970 vandals had reduced the Playhouse to almost an empty shell. Grass and weeds grew between the cracks in the sidewalk and on paths leading to the theater. Windows were broken and glass particles were everywhere.

The Pasadena Playhouse had friends who were determined to bring the once proud Playhouse back to glory again. Don DeFore, actor and graduate, put together a group to buy the theater back from the Bank of America but ran into trouble. Kevin Tighe, a television actor, brought a crew and shot an episode of "Emergency" there. He had gotten his professional start at the Playhouse, as had many other actors and actresses.

Raymond Burr fought the hardest and longest of any of the alumni to try to get the theater going again. He approached a friend, Dr. Burns, president of the University of the Pacific. He hoped Burns could arrange to have the Pasadena Playhouse made part of the University at Stockton, California, as their graduate theater school. Raymond also wanted to develop a mathematics and theater science program. He planned to get famous actors and theater and Hollywood professionals to come to lecture and exchange ideas and present a Sunday seminar program. The Playhouse could make videotapes for educational television, which might open doors for grants. Raymond had great ideas and perhaps all systems might have gotten the go-ahead signal—if Dr. Burns had not dropped dead.

It was a year before they could choose a new president. Meanwhile, the acting president could not do anything to help the Pasadena Playhouse. By the time the year had passed, interest in Raymond's ideas had dwindled.

With the death of Gilmor Brown, the Pasadena Playhouse, in a sense, died too. Gilmor's ghost was rumored to haunt the old theater. His oral history is incomplete, never mentioning Raymond or any of his famous students. Over four hundred students, teachers, and friends attended Gilmor Brown's funeral.

Besides Raymond Burr, the Pasadena Playhouse graduated many other actors and actresses, such as Robert Young, Robert Preston, Carolyn Jones, Joanne Worley, Barbara Rush, and Charles Bronson. William Holden's real name was William Beedle, and in one of the plays he acted the part of an old man. A Hollywood producer went backstage to meet Holden. The meeting led to Holden's role in the film *Golden Boy* in 1939. For many students, the Pasadena Playhouse was a ticket to fame and fortune. For a great many others like Raymond, just being there was enough.

Years later, in April 1984, Raymond wrote the foreword to author Diane Alexander's book about the Pasadena Playhouse. Alexander's book tells the history of the Pasadena Playhouse and its struggle to survive. Raymond addressed his words to the late Gilmor Brown and thought Brown would be pleased with her book.

Maude Prickett Cooper, a well known character actress in early films, was active in the Pasadena Playhouse. She states in her oral history,

> When I was at the Greek Theater, Raymond Burr at the time had become "Perry Mason" to the nth degree.
> We tried to find some weeks available for him to do the play *Anne of the Thousand Days* again, not only at the Greek Theater but the Biltmore and the Curran Theater in San Francisco as well. He was so busy and knocked out from doing "Perry Mason" episodes that we couldn't find the time available. We had two or three sessions in which we tried to align time, because to me he just played Henry VIII to a degree of perfection. He was just wonderful in it.

Raymond feels *Anne of the Thousand Days* was his most exhilarating legitimate experience.

"The happy news is," said Raymond, "the Pasadena Playhouse will open in 1986 and many special events will once again take place there." Many of the theater's former students showed up for the grand opening: Dana Andrews, Buddy Ebsen, Jamie Farr, Barbara Rush, and a host of other people. The Pasadena Playhouse in the 1990s plays to capacity audiences, with many of the former students appearing in plays they did not have a chance to do when the theater was in its heyday.

Raymond had attended the Playhouse reunions but his heavy schedule had precluded his participation in any of the meetings. He was once awarded the Man of the Year Award, but despite repeated notifications, the plaque remained in the trunk of someone's car for three years before he could be induced to come and get it.

In James Brough's 1956 book about Hedda Hopper, he quotes her as saying this about Raymond Burr:

> I had Raymond Burr literally at my feet when I first met him. I had lunch most every day in the Garden of Ivar House; a restaurant long since demolished.
>
> One day a husky fellow was laying bricks in the patio where I was sitting. I had to keep moving my chair to make room for him to work. Finally I looked down into a handsome face and a very large body.
>
> "You don't look like a bricklayer to me," I said.
>
> "I'm not. I'm an actor," he said.
>
> "Then what are you doing this for?"
>
> Hedda said, "If looks could kill I wouldn't be here! He was s—o mad! He quit his job that night and never laid another brick."
>
> Raymond said, "I told Hedda to move her damn feet because I was working in cement. At the time I was earning a living building a wall and she wouldn't move her feet out of the way. I didn't know who she was then.
>
> "Everytime I did a play at the Pasadena Playhouse she or one of her people always came to see me and she said she saw all my movies. I loved her. Everybody called her hardboiled, but I got to see the other side of her."*

Later, in 1957-58, when Hedda's son, Bill Hopper, played Paul Drake in "Perry Mason," Hedda Hopper and Raymond Burr became very good friends. Hedda wrote about Raymond a number of times in her newspaper gossip column. When he decided to quit the "Perry Mason" series, he gave the news to Hedda, not Louella Parsons.

**James Brough and Hedda Hopper, *The Truth and Nothing But* (New York: Pyramid, 1963), pp.237–238.*

Raymond realized he was not getting farther than the Pasadena Play-house. The producers, directors, and agents never approached him for a movie role or gave him the film contracts many of the other students were getting. Raymond decided to go back to England, even though World War II was active. As a Canadian citizen, he had not joined the U.S. forces yet. He did not know he was about to meet and fall in love with Annette Sutherland.

IV

England: Love, Then Tragedy

Raymond returned to England to learn and act in more Shakespeare plays. In the course of pursuing his career he met a young Scottish actress, Annette Sutherland. After a few dates they found themselves falling in love. The year was 1942, and they were both 25 years old.

Knowing time was important in war torn Europe, Raymond and Annette did not waste time on a lengthy courtship. Several months after their meeting, they were married. There was no chance for a honeymoon, as Annette was in a touring company and Raymond was again touring with Shakespeare plays. Not long afterwards Raymond gave up his troupe and joined Annette. He took whatever roles he could get and went with the company to Spain, where Michael Evan Burr came into this war-clouded world of 1943.

Great Britain was now in a full-scale war with Germany. Raymond tried to persuade Annette to leave the touring company and return with him to America, where she and the baby could be safe. Annette insisted on fulfilling her contract, however, so they compromised. Soon after Michael Evan was born they returned to England long enough to leave him with her parents, who lived quite a long distance outside of London. They thought the baby would be safe with his British grandparents until Annette completed her contract and could pick up Michael and join Raymond in America.

Raymond returned to America and wrote to Annette constantly, begging her to join him. Britain was now under heavy bombardment. His last letter from her was from Spain, telling him she was returning to England to pick up Michael and would meet him in the States shortly.

The week of June 1, 1943, turned into a nightmare for Raymond. He was in a play at the Pasadena Playhouse when word came that his wife had perished along with the passengers and crew of a *commercial* flight from Lisbon, Portugal, to London, England.

An Australian Sunderland flying boat shot down three of eight German junker 88s that attacked the plane Annette was on while they flew on

19

antisubmarine patrol over the Bay of Biscay. British pilots on patrol duty noticed an increase in enemy offshore activity and attributed this to an attempt to engage all planes bound for Great Britain. A second British civil plane had been attacked on the Lisbon run in April 1943. The Nazis also attacked a KLM DC7 which was painted with camouflage paint.

Leslie Howard was also on a plane en route *from* Lisbon to England on June 3, 1943. A Nazi sky raider shot down the Howard plane; the Nazis thought Winston Churchill was on the plane, but the prime minister was safe in England. No one by the name of Annette Sutherland Burr was listed as a passenger on the plane, yet down through the years, every newspaper or magazine article always repeats the same mistaken information that she was on this plane. Annette's flight was a regular, commercial airliner, with no one famous on board.

Raymond flew to England, Spain, and Portugal to find out more about the crash. He had little to go on, and the authorities could not give him any more information than he already knew. Apparently no bodies were ever found, and in the ensuing years no other information or clues have turned up.

A saddened Raymond Burr visited his son. He asked Annette's parents to take care of him and promised to send whatever he could for his care. He felt it was best to leave Michael with the people who loved him, especially since he did not know in which direction his future would be going.

Raymond returned to the Pasadena Playhouse and plunged into acting in plays, trying to forget the tragedy. He was the production coordinator for *The Great Magician* and acted in *Othello, The Jest, Arsenic and Old Lace, Jason, The Intimate Strangers, Colonel Satan,* and *Monsieur Beaucaire.*

Taking a leave of absence from the Pasadena Playhouse, he tackled New York once more. He telephoned Lenore Shanewise from New York, asking her to direct him in a play the Theatre Guild wanted him to do. Lenore refused to come to New York, and Raymond never did the play.

In New York he was in the lobby of the Algonquin Hotel when he was called to the telephone. He was instructed to come to a room upstairs, where a stage producer met him at the door.

> A strange man opened the door to a Central Park South beautiful apartment. He told me he was having dinner with his family and would bring me a scene to read. So I read the scene and then he sat down and read the entire scene with me. He said, "That's extraordinary. You are exactly what we want! I am going to direct the play and I give my approval and the producer will give his approval, but there is one other voice and I called him on the phone. He lives about two blocks from here and he will be here in twenty minutes. Please wait. We will have you meet him," and he went back in to his dinner.
>
> About twenty minutes later the door opens with a key and the man says

"Ah, ha, it's you!" It was Phillip Merivale, my childhood idol. I was completely undone, and at the time I could not have read my own name, let alone read a scene for him at that moment!

He turned to the director. "You like him?" The director said, "Yes, very much" and "He's marvelous; exactly what we want."

Phillip said, "I like him. We won't have to read young man, it won't be necessary, I know you already."

We had never met of course.

He had never seen me in a play, but it was my biggest moment.

We had eleven days to rehearse the play before it was to open on Broadway. It was a costume play by Patrick Hamilton and a very good play except there were no women in it! Stuart Cheney at the time was one of the best costumers and scenic designers in New York. Everything was gorgeous!

Raymond was cast in the part of Voulain, the friend of the blind Duke, played by Phillip Merivale. *Duke in Darkness* turned out to be the turning point in Raymond's career, though he did not know this at the time.

One day while he was at rehearsal he was locked out of his hotel room. His luggage was held by the management, and he rehearsed for 14 days wearing the same clothes.

The rehearsals lasted two months in late 1943. The play opened on Broadway, January 4, 1944.

Opening night I went back to my room feeling sorry for myself, so I went to bed. About five o'clock in the morning a man came in, an engineer, whom I'd never met. He came in with the first of the reviews of the play and brought me some coffee. He proceeded to reveal which were the good reviews, and about two hours later the housekeeper of the hotel along with two other people came in bringing me breakfast and other reviews. So at ten o'clock I got up and I could walk the few blocks to the theater. They were changing the signs and the photographs too! I thought, my God we've already closed after one night of the play! I looked up and at that time they brought out a big picture, full size, and it was me! They were changing *Duke in Darkness*, starring Phillip Merivale, who was *the* only star, to *Duke in Darkness*, starring Phillip Merivale and Raymond Burr. It was astounding because they had to call him in the middle of the night and ask him for permission to change it. It didn't do any good because not long afterwards we did close, but it was just a fantastic experience. Later on we did a picture together in Hollywood.

This heavy French drama, with no women in the cast, closed in April, and the reviews were not good.

However, John Chapman of the *Daily News* said, "Raymond Burr, a newcomer to the New York stage, is extremely effective as the patriot Voulain. His performance is uneven and frequently rough but he has fire and intensity." Another reviewer told readers to "remember Raymond Burr.

I heartily recommend for further use in the theatre one Raymond Burr, who plays the friendly plotter with physical charm and dramatic intensity." Ward Morehouse said of him, "There is plenty of fire in the playing of Mr. Burr as the plotting Voulain." Robert Coleman remarked, "Raymond Burr creates a favorable impression. He is good looking and reads lines well— exceptionally well. We wonder how the Hollywood talent scouts ever let him escape East from Pasadena and other Western drama centers."

Lester Sweyd, a theater buff who had been a child dancer on Broadway years before, saw *Duke in Darkness* and advised an agent he knew to go see this young Burr perform in the play. Elizabeth Van Cleve saw Raymond's performance and helped secure an exclusive contract with Frank Ross at RKO Studios.

After *Duke in Darkness* closed, Raymond was at liberty. He stopped in Denver to perform in eight plays for the Elitch Gardens Theatre during the summer of 1944. Raymond's costar was Martha Sleeper, an actress who gained fame in early live dramas on television. Another actress in the cast of players, Ruth McDevitt, gained fame years later in the "Mr. Peepers" television comedy with Wally Cox.

Raymond debuted at the Elitch Gardens as the male lead in *Another Love Story*, on July 2, 1944. This play was followed on July 9 with a Booth Tarkington comedy titled *The Intimate Strangers*. The next comedy was *But Not Goodbye*, on July 16.

Raymond had the physique of a fullback and portrayed the role of the eternal All-American tramp athlete "The Wreck" in *My Sister Eileen*. This was followed by two comedies, *Janie* and *The Doughgirls*, and a drama, *Tomorrow the World*, in which a very young Joyce Van Patten, sister of television actor Dick Van Patten, had a role. A Rachel Crothers comedy, *Let Us Be Gay*, ended the series, and it was time for Raymond to report to RKO Studios.

Frank Ross told Raymond he was preparing him for the leading man role in his new film, *The Robe*. His instructions to the young actor were, don't be seen in nightclubs or drinking and, most of all, avoid getting unwarranted publicity of a derogatory nature—*The Robe* was a biblical film with a serious religious theme.

Raymond was under contract to Frank Ross from March 18 until September 10, 1946, but had been under a standard contract with RKO beginning in late 1944. His salary was $150 per week, for which he sat around, doing nothing until he got his first role, a walk-on part in *Fighting Father Dunne*, starring Pat O'Brien, in 1945. He played the district attorney who sends Darryl Hickman to the electric chair. The part lasted for a fleeting moment on screen, and he had no dialogue—most of his scenes landed on the cutting room floor.

Meanwhile, Raymond returned to the Pasadena Playhouse, and Lenore

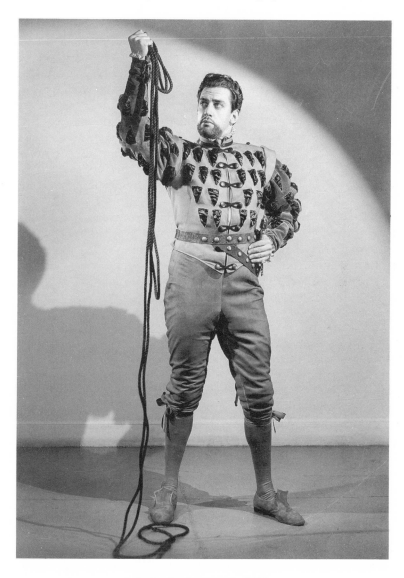

Duke in Darkness, 1944.

Shanewise directed him in *While the Sun Shines*. Sally Cooper and her step-brother, Jack Merivale, had parts in the play and their names are listed in the playbill under Burr's. This play opened June 12, 1946, and on December 1, 1946, Raymond directed and acted in a play titled *Murder Without Crime* at the Playbox Theatre, where Raymond had recruited helpers to paint the theater inside and out many years before. At the bottom of the

Raymond acted in and directed *Murder Without Crime*, 1946. Courtesy The Huntington Library, San Marino, California.

playbill it notes, "Raymond Burr returns to the Playhouse after two years away. He was an associate director on the staff, left for a major role on Broadway in *Duke in Darkness* and then came West under contract to RKO Radio Pictures ... he is now under their contract!"

Raymond's original biography from RKO no longer exists. The studio has changed hands many times since around 1958, and records are lost or buried in a warehouse somewhere. The biography was full of false information, dreamed up by press agents of the day, which has nonetheless been printed over and over again. Raymond learned the hard way that when you are under contract to a studio, especially the first contract, you have to take what the studio bosses dictate. He came to the conclusion early in his career that it was better *not* to confirm or deny—or even read—anything, whether true or false, about himself. Soon after it was printed, any article would be forgotten and buried in a clipping file.

Not used to sitting around waiting for work, Raymond kept after the studio to put him in a film or cancel his contract. Raymond was tall, handsome, and a slim 185 pounds. With typical studio logic, RKO cast him as a young naive gangster, and his movie career began.

V

Film Career

As the sun slowly sinks in the West, the lovers ride off into the sunset. This was the way most Hollywood films of the thirties, forties, and fifties ended.

Never did this happen to Raymond Burr in the movies he made during those years. Usually he got punished to atone for the vicious acts he committed against the hapless hero or heroine. He never got the girl, he never won a battle, he never triumphed.

Instead, he was beaten, burned, blown up, choked, chastised, crushed, poisoned, or imprisoned. If he did not meet death in this fashion, he was shot or stabbed in the back. He rarely got the chance to use any weapon he carried to defend himself. Raymond was a target for a gunman shooting at him from a helicopter. He was shot by the hero while riding a galloping horse and as he tried to escape in a speedboat. He fell or was thrown off cliffs, mountains, docks, tall buildings, and fell or was pushed down flights of stairs. He was stomped to death by a herd of stampeding elephants.

Raymond was given a small role in Lawrence Tierney's *San Quentin*. His job was to bring groceries to escaped murderer Barton MacLane, who was hiding out in a lodge in the woods. Caught by the police, he was led away looking bewildered, in handcuffs.

There was still no word as to when RKO would start filming *The Robe*. A script was not ready yet, and the biblical theme was too difficult to put on screen, according to the people who were trying their best to come up with an excellent film.

Raymond was given a bit part in the film *Without Reservations* in April of 1946 and was paid $250 a week. He speaks not a word of dialogue in the film but dances twice with the star, Claudette Colbert. In the first scene he wears a Navy uniform and in the second scene he is seen in civilian clothes. The third scene shows Raymond and Claudette, in sports clothes, riding bicycles. A photograph of Raymond is used in a newspaper John Wayne is reading. The caption under the photo says, "Paul Gill, Actor." Wayne is supposed to get jealous when he reads the article about the actor and Claudette seeing each other. All Raymond's scenes are almost at the end of the film and last fewer than five minutes on the screen.

Meanwhile, *The Robe* continued to be postponed for one reason or another until RKO finally gave up on it and sold the rights to another studio. Three years later *The Robe* reached the screen with a young Welshman, Richard Burton, in the leading role. Raymond says, "Somewhere in a Hollywood costume shop there is a large suit of armor that has never been worn. It was designed and fitted for me, but I never got to wear it. I regretted the studio dropping the idea of making the film and my chance to star in it. Richard Burton and I went along different routes, career-wise."

During 1946, Raymond received his official discharge from the Navy as a lieutenant commander. He did counterintelligence work during World War II and wound up in an Australian hospital with injuries when the Navy ship he was on became a target of Japanese kamikaze planes off the coast of Okinawa. He was seriously burned and had to be operated on six times for shrapnel in his back and shoulder. In later years pieces of shrapnel surfaced from time to time, requiring more operations to remove them.

Raymond had never elaborated on his World War II experiences and it was not well known that he received the Purple Heart for his injuries. He was in the Navy only a short while when the incident happened and stayed in the Naval Reserves until his discharge.

After Raymond finished his part in *Without Reservations,* he became more and more frustrated because roles were few and far between. He tried to break his contract with Frank Ross and RKO. In his frustration, Raymond began to overeat until he weighed 230 pounds. Because of his huge build, or in spite of it, Raymond was given his first really good part in another version of the Western *Code of the West* (there had been several earlier versions, including a silent film). Raymond played the gang leader.

This film was released on February 21, 1947, and was billed as a Western with music. One reviewer (*Variety*, February 21, 1947) said,

> There is no law in the whole Arizona Strip that can stop Raymond Burr and his gang of varlets.
> They round up all the acreage because the railroad is coming through Rainbow Valley, repeatedly sung by one of the cowpokes. The gang keeps pulling up stakes and violating the "Code of the West," making citizens mad as hell.
> Ain't much they can do about it, cause Burr has all the law officers on his payroll.
> Burr and his henchmen cook up plenty of skullduggery before hero James Warren rides to the rescue and puts Burr in the pokey, along with his entourage. The wave of lead poisoning stops when a federal judge comes to town and makes it all legal!

Finally, Raymond won his release from his contract—RKO did not have parts for fat men. He was not out of work very long. His gamble paid off when he free-lanced, working for any studio that would hire him on a picture to picture basis. Between assignments, Raymond recorded radio shows for the armed forces. He acted in dramas and comedies, hosted shows, and played lovers, villains, and straight men for well known comedians. Between times he kept up his stage work at the Pasadena Playhouse.

Raymond was given a very good part as the heavy in a film titled *Desperate*. Steve Brodie was the star and Raymond, the villain, hounded him throughout the film. Raymond blames Brodie for his brother's death in a shootout with police. Brodie finally has enough and pursues Raymond to the top floor of a tenement house. There, in self-defense, Brodie shoots Raymond, who clutches his heart and falls over the banister to his justifiable death.

Raymond's movie career was beginning to take off but he was typecast as a vicious gangster for the next few years. His next assignment was for Columbia Pictures, playing a henchman of John Ireland in a film called *I Love Trouble* and beating Franchot Tone unmercifully with a blackjack. Roy Huggins wrote the screenplay and years later produced some of Raymond's "Ironside" series.

Columbia Studio's biography said Raymond was a rave with the girls at RKO. He was 6 feet 2 inches tall and a brawny 190 pounds (that was *before* he gained a great deal of weight), with curly black hair (it was dark brown), blue eyes, and an engaging grin.

A second chance to appear with Claudette Colbert gave Raymond the opportunity to be on the right side of the law for a change. This time Don Ameche was the villain in *Sleep, My Love*. Raymond played detective Lieutenant Strake, who could not believe Ameche was trying to kill Colbert by driving her insane.

After this film was finished, Raymond took time out for the week of January 22, 1947, to appear in a play with Elizabeth Bergner. Bergner was at the height of her career then. The play was called *Miss Julie*. Raymond played the butler and costarred with Bergner at the Forrest Theatre in Philadelphia, Pennsylvania. The reviews praised Bergner but never mentioned Raymond.

Back in Hollywood, Raymond signed for two films for the Eagle-Lion Studio. In the first film, *Raw Deal*, Raymond was a vicious mobster who delighted in throwing acid on Cara William. He also tormented Marsha Hunt, Claire Trevor, and Dennis O'Keefe. Finally, Raymond met his demise by backing into and falling out a window. He caught his foot in a wire on the floor, that tripped him and caused the bottle of acid he held in his hand to spill on himself. His screams can be heard as he falls to his death.

Desperate, with Steve Brodie and Raymond Burr, 1947.

The second film for Eagle-Lion was titled *Ruthless*. Zachary Scott was the star, and Raymond portrayed his father, Pete Vendig. This was a small but important part near the beginning of the film, when the 12-year-old son seeks his father's help and is turned away. The episode transforms Scott into a ruthless man who stops at nothing to obtain everything he wants.

Columbia Pictures signed Raymond for a good part in *Walk a Crooked Mile*. Louis Hayward was a Scotland Yard detective and Denns O'Keefe an FBI man. Raymond was a Russian spy, Krebs, who kills an FBI agent.

Years later, when interviewed on the "Merv Griffin Show," Griffin held up a photo from the film. Raymond exclaimed, "No! No! That was not the title of the film! That was titled, *The FBI versus Scotland Yard*. I wore a Van Dyke beard and a pulled down brimmed hat. I had a camera and walked all over the factory shooting pictures. No one questioned why I was there or what I was doing! In the end, after I beat up and torture Louis Hayward, Dennis beats me up and finally kills me."

Paramount Studios put out a biography on Raymond filled with falsehoods and half-truths. One error listed Norman Burr as his brother instead of his nephew. Norman was one of the five children of brother James Edmond Burr, and Raymond was helping Norman try for an acting career.

Every day Raymond was not on a soundstage at the studio, he could be found at the Pasadena Playhouse as an actor and teacher. He also continued doing the radio broadcasts in between all his other jobs. Since he got paid for the lines he spoke on the air, he was able to run from studio to studio if the radio shows were done in the same building and could make a number of radio shows in one day. Raymond made over five thousand broadcasts over the years, but quite a few never mention him in the cast of characters.

One day in 1947, coming back to the Pasadena Playhouse from one of his radio assignments, Raymond met Isabella Ward on the street. She was visiting the Playhouse, hoping to meet old friends and classmates.

Isabella and Raymond renewed their friendship, began dating, and shortly afterward, Raymond proposed marriage. The wedding took place on January 10, 1948, in the Bakersfield, California, home of Raymond's sister, Geraldine. After a small wedding reception of family members and the minister and his wife and no honeymoon because of Raymond's commitments to the film studio, the Playhouse, and his radio broadcasts, the newlyweds settled in the basement apartment in the house Raymond had rented years ago for his grandparents and his mother. He had promised them when he made enough money he would rent a house big enough for them all, and he found such a house in the Los Feliz Park area of Los Angeles. The apartment opened onto a patio, and Isabella and Raymond soon found out they had no privacy. They tried to make the best of the situation until they could find a place of their own.

As husband and wife, Raymond and Isabella acted in a play based on the life of the artist Paul Gauguin. Stephen Longstreet and Catherine Turney wrote the play, which opened May 26, 1948, at the Playbox Theater. Raymond studied everything he could find about Paul Gauguin, even coming into possession of one of his letters. Isabella portrayed Mette, Paul's wife.

Bob Telford, actor and director, heard about Raymond's performance as Paul. Bob said, "A friend of mine stage managed *Gauguin* and came away saying, 'Jesus, that's the greatest sonofabitch I have ever seen! He's going through the back of the building some night. He is frightening and they are terrified of him.'"

Raymond *did* go through the back of the building one night. In one scene he was to fling himself on a cot in despair and did so with such force that the cot and Raymond flew across the stage, sailing into the cardboard set into the back of the building, where it stopped with an astonished Raymond Burr still lying on it.

Though there was harmony on stage between Isabella and Raymond, they both realized their marriage was not as happy as it should be. Deep emotional problems, student-teacher temperament clashes, and the lack of

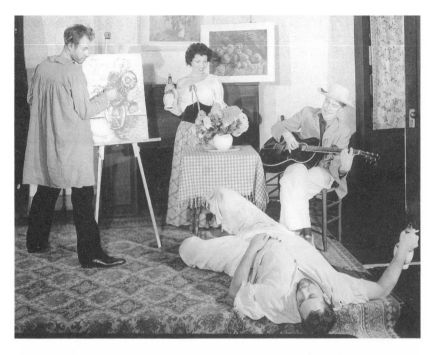

Gauguin, 1948. Raymond and his real-life wife, Isabella Ward, played Paul and Mette Gauguin. Courtesy The Huntington Library, San Marino, California.

privacy did not help the situation. Raymond had gained so much weight back, and the demand for his services increased while Isabella was not getting the assignments she hoped for.

Sometime in late June 1948, Isabella decided she had had enough and left Raymond. They had been separated for four years when an item appeared in the *Los Angeles Daily News* on August 22, 1952, stating she had instigated divorce proceedings in Baltimore, Maryland. Raymond did not contest the divorce, and when it became final, Isabella returned permanently to her home state of Delaware.

Near the end of 1948, Raymond had started to film his part in a costume drama for Warner Brothers studio. This Errol Flynn color film was called *Adventures of Don Juan*. Raymond's role was Captain Alvarez, whom Flynn eventually kills in a duel. Flynn caused many delays on the film because he showed up drunk, sick, or not at all.

Because of the delays, Raymond was able to film his part in *Bride of Vengeance* for Paramount Studios. Formerly called *A Mask for Lucretia*, this costume drama had a large and distinguished cast including John Lund, Paulette Goddard, and MacDonald Carey. Portraying Michelotto, Raymond was the henchman for Carey. For his loyalty Carey shot him in the back with a crossbow and arrow—proving he should never turn his back on another archvillain.

Errol Flynn continued to delay the *Don Juan* film for months, so Raymond reported to his alma mater, RKO, for a film with Dick Powell. Powell had given up his singing career to take dramatic roles, and *Stations West* was a good Western film with Agnes Moorehead and Jane Greer. Raymond portrayed a crooked lawyer, Mark Bristow, a cowardly, spineless gambler who owed Greer a lot of money. Trying to ride out of town to escape Powell and Greer, he is gunned down by another villain, Gordon Oliver.

Pitfall was the second film Raymond made with Dick Powell, this time for United Artists. The film was released in 1948, a few months prior to the finally completed *Adventures of Don Juan*. Raymond was up to 310 pounds and portrayed a burly private insurance detective named MacDonald. *Pitfall* turned out to be an excellent film for Raymond as a menacing hulk of a man who tries to possess Lizabeth Scott. He tricks Dick Powell into killing her boyfriend, who acts like a burglar outside Powell's home. He threatens Dick's family, tries to force Lizabeth to come away with him, relentlessly pursues her, and cunningly and brutally handles her until she shoots and kills him. Raymond was so believably rotten, that some audiences booed him and cheered when Lizabeth killed him.

Audiences now took notice of Raymond as a portrayer of vicious, vindictive villains, and he made $100,000 per year for his cruel, snarling portrayals of mean characters! Despite his huge size, he was in demand more than ever as a villain.

Alas, it was back to the small parts again when Orson Welles made a dreadful film called *Black Magic* in 1949. Since Welles did everything on a grand scale, the film was shot on location in Rome and Raymond portrayed Alexander Dumas, Jr., in one scene at the very beginning and another at the end of the film, which Gregory Ratoff directed. The film filled a double feature bill in local theaters throughout the country, receiving bad reviews wherever it was booked. Raymond was rarely mentioned in the newspapers; Orson Welles received all the attention.

One of the highlights of the trip to Rome was an audience with Pope Pius XII, and the second was a trip to England to see his son, now seven years old. The visit was a short one due to Raymond's film commitment in the States. Republic Studios wanted him for their next film.

Hillary Brooke became Raymond's next victim in *Unmasked*. She tried to blackmail him, and Raymond choked her to death, then cleverly covered up the murder by arranging for someone else to take the blame. The authorities found out, of course, and he was imprisoned for his crime. A critic reviewing this film stated, "Raymond Burr should be in 'A' pictures, he is that good!"

Pitfall, 1948.

This was also a low budget film churned out for the double feature theaters. In the 1950s, a moviegoer got two feature films, a newsreel, a cartoon, coming attractions, and a children's serial—on Saturday matinees and all for the admission price of less than 50 cents.

Universal Studios hired Raymond as a gangster in another B picture, called *Abandoned*, about the baby adoption racket. Gale Storm becomes involved when she tries to locate her sister's baby and hands over a huge sum of money to Raymond, who puts a baby in her arms. The baby is not her sister's child, however. The rest of the mob finds out about the double dealing money scheme and proceeds to beat and torture him to death, with Mike Mazurki choking and kicking him. Dennis O'Keefe was the star of this film, but the shocker was the gang leader, who turned out to be a much beloved stage and screen actress, Marjorie Rambeau.

Raymond's performance often stood out above that of the star's or any

Abandoned. **Mike Mazurki choking Burr.**

of the main players', and the class B films continued for several more years. Another example of this typecasting was in a film titled *Red Light*. The title referred to church candles; Raymond killed a priest, whose brother was played by George Raft. Short tough guy Raft slapped 6-foot-2-inch Raymond Burr, knocking him onto the floor, which was not easy, considering Burr was still extremely overweight. Raft chased Raymond to the rooftop of an industrial building, where a huge neon sign lit up the night and the two men. Raft aimed a gun at Raymond, who was backing away from him trying to escape his wrath. Unaware how close he was to the neon sign, Raymond backed into the sign and was electrocuted—a fitting punishment for the priest killer who had left a hotel Bible opened to the verse "Vengeance is mine; I will repay, saith the Lord."

Someone wrote a fan letter to a magazine with advice to Raymond Burr. Apparently the fan had seen him in *Pitfall* and was impressed with his performance as the young villain. Should Mr. Burr reach stardom, he hoped he would not be foolish enough to reduce his weight. His build and personality made him an excellent villain, since youthful character actors were not too plentiful, while slim, pretty-boy heroes were a dime a dozen.

Raymond's girth matched Andy Devine's: they both weighed in at over three hundred pounds in a film called *New Mexico*. Both were miscast as cavalry soldiers in this Western saga. Lew Ayres was the commanding officer who sent them on patrol to fight Indians. Marilyn Maxwell and Dorothy Patrick had little to do except look pretty and get in the way of the fighting men. Raymond was outstanding as the surly, despicable sergeant who caused trouble for everyone.

Universal Studios decided their villain should wear a white suit, black shirt, and a white tie as a drug smuggler south of the border in Mexico. In *Borderline* (1950), Raymond is chased all over Mexico by Fred MacMurray and Claire Trevor as federal agents. Raymond's shipment of dope is highjacked, and he is trying to find out who in his organization has committed the crime. The comic relief ensues when MacMurray and Trevor chase Raymond, who in turn is chasing his highjacker. Trevor does not know MacMurray is a federal agent, nor does he know she is. The two of them get together before the final reel, capture Raymond, and justice triumphs for all.

Peter Lorre had made an excellent film titled *M* but the remake, using the same title, was anything but good. The best thing about *M* was the huge cast of stage and screen actors who were wasted in small parts. Raymond was a good gangster for a change, with Luther Adler, Martin Gabel, David Wayne, Norman Lloyd, Steve Brodie, Howard De Silva, Glen Anders, and Walter Burke acting as gang leaders or small time mobsters out to capture a child molester played by David Wayne. They all were determined to capture Wayne and deal with him before the police did. Raymond was the payoff man, and for once was not killed in the final reel.

Another film in the B category was *The Whip Hand*, an average suspense thriller with Elliott Reed as the leading man. He finds mysterious things going on in a tiny village near a lake. Reed stumbles on a clue telling him that the Nazis have now turned communist and are experimenting with germ warfare. The FBI arrives in the nick of time as Burr and his cohorts try to capture Elliott escaping in a speedboat.

Bride of the Gorilla, **with Barbara Payton and Raymond Burr.**

Raymond was *not* the villain in *Thunder Pass*—John Carradine is selling guns to the Indians. Dane Clark, Burr, and the settlers are mad as hell until Raymond shoots Carradine and peace comes to the pass at last.

Early in 1950, Raymond went on a strict diet and managed in about a year to slim down to the 185 pounds he was when he first came to Hollywood. He *still* was not getting the leading man roles even though he was back to the leading man type: tall, handsome, steel-blue eyes, dark brown wavy hair, and a mustache.

The mustache was added for his role as a corrupt politician in MGM's *Key to the City*, starring Clark Gable and Lorettta Young. Gable and Raymond are former dockworkers. Toward the end of the film they fight using stevedore hooks. Clark, the hero, ends the fight by knocking Raymond into a huge fountain.

Alas, *Bride of the Gorilla* was another so-so picture and the beginning of a series of low budget horror movies. These were mild compared to the horror films that were made many years later. The thin plot had Raymond looking in a mirror and seeing himself as a gorilla. A native hag had poisoned and cast a spell over him so he looked and acted like a gorilla. He went on a rampage in the jungle every night while his bride (Barbara Payton) tried to figure out why he disappeared and came back the next morning exhausted. One night as a gorilla doing a lot of butchering, Raymond is killed by Tom Conway and Lon Chaney, Jr., who hunt for the huge beast only to discover their friend turning back into a human being one last time.

Still working for independent producers, Raymond had a secondary role in *FBI Girl*. The audience was shocked when he socked Audrey Totter in the jaw to knock her out. A smooth, cagey villain, he was pursued by FBI agents George Brent and Cesar Romero. Raymond tried to escape from both of them in a speedboat, shooting at the helicopter, missing it every time, while Brent and Romero, using machine guns, filled him full of lead.

Totter and Raymond dated during the making of this film and she says, "He was a fun date; a delightful gentleman with a rare wit. Later I appeared on his 'Perry Mason' and 'Ironside' series. One day when I came on the 'Perry Mason' set, there was a huge blown-up photo of the cast of *FBI Girl*, displayed for all to see. The photo was Ray, Cesar, George, Tom Drake and myself walking arm in arm, bigger than life but 100 years later!"

Raymond made an excellent living for years by dying in films. He played these characters so well there were false rumors he was barked at by dogs, stoned by brats, avoided by some women and adored by others, glared at by men, and hissed or booed by the theater audience because he acted with such intensity. Also depending upon what year his films were released, Raymond was slim, overweight, or huge. Not all his films were released in the year they were made.

Frank Sinatra killed him in *Meet Danny Wilson* by shooting him in the back as he clung to a pole in a ballfield. Errol Flynn threw him down a flight of stone steps during a terrific fight in *Mara Maru*, and Robert Ryan shot him at point blank range in the Western *Horizons West*.

Anne Baxter *thought* she had killed Raymond by hitting him over the head with a vase in *Blue Gardenia*. He got a little too rough in one scene where they struggled, and Baxter suffered a torn ligament in her leg, delaying production until she could walk again.

***Horizons West*, with Rock Hudson, Robert Ryan, and Raymond Burr.**

Yvonne De Carlo portrayed a French intelligence agent and Raymond an Arab chieftain in *Fort Algiers*, made in what was then a new process, wide screen stereophonic sound. Raymond riding an Arabian horse at full gallop led his band of cutthroats against the French Foreign Legion and was killed in the battle.

Richard Greene played twins—one good, one bad—in another remake of *The Corsican Brothers*. Renamed *The Bandits of Corsica*, it starred Paula Raymond as the love interest between Burr and Greene. Greene, as the good twin, killed Raymond in a duel.

Raymond weighed around 185 pounds when he made *Serpent of the Nile*, for Columbia Studios in 1953. Rhonda Fleming portrayed Cleopatra to his Marc Antony. His dark brown hair was curled, and he wore a toga of white and silver. Carrying a shield, he made a dashing hero. He ignored the advice of his friend (William Lundigan) when informed Cleopatra was using him to carry out her schemes. When he realized his friend was right, he committed suicide by stabbing himself. This was a poorly made film and shows up quite often on television.

Poor Raymond was trampled to death by a herd of stampeding elephants in *Tarzan and the She-Devil*. Burr beat Tarzan (Lex Barker) with a bullwhip and got his just deserts for creating mayhem in the jungle as an ivory poacher.

Raymond and Lucille Ball were villains in a Supercinecolor Arabian Nights fantasy made for Columbia Studios as a Saturday kiddie matinee. In *The Magic Carpet* Raymond was dressed in flowing robes and wide accordion pleated pantaloons, which made him look twice as big as he really was. Ball tries to outdo Raymond as a villain when they both try to find out if John Agar is the mysterious prince who flies around on a magic carpet. Agar and Patricia Medina, with the aid of the carpet and a lot of derring-do, kill Raymond with a scimitar—but at least Raymond got to kiss Lucille Ball several times before his demise.

When shown some old stills on the "Merv Griffin Show," Raymond revealed some information about the film:

> Lucille had a commitment with Columbia Pictures, at the time, for $100,000, to do comedy. Harry Cohn said, "We have a script for you until...." Without even looking at the script or finding out what the story was about, Lucille said she would do the film. Turned out she got paid more than half of the original budget for the film, and the producer almost killed himself! She played a bad woman, a villainess, but we had a great deal of laughs during rehearsals for this film.

No one noticed a much thinner Raymond Burr in a Robert Mitchum film called *His Kind of Woman*. Jane Russell and her sleepy-eyed costar appeared in this sultry action thriller made for RKO. Sure enough, Raymond was cast as a Luciano-type gangster trying to return illegally to the United States. His lookalike, Mitchum, was hired at great expense so Raymond could have him killed in order to assume his identity. Jane Russell pretended to be a rich woman trying to snare a rich husband. Mitchum woke up long enough to gun down Burr and get the gal in the last few minutes of the film, but Vincent Price, playing a ham actor, stole the picture from all three of them.

United Artists released a Marx Brothers comedy, *Love Happy*, with Raymond portraying a gangster henchman of Ilona Massey. Harpo Marx chased Raymond up a flagpole while two other Marx Brothers chased Massey and other females. The film taught Raymond timing and ad-libbing, because he never knew what the Marx Brothers would do next. This film was not the best of the Marx Brothers' work and did nothing to further Raymond's career.

Raymond's most praiseworthy performance is often considered his role in George Stevens's *A Place in the Sun*. He portrays a ruthless district attorney, unrelenting in his interrogation of Montgomery Clift. In a series of climactic scenes, he cruelly probes Clift to get him to admit he planned Shelley Winters's murder. Standing in a rowboat, he demonstrates how Clift killed her by raising an oar high above his head and, describing the vivid details, bringing it down with such force it snaps in two. The action stunned

Raymond Burr and Lucille Ball play a villainous pair in Columbia's Super-cinecolor fantasy, *Magic Carpet*.

the jury and the crowded courtroom into a horrified silence, and Montgomery Clift was found guilty of murder.

Most of the publicity for *A Place in the Sun* centered on the young, beautiful Elizabeth Taylor and the moody Clift. Raymond's fine performance was singled out, however, and at least this one was an A category film.

For every good role like that in *A Place in the Sun*, however, many other mediocre film roles would follow. Raymond did not get another decent role until 1953, when he signed a contract to appear in the Alfred Hitchcock film *Rear Window*.

Gang leader Raymond Burr fights invading law officers, aware that his evil game is up. A scene from RKO Radio's *His Kind of Woman*, which costars Robert Mitchum and Jane Russell.

Before he reported for work, though, Raymond took off for Korea to spend about six months with American service personnel. He had started these trips in 1951, soon after the war started. Raymond would arrive at a military post and ask the men whether they would like him to entertain them or just sit and talk about things going on at home. He wrote sketches and used volunteer GIs as the actors, sometimes joining the cast himself.

He preferred talking to the men in the trenches rather than to the top brass, although at the end of his visits he would ask if he could help the brass in any way.

Trying to get away from all his villain roles, Raymond performed in many radio programs dealing with religious stories. He played Christ in one episode of "Family Theater," a Catholic radio show, and played Peter in an early filmed television show. Raymond was spent a great deal of time over the years doing projects for the United Jewish Appeal. He was very proud of knowing the Talmud, Koran, and the King James version of the Bible and recorded parts of the Bible in Yorkshire, England, and also in this country. Raymond attended Christian Scientist churches, among other religious organizations, and since childhood had a deep respect for all religious groups.

Between his appearances on the stage, in films, and on early live television shows, Raymond continued to perform in many radio dramas and comedies. This is how he met Jack Webb in 1947, and the two men joined forces in several famous radio shows.

VI

"Pat Novak for Hire"
and "Dragnet"

A radio show called "Pat Novak for Hire" began broadcasting from San Francisco in 1946. Jack Webb had been playing the part, which propelled him to fame as radio's tough guy. After he had played Pat for several months, Webb had to turn the role over to Ben Morris and leave for film assignments. Fans wanted Webb back in the part, however, so Webb and writer Richard Breen did a summer series in 1947, which they called "Johnny Madero." Although the show was almost a copy of "Pat Novak," the public did not buy it and demanded Webb return as Novak. In the meantime, Webb bought the rights to the show, rewrote the scripts to fit his personality, and started searching for an actor to play his adversary. Raymond Burr got the part of Lieutenant Hellman, a brutish police inspector who wanted to lock Pat Novak in jail and throw away the key.

The new version was picked up by ABC and ran coast to coast, starting on February 12, 1949. The show began where the original left off. The script was filled with clichés, and bits of what was even then considered purple dialogue—"The street was deserted as a warm bottle of beer"; "A car started up down the street, and the old man couldn't have made it with a couple of aces"; "I caught a glimpse of the license plate in a dull, surprised way, the way you grab a feather out of an angel's wing"—tumbled out half a dozen a minute.

Jocko Madigan, played by British actor Tudor Owen, was Novak's assistant—wharf bum, ex-doctor, and boozer, but honest guy. Owen, plus Burr, plus Webb helped make the series a success, and the show ran for 27 episodes. Other well-known cast members included Ted De Corsica, Vic Perrin, Herb Butterfield, Betty Lou Gerson, Lurene Tuttle, Virginia Gregg, and Lee J. Cobb. Raymond remembered all these people through the years and employed them later in his various projects.

"Pat Novak for Hire" led to another success for Jack Webb. While he was working and acting in "Pat," he was also involved in writing and producing another radio show. Consequently, after the last episode of "Pat Novak" was heard on August 3, 1949, "Dragnet" had already made its debut, on July 7, 1949.

Dum-De-Dum-Dum. The theme music, composed and conducted by Walter Schumann, became as familiar as Mom's apple pie. It was usually heard at the end of the show, when the announcer stated, "The story you have just heard is true. Only the names have been changed to protect the innocent."

There were trademark lines lines throughout the 30 minute show: "My name's Friday, I'm a cop"; "Just the facts, ma'am." Webb talked in a monotone voice, as if everything was a dull routine and he was tired of chasing down clues that did not fit the case.

"Dragnet" was the story of mundane police work and the details of tracking down criminals. The sponsor was Fatima cigarettes, and the show was heard on the NBC network. James E. Moser, John Robison, and Frank Burt, all wrote excellent scripts based on actual files in the Los Angeles Police Department. Sound effects were done by experts Bud Tollifon and Wayne Kenworthy.

The police chief was played by Richard Boone, and Raymond Burr was the chief of detectives Ed Backstrand, Thad Brown, or one of several other names used for his character. His film, stage, television, and other radio show commitments kept him from appearing. Barton Yarborough played Ben Romero but died of a heart attack after the second episode was filmed for television. Raymond played his chief of detective role, Thad Brown, in the first episode filmed for television, titled "The Human Bomb" making its debut on December 16, 1951. The show previewed on the "Chesterfield Sound Off Show Time," and the rest became history.

Raymond had to leave "Dragnet" after that first episode was on the air because he was playing Henry VIII in *Anne of the Thousand Days* and the John Barrymore role in *Twentieth Century* for the Pasadena Playhouse, between all his other commitments.

He had asked his friend Lenore Shanewise to find a play for him to do at the Pasadena Playhouse that would belong solely to him. She told him, "Raymond, I don't have to hunt, as I know exactly the play that will be right for you." The play was *Anne of the Thousand Days*, with Raymond as Henry VIII. Of course he looked exactly like Henry VIII at that time, and the part was just right for him. "He was perfect in appearance for the role, as Raymond had a voluptuous face and he was really a great success in the role. It was one of my most gratifying experiences and his too."

Maude Prickett Cooper, one of the most famous actresses to come out of the Pasadena Playhouse, had this to say about Raymond Burr. "I can't neglect what was probably one of the most attractive productions in the Playhouse history in which a young man by the name of Raymond Burr really came into his own. Ray was a great Henry; just a perfect Henry VIII."

Adding to the production's appeal was the work of a young designer, Edward Stevenson, a graduate of the Playhouse's technical staff. He designed unique banners that were used as the entire background for the scenic portion of the production.

> One of the things we did in that production was the use of the false boxes. A false box was used for Henry VIII's office chamber. The false box on the right was the Tower of London, where Anne was. The intervening scenes would take place on the main stage so it didn't take up the time to make scene changes.
>
> Raymond wasn't too sure that he wanted to do it that way, but in rehearsals he finally said, "This was the *only* way to do it!" Raymond was perfect in appearance for the role, and I agree with Lenore that he was a great success.

Then, for a week, Raymond found time to play George Washington in *Valley Forge* at the Playhouse, with fellow actor Patrick T. Miller. Miller recalls an incident with Raymond Burr when they shared a dressing room.

> For a man who stayed busy in films, radio, and television, Raymond was selfless in devoting a considerable amount of time in services to Gilmor Brown and the Pasadena Playhouse during the heyday of that wonderful theater. Painting the Playbox Theater for Gilmor was such a contribution and went unknown as far as the general public was concerned. Burr's many noteworthy contributions to the Playhouse as an actor were well known too, and warmly appreciated by the theatergoing public.
>
> Raymond has an unusually powerful presence which fills the stage, the wings, and goes through the audience all the way back to the last row. His emphatic projection of any thought or mood is so powerful that anyone present gets the idea full-blown, loud and clear.
>
> This power was demonstrated to me in the course of the production of Maxwell Anderson's *Valley Forge*, at the Pasadena Playhouse during the Great American Festival of 1952. Ray Burr was in the role of George Washington, of course, and I played the part of General Conway, a very unsavory, sententious, angry, and bitter man, with some attitudes that neared treasonable.
>
> One particular scene concerned an argument between Washington and Conway.
>
> The conflict reached a high point when Conway bellowed forth with an odious statement that was clearly traitorous. Ray Burr, in furious shock, held a moment, and then advanced three steadily paced steps toward me. He then stopped, regained his control, and delivered the next line. *But it was during those three steps that the ire of General Washington came through so awesomely.* On opening night, Ray hit his stride, and during those three steps toward me I could almost hear General Washington saying, "You traitor! ... I am going to tear you limb from limb!"

As I perceived this dreadnaught bearing down on me, I felt a moment of panic and took one slight, almost imperceptible, step backwards in retreat, then held, and continued the scene. I received many compliments on my performance as Conway, especially for that brief moment when I flinched in retreat. But I know . . . and now you know . . . that it was the power of Raymond Burr I must thank for those compliments.

Another colleague of Raymond's at the Pasadena Playhouse was Bobker ben Ali. His association with Raymond began in the early 1950s.

Although Raymond is a very genial person, he is also quite private and disinclined to speak readily about his personal life and relationships. He is quite correctly described as a "workaholic," but one who leaves no room for personal chit-chat or trivia. During the 1950s, I directed Raymond in two mainstage productions: Maxwell Anderson's *Valley Forge* in 1952 and Ben Hecht–Charlie MacArthur's *Twentieth Century,* also done in 1952. A season or so later I played Thomas Bolyn to Raymond's Henry VIII in Anderson's *Anne of the Thousand Days.* These, of course, predated Ray's success in TV.

As to anecdotes or practical jokes about him, I'm afraid I draw a blank, I do recall that he was exceedingly convivial and often took the companies of players in his productions to after-the-show dinners—even when he could ill afford to do so. But that never seemed to disturb him.

I recall with the vividness of an epiphany my first encounter with Raymond—who had been in, out, and around the Playhouse and Playbox for years, although I had never met him. The time of our meeting must have been about 1948, as I seem to associate it with the mainstage production of *Angel Street.* In any case, I was standing just inside the alley fire door in a small hallway that led to the stage door from outside the theater.

Most of the players entered the building through the fire door, which is what Raymond Burr did that night, bringing us suddenly face to face. He was dressed in a dark business suit and wearing a trench coat (if memory serves). He was slim as a ballet dancer that year and had these luminous blue-gray eyes that always seemed somewhat puzzled or surprised or startled. They had the same qualities when I met him a year ago, after a long period of no contact. The eyes were the same as ever. Of course at the time of our first encounter we didn't know each other. I recall that Raymond asked me some sort of question—had Gilmor Brown just come through the hall? (or some such question). I didn't know. Then Burr was instantly off, disappearing into the elevator most likely. Well, I was awed by this brief encounter. Burr's looks and vitality were stunning!

The next time I saw him however, he had undergone a kind of miraculous transformation. You must understand my personal conjecture runs high with virtually no confirming proof. I saw Raymond Burr next in almost the same place as our first encounter and I hardly recognized Burr for himself. It was apparent, moreover, that the new Raymond Burr had grown quite obese.

I, of course, have always felt that Ray did it by design, making himself over for those proliferating opportunities. I have no evidence to prove this other than my personal observation and conjecture.

But there is one thing more. Over the years Ray has many times lost and gained back this enormous weight. He's gone from fat to thin like a leaky tire periodically refilled. This could have had something to do with his health problems from time to time. My personal observation is that the heavy Raymond Burr has generally dominated the thin one. I have wondered whether this was on purpose for the screen roles or whether it may have gotten out of hand. I'll probably never know for sure.

Bobker ben Ali was a teacher in two community colleges and says Raymond's devotion to the Pasadena Playhouse and the Playbox Theater was really his devotion to Gilmor Brown and Lenore Shanewise, two people he dearly loved.

Raymond always felt Lenore Shanewise made a mistake when she did not grasp the opportunity to try her luck in New York as a director or producer of stage plays. He loved her very much and was sad when, in the late sixties, she moved away from Pasadena and settled in Laguna Beach, California.

Wondering what to do with her antiques, Shanewise remembered Raymond was a collector. She telephoned him and asked if he would be interested. Ray came over immediately, looked at them, and said, "I'll take all of them, including that portrait of you by painter Harold Streator."

Shanewise felt the portrait should belong to the Playhouse, however—if the Playhouse wanted it. She wrote Raymond a note stating she would like to have something to show that she had been some use to the Playhouse and had achieved some career accomplishments and would appreciate it if he would allow the Playhouse to have the portrait. Thereafter, the painting had a note attached to it stating it was on loan to the Pasadena Playhouse from Raymond Burr. The painting was one of his prized possessions.

In her oral history, Shanewise said,

> I had been in London and Europe and when I returned, Raymond said he had a role for me in one of the "Perry Mason" episodes. At the time I was staying in his Malibu home, that particular day. When Raymond came home he handed me his script.
>
> He said, "Lenore, if the producer approves of you, you're to play this role in 'The Case of the Fiery Fingers.' I played in several episodes and later when Raymond did his 'Ironside' series he used me in episodes of that too.
>
> He also promised to take me on a trip to his Fiji Island of Naitamba someday. I was one of eight people he invited to spend ten days at Pink Sands, Harbour Island, in the Bahamas. After that I went to South America.

Lenore died December 22, 1980, in a nursing home, at the age of 91.

Raymond, between film assignments, continued to make radio broadcasts during the daytime hours and appear in plays at night. Among the many other radio shows he did were "CBS Workshop," "Actor's Studio," "The Whistler," "Line-up," and "Dr. Kildare." Many times he disguised his voice so well it is difficult to prove he acted in them. Raymond worked for the Screen Director's Playhouse, first on radio and later on television. "Chicago Deadline" was broadcast with Alan Ladd playing his original role, and Jim Backus and Raymond Burr. Burr spoke only a few lines in this 30 minute show. "The Fighting O'Flynn," with Douglas Fairbanks, Jr., followed this one on April 7, 1950. Both tried to speak with Irish dialects. Then Raymond portrayed his original character of MacDonald in a 30 minute version of "Pitfall" for the Screen Director's Playhouse.

"The Line-up" was another successful radio show that aired from July 6, 1950, until 1953. The dramas, built around a police line-up, were fast, furious, and realistic. Raymond disguised his voice many times as he portrayed a variety of characters in the line-up or a detective or policeman questioning a suspect. Even in this half hour show, Raymond might have only a line or two of dialogue.

Other well known actors and actresses that played in "The Line-up" were Jeanette Nolan, Sheldon Leonard, and Bill Johnstone, who played Lt. Ben Guthrie. Wally Maher played Sgt. Matt Grebb, Ben's hotheaded, gruff sidekick who instructed the suspects in the line-up in a bored, monotone voice. The writers for this show were Blake Edwards, who later gained fame as a film producer, Morton Fine, and David Friedkin.

Jaime Del Valle was the producer and director who gathered his ideas for the scripts from newspaper stories and trips with the police on their beat. Writer Elliott Lewis was also a producer of this show, and the music was handled by Eddie Dunstedter.

Raymond performed in a few "Dragnet" episodes during 1950 but finally had to give up this series too, as he began to work in live television. Now, along with his other commitments, Raymond performed in many television dramas. One such drama introduced the daughter of Robert Montgomery, Elizabeth Montgomery, who made her debut in "Top Secret," with Raymond playing the lead in this episode of "Robert Montgomery Presents."

Jean Pierre Aumont recalls in his autobiography about the time he appeared in live television with Raymond Burr. They were doing "Crime and Punishment," and it was condensed into 26 minutes of air time. Aumont played Raskolnikov, while Raymond played Porphyre. Just as Aumont was to stab Raymond as the old usurper, a man stepped before the camera and nudged him aside to advertise Chesterfield cigarettes. Jean was then pushed back in front of the camera, where he continued to stab Raymond.

For "Stars Over Hollywood," Raymond did two productions and several short subjects for "ABC Dramatic Anthology." By now, most productions were on film, and very little live television was done anymore.

"Schlitz Playhouse of Stars" was an excellent television show, and Raymond, in between film assignments, appeared in quite a few plays over several years, including *The Ordeal of Dr. Sutton*, with Marilyn Erskine, shown on July 1, 1951. The public relations firm that handled the account destroyed all their records up to 1955, however, and no photos or press copies exist.

Raymond did plays for the "Gruen Playhouse," produced by ZIV-TV, plus other shows for different sponsors. One play, *The Mask of Medusa*, was done for "Twilight Theatre," and featured Steven Geray in the cast.

Raymond then took some time off to go to England to visit his son, now ten years old. He decided to bring the boy and Annette's parents to America and traveled around the country with them whenever he could get away from the film studio. He really got to know Michael Evan in the few months they had together. The excitement of a child's discovery of new and different things was new to Raymond.

Suddenly, however, Michael lost interest in everything and seemed tired all the time. Raymond thought perhaps he was homesick for England, but it was more than that. The doctor broke the news to Raymond and the grandparents that Michael had leukemia. He took Michael and the grandparents back to England, where shortly afterward Michael died at the age of 10 in 1953.

A saddened Raymond Burr returned to America, hiding his grief by going back to work. Fay Bainter was his costar in a television play for "Lux Video Theatre" titled "Shall Not Perish," a war drama. "The Immortal City," a Vatican film, was narrated by Raymond and was released to controversial reviews.

Raymond then signed for the lead in a Joe Parker production about Israel. His costar was to be Jeff Chandler, but *The Key to "54"* was never made under that name for 20th Century–Fox.

Meanwhile, Raymond's manager tried to put a package deal together to produce 26 films in the Philippines, Japan, and India, including 52 half hour telefilms for the "International Story Theatre." Due to the lack of financial backing, the project never came to fruition.

After hosting the Academy Awards telecast in 1953, Raymond left immediately for Korea. He joined an all-soldier entertainment unit and spent 25 days touring hospital and military installations throughout Japan, Italy, North Africa, Turkey, Greece, Israel, Spain, Azores, England, and France. Upon reaching England, he tried to get a play he had written, *Tell Her It's Adam*, produced. He had dreams of starring in it, but could get neither the backing nor a theater to stage the play and silently buried the manuscript in his suitcase. When he got back to the States, he put the manuscript away with other forgotten dreams.

Once Raymond got back to California, Paramount Studios signed him for a part in a Bob Hope farce titled *Casanova's Big Night*. Costumed in a frilly outfit of satin and a curly wig, Raymond was quickly disposed of in the first ten minutes of the film when he got in the way at the wrong time and Hope accidentally killed him with a sword.

For 20th Century–Fox, Raymond made *Gorilla at Large* in 3-D. The reviewers panned it, but Raymond played a good guy for a change. Anne Bancroft, Cameron Mitchell, Lee J. Cobb, and Lee Marvin were the other players. A rampaging carnival gorilla got loose and found his way to the top of a rollercoaster, where fireworks burst all around him. The audience was made a part of the action on the screen and was supposed to experience thrills and chills. The idea worked for a while, but the audiences did not like wearing the cardboard glasses. After a few more 3-D films were made, the process faded into oblivion.

One day Raymond was asked to appear on a Hollywood soundstage. He was given a script and sworn to secrecy about it. Raymond was paid $10,000 for about 24 hours of work on the film, and when completed, the film was flown to Japan, where the rest of the film had been shot, and his scenes were inserted. There were two versions, one in Japanese and one dubbed in English. All the precautions were taken because most of the film was made with miniature sets and was a spoof of the horror films being made by practically every studio. Monster movies were big box office attractions and moneymakers that year. Raymond was the only American in the film *Godzilla*. In later years, this film came to be considered a cult classic horror film and still shows up often on television.

Years later, Raymond told a reporter,

> The first *Godzilla* was done in the USA. The producers bought the rights to the Japanese picture, cut it, edited it and shot my scenes in a tiny studio on Los Angeles's Vermont Avenue. We had every scene in that small studio, including the mountains, the climbing scenes. The hospital scenes, the hotel scenes, with me looking out the window watching *Godzilla* destroying Tokyo. It was all done in that one little studio.

The producers hired Japanese-Americans to help blend Raymond's scenes into the action with the original Japanese cast. He was worried about working against the language barrier. The producers assured him that the actors would be Japanese-American.

"Well, 99 percent of them didn't speak English," Raymond said. "I almost went out of my mind!

"I wanted them to give me part ownership of the picture, but they refused."

VII

Rear Window, *and* the Roles Get Better

Raymond had made 38 films by the time he filmed *Khyber Patrol*. He played an East Indian again and tried to steal a new invention, the Gatling gun, from Richard Egan, the hero. Raymond is killed by the gun in a battle with the hero and his loyal troops.

Rear Window was the only time Raymond worked with the great director Alfred Hitchcock. He had signed a contract to act in the film, but before he reported for work, he went to Korea. When he returned to the States, he filmed his scenes, and the picture was released in 1954.

His role was a powerful one. Throughout the film the viewer sees him only through the eyes, or the binoculars, of Jimmy Stewart. Most of the time the audience *sees* but never *hears* Raymond speak, until the end of the film.

James Stewart is confined to a wheelchair with a broken leg in a cast up to his hip. To while away the hours he uses his binoculars to spy on his neighbors across a courtyard and discovers a man (Raymond Burr) planning to murder his nagging wife. Grace Kelly is caught in Raymond's apartment taking his wife's ring as evidence. The police reprimand her and let her go. Raymond, however, realizes who is spying on him and goes to Stewart's apartment, where Stewart sets off flashbulbs to blind him. Raymond tackles Stewart and pushes him out the rear window, causing the other leg to break in the fall. Wendell Corey, the detective, arrests Raymond for his wife's murder.

For this role, Raymond had to be padded, since he had lost some weight while traveling in foreign countries. His hair was bleached white and cut very short. He wore gold rimmed glasses and stooped like a worn-out salesman who carried two heavy suitcases when he made his rounds. Raymond finally received recognition for his powerful and chilling performance. He received rave notices for his portrayal of the wife murderer.

Right after the film opened all over the country, Raymond went to Europe, where character actors are often more revered than the stars, and

Raymond Burr the wife murderer as seen through the binoculars of Jimmy Stewart (*Rear Window*, 1954).

was mobbed by fans who had seen it. Raymond told an interviewer, "In Germany I found myself with the same billing as Jimmy and Grace and did a great many interviews. They would announce me as Raymond Burr in Alfred Hitchcock's *Rear Window*. I heard it in France, Germany, Italy, Portugal, England, Spain, and some parts of the United States; everywhere I went." Years later, when the movie was released in reruns in theaters and on television, the same thing happened to Raymond, only now the adoration was worldwide.

During the filming of the movie Raymond and Hitchcock could be seen huddled in animated conversation. They would look at one of the actors in the cast, then continue their conversation with a smile or a hardy laugh. No one knew what was so funny or what the mysterious conversations were about. They were playing a practical joke on the rest of the cast, as it turned out.

Raymond recalled a practical joke he played on Hitchcock:

> At Universal Studios I was given Rock Hudson's old dressing room, which had been redecorated and made into a bungalow in case I wanted to live in the studio while making the early "Perry Masons."

That bungalow was right next to Hitchcock's old complex and my kitchen looked on the place where he parked his car. They had tours going past my kitchen and one day I suddenly had an idea. I had a big cutout made of Hitchcock. It took three weeks because it was a life size blowup. Then I fixed the shutters so that his hand looked poised like he was waving. Another three weeks were needed to light the blowup so it was perfect. I had the tour guides say as they went by, "Look! There's Alfred Hitchcock in Raymond Burr's rear window." Finally, about six months later, I got a note from Alfred, from next door saying, "Raymond, it's been six months, I think it's enough!"
So I took it down, but it was just great.

Raymond severely injured his leg in a chase scene in *Passion*. While he was being treated at the hospital, the script was rewritten to explain his limping. This time he portrayed a Spanish policeman in old California. Cornel Wilde's "passion" was to hunt down the killers of his entire family. Yvonne De Carlo played twins: Wilde's dead wife and his sister-in-law. De Carlo and Raymond pursue Wilde and the other villains into the Sierra Madres. The colorful scenery was beautiful but the screenplay was weak, wasting the talents of many fine actors and actresses.

At Christmas 1954, Raymond was about to leave for the Alaskan bases where U.S. armed forces were stationed when Minerva came to tell him she was rejoining his father and they had decided to remarry. Raymond was overjoyed; he knew they had been in touch with each other over the years. Son Edmond had been the instigator in this reunion. They were remarried in Seattle, although Minerva and William understood why Raymond did not attend the ceremony: he did not want to spoil the happy moment for them by bringing with him the inevitable reporters and photographers. They returned to New Westminster, British Columbia, to live in their ancestral home. William's mother had died at the age of 102, and he had inherited the home. In later years when they could no longer maintain the home, William decided to sell the hundred year old house and move into an apartment.

Sometime during 1954, Raymond met and fell in love with Andrina Laura Morgan. Andrina was not an actress nor was she interested in show business. When Raymond was free of filming for a length of time, the couple were married, and they made elaborate plans for a honeymoon.

Suddenly Andrina took sick. Once again Raymond received the bad news from the doctor: His wife had cancer. Andrina had been the picture of good health before they were wed. Sadly, the cancer spread quickly, and Andrina died.

Once more tragedy struck Raymond a powerful blow. He never married again, although there were other women in his life. He shied away from commitments, fearing another death blow to someone he dearly cared for. He also kept to himself about women he had dated. In later years he was

asked to tell all in a book about the
women in his life. He said only that
he had had contact with many
women all his life and loved some
of them deeply.

Raymond concentrated on his
work, becoming more absorbed in
the roles he portrayed. He played
them with such intensity and energy
that the audiences were torn between hating him or sympathizing
with him. More and more, Raymond transformed himself into the
character he was portraying.

In the films where Raymond
portrayed characters who were
Asian, Arab, East Indian, and the
like, he usually wore a sword or a
dagger of some type in the waist-
band of his fancy trousers. When it
came to a showdown in hand to
hand combat, however, he never
got a chance to use the weapon in
self defense. Inevitably, he would
be killed before he could reach for
it.

For every excellent, meaty role
Raymond had, a couple of bad
films would surely follow. A case in
point was *They Were So Young*,
starring Scott Brady. Raymond, as
usual, is the villain in a South American port. This time he uses women,
disguised as models, as slaves.
Murder and mayhem contribute to
the flimsy plot. He is caught by the
hero and pays for his crimes, but at
least he is not killed by the end of the movie.

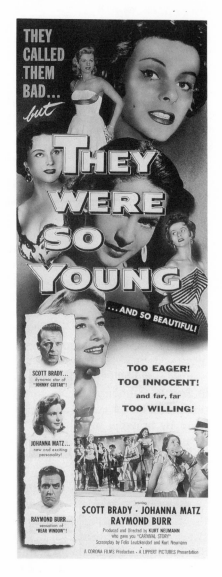

Poster for *They Were So Young*.

The next dud to follow that one was a remake of *The Major and the
Minor*. The original had been an excellent movie with Ginger Rogers. This
film, titled *You're Never Too Young*, featured the team of Dean Martin and
Jerry Lewis. Raymond, the gangster, robs a hotel of some diamonds and
hides them in Martin's pocket. Somehow they wind up in Lewis's pocket,

and Raymond chases the pair all over the place. He pursues Lewis through a train, a girls' school, musical numbers, and a funny motorboat chase. The film ends with Lewis up a tree and Raymond in jail.

From a comic role to a nasty role again, Raymond took on Van Heflin in *Count Three and Pray*. Filmed in wide screen Cinemascope, this costume drama takes place after the Civil War ends and the soldiers return home to start life anew. The beauty and the majesty of the land and closeup background scenery appear in vivid Technicolor.

Raymond played a bitter, snarling individual who vented undue cruelty on Van Heflin. He wore a leather glove on the wooden hand he had lost in the war and took great pleasure in having his men beat Heflin severely and often. The townspeople finally get enough courage to turn against Raymond and rally around the bloodied but undefeated hero. A young Joanne Woodward portrayed a backwoods teenage tomboy who steals the movie from Van Heflin and Raymond. Raymond got the girl at the end of the film—not the girl he wanted, of course, but the one he is forced to marry.

That meaty role was followed by a mediocre one in a Ray Milland film, *A Man Alone*. Milland tried to produce, direct, and act in this run-of-the-mill horse opera and wound up with just a tired Western. Even with Ward Bond and Raymond Burr trying their best, this one became a second feature on theater marquees. Raymond the villain went to jail, Milland got the girl (Mary Murphy), and Bond went back to being sheriff.

Between 1955 and 1956, Raymond was gaining weight again; when he played Jumbo Means in *Great Day in the Morning*, he really looked the part. Raymond was as mean as his name implied in yet another Civil War saga. He wreaks havoc upon Robert Stack, the hero, and Virginia Mayo. He threatens Ruth Roman, and anyone else who gets in his way, with his pistols. He kills Roman and for his crimes is run over by a gold laden wagon. As he lies under the wagon, it is blown to bits from dynamite thrown to prevent the gold getting into the wrong hands.

Raymond was a nasty bank robber in *The Secret of Treasure Mountain*. He fought with everyone in the film, including the star, William Prince. He battles fiercely with a Native American actor and in one ferocious clash, Raymond loses his balance and falls off the mountain to his death.

When he started to film *A Cry in the Night*, Raymond dated his costar, Natalie Wood. She was 17 and he 38 when the romance started to gather headlines and unwarranted publicity in fan magazines and newspapers. Raymond taught her to enjoy good music, books, and plays, and they enjoyed each other's company at Hollywood parties. Raymond said years later, "I took Natalie out on dates. I was very much attracted to her and I think she was attracted to me. Maybe I was too old for her, but pressures were put on both of us from the outside and the studio. It finally got very awkward for us to go around together."

The studio tried to break up the romance because they wanted to keep Wood's sweet, all–American girl image. In real life, she dated Nick Adams, Robert Wagner, and others. In an interview, Raymond said he did not think she would marry Wagner, but the studio pressured Wood and Raymond to break up their romance. Deeply hurt by this command, they parted as friends after the movie was completed and about to be released all over the country.

In the movie, Raymond played a psychopath who watches Natalie and her boyfriend (Richard Anderson) as they sit in a car in lover's lane. Raymond knocks out Richard with his lunch pail when they catch him watching them, then picks up Natalie and socks her in the jaw, knocking her out, too. They hide in an abandoned brickyard while her father (Edmond O'Brien) rants and raves about teenagers in parked cars at lover's lane. The police, led by Brian Donlevy, hunt for the two of them. When Raymond is finally caught, O'Brien beats him up while Raymond screams for Mom to come help him. Raymond expressed emotion with his hands and eyes, readily understood by the audience to the degree he conveyed sympathy rather than hatred. Actor Alan Ladd produced this film and narrated the beginning and the end of the movie.

Not long afterward Natalie Wood married Robert Wagner, and eventually divorced him, married someone else, divorced him, and remarried Wagner. Both remained friends with Raymond until Wood's tragic death. She had a deep fear of water, and it is ironic that she met her death by drowning, trying to get into a dinghy that was tied to the yacht she and Wagner owned. The newspapers were full of headlines and stories of Wood's drinking and arguing with Wagner and another actor on the boat. In a huff, she had decided to go ashore and back to their house. Her body washed up on the Catalina shore the following morning.

After Raymond and Wood were forced to break up, he dated other actresses such as Debra Paget and Pier Angeli. Fan magazines, newspapers, and cheap tabloids brought up their romance from time to time, but Raymond remained friends with Robert Wagner and appeared in a cameo role in one of Wagner's television series.

In his next film, Raymond was back in jail again. Wanted posters, offering a big reward for him, were plastered all over the territory. Desperado Burr escaped the jail, killing a few innocent people who got in his way. Hugh O'Brien played a Wyatt Earp–type character in *The Brass Legend*, chasing Raymond on foot and on horseback. Each kept shooting at the other, but somehow always missed. Both finally wound up on top of a hill, exhausted. One final shot by each of them kills Raymond and wounds O'Brien. Not a spectacular Western, but it was well acted by both men.

Before Raymond would start another film, he flew to Canada to visit his parents. Minerva had undergone several operations on her legs. After

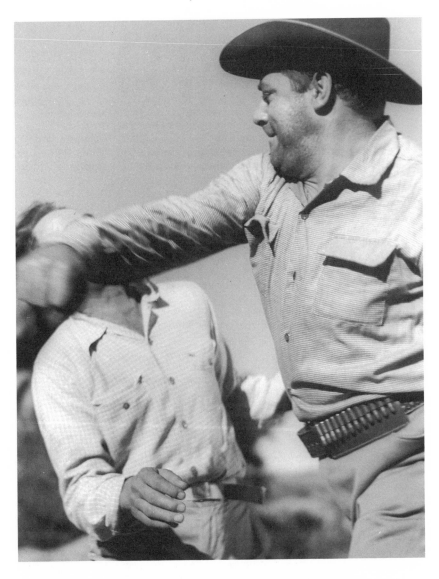

William Prince is clouted on the jaw by bulky Raymond Burr in this scene from Columbia's *Secret of Treasure Mountain*.

she left the hospital, she spent a great deal of time in a wheelchair until she was well enough to use crutches and later two canes. Although she had lost her sight due to diabetes, an operation had restored it and she wore thick glasses. She had also suffered a stroke.

Raymond told Valerie Sutherland in a Paris interview in December

1989 that he didn't believe in socialized medicine as practiced in Canada. He detailed the care his mother and father were given.

When my mother had a stroke and she was taken through the system, I let it go because she had gone back to Canada and remarried my father years before. She wasn't being cared for properly. She was a woman that never should have lost complete control of one side, her face or the rest of her body. Never! The stroke was not that bad she did because they left her and there were no rehabilitation centers there. This is Vancouver, British Columbia, where the medicine is supposed to be as great as Toronto and they have a two year residency, all those things.

The apartment became too confining for a wheelchair, so I found a cottage at Boundary Bay for them, all on one floor with a chance to go outdoors and tend to their flower garden. Satisfied they could get along without me and were in control of their lives, I returned to California.

I finally brought my mother to California and my father finally came down and they lived their final ten years with me. I saw to it she had rehabilitation at a time when it was very difficult and very painful for her, but she walked! Not very well, but she was out of her wheelchair, which made a difference to someone who had to be wheeled and sometimes carried to the bathroom and was not able to use her side. It meant having someone who wasn't always qualified to care for her. Then she suffered another stroke but was healed with the medicine and the treatment she got.

Then she got cancer and managed to live four more years. It was a miracle she lasted as long as she did. I was happy she was in California when she died January 31, 1974, and she is buried in California.

My father went back to Canada. He never had been in a hospital in his life until he was 90 and had his first operation. He didn't do very well so he had another operation. Then—he had another operation to fix those other two! That's stupid! Then he became very ill and wasn't going to live.

I would go up to Canada to see him each time he was sick no matter where I was in the world.

My mother was the one who gave her life to us and my father. My father was a marvelous human being but he was duped by his family and his mother. He stayed where he was, living with his mother, stayed with the same firm, the same town. He was solid. We were not. There is no bitterness because of his life-style. My mother sent me up to Canada to see him every single year. He didn't pay for those trips. She did. She never wanted me to lose sight of the fact he was my father. His relatives came first before my brother or sister or my mother. He didn't want to be in the United States. They had a reasonable time together. Not a great time—it should have been a marvelous time for them.

My mother had gone so far education wise, world wise, and knowledge wise. She had done so much with her life and he had stayed exactly the same.

My mother and I had a very unusual arrangement. We were not only mother and son but great friends. I'm the only one of the three children that stayed with her constantly during the depression years when food and money were scarce.

After ten years in the business, Raymond finally reached stardom. In 1956 he made *Please Murder Me*, with Angela Lansbury, and was once again slim, handsome, and the good guy!

For the third time he portrayed a lawyer, this time defending Lansbury against murder charges. Through legal trickery, he proves she did not kill her husband (Dick Foran) and manages to get her acquitted. He falls in love with her and proposes marriage, only to find out she is two-timing him and bragging how she killed her husband. He knows he can not bring her to trial again for the same murder. So he ruthlessly sets out to torment her so successfully she falls into his trap. He forces Lansbury to kill him, but not before he leaves enough evidence and a tape recording of their conversation for the police to find her and convict her of *his* murder. This well-written screenplay provided an excellent part for Raymond and the beginning of a new image.

Alas, this good film was followed by another so-so one, *Ride the High Iron*. Don Taylor and Sally Forrest play the love interests in this film. Raymond had top billing, but the two young players took over the film. He portrays a public relations man being paid to keep Forrest's name out of the headlines. He hires Taylor to keep her in tow and regrets this when she begins to fall in love with him. All three were wasted in this drawing room drama. Taylor gave up acting to direct television and theater films. Forrest faded into oblivion after making a few more low-key films.

Raymond, however, went on to bigger and better roles in many films and great parts in radio plays.

VIII

Radio Shows, Movies End, Quest for "Perry Mason"

Lester Salkow, Raymond's agent, set up a company they called Bursal Productions. They planned to make three independent films in which Raymond could star. *Listen World* was based on a script about Korea written by Raymond. He also wrote the other screenplays in treatment form: *The Black Wind* and *The Day the Sky Went Out of Its Mind*. He planned to play two sympathetic characters and a "heavy." Hoping to get financing, Raymond came to New York to sell his ideas. He did not succeed in this venture, and the films were never made. Meanwhile, he continued broadcasting on radio shows.

One of the great shows on radio during the 1956-57 season was the "CBS Workshop." It was called "Theatre of the Mind," dedicated to the human imagination. William Conrad was the announcer. One special episode was done by Sen. John F. Kennedy.

One of the best broadcasts Raymond did for the "CBS Workshop" was called "Silent Witness." His voice is the only one heard throughout the half hour drama. Sound effects play an important part in this piece. Raymond is a lawyer questioning a woman who has witnessed a murder. She is in a state of shock and cannot speak to him. As he questions her, she writes her answers on a piece of paper. Raymond then reads her answers aloud to the jammed courtroom. Summing up the case, he insists she disclose who the murderer is. Her pencil breaks, dropping from her trembling hand. He hands her his pen, which has green ink in it. Suddenly she writes, "You are the murderer!"

Another memorable play for the "Workshop" was titled *Gettysburg*. Raymond narrated this powerful drama and acted the part of a general conferring with other key generals as well as addressing the troops camped at Gettysburg.

As if Raymond was not busy enough making these shows and films, he took on a new radio series for CBS. "Fort Laramie" was a transcribed series produced a week or two in advance of the actual air date. It began on January 22, 1956, and ran for 38 episodes, with two excellent ones repeated.

The final episode was broadcast on October 28, 1956. Raymond portrayed Capt. Lee Quince of the U.S. Cavalry. The Indians were portrayed as human beings. The dramas were about life on the Wyoming frontier. Sound effects were done by perfectionists who had also worked on the radio version of "Gunsmoke," with William Conrad.

Norman MacDonnell produced both radio shows. He also narrated the "Laramie" show. Raymond read most of his lines seated in a wheelchair; he was recuperating from an operation on his leg to correct an earlier injury sustained while he was making the film *Passion*. No one suspected Raymond was doing love scenes with Virginia Gregg for the episode "Willa's Romance" from a wheelchair. Nor did the audience ever know he led his troops out of Fort Laramie into the wild frontier from a wheelchair.

"Climax" was a live television show broadcast from Hollywood's CBS-TV studios. Raymond did "The Sound of Silence" on March 1, 1956, with Jean Pierre Aumont and Lloyd Bridges. On May 24, 1956, Raymond acted in "The Shadow of Evil" with Jan Sterling and Richard Boone. "Savage Portrait" followed on December 6, 1956, with Joanne Woodward and John Cassavetes.

Then one day in April 1956, between all his activities, Raymond heard tests were being made for various roles for a television show to be called "Perry Mason." He made the tests along with hundreds of other actors. Gail Patrick Jackson wanted him for the role of prosecuting adversary. Raymond asked if he could also make a test for the Perry Mason role. He was told to lose weight and come back. Dieting strenuously for the next few weeks, Raymond got his weight down to 210 pounds. He was 40 years old, and was picked out of the 50 finalists who auditioned. Raymond had not planned on auditioning for the Perry Mason role, but for the part of Hamilton Burger, the district attorney.

David L. Stanley of Oakland, New Jersey, recalls the dinner he and his wife enjoyed with Raymond the night after the auditions.

> "It was a most interesting audition," was the way he opened the conversation with me and Patricia. We were having dinner at a restaurant in San Pedro, California. Ray was complaining the sauce on his shrimp cocktail was too hot while continuing to tell us what happened.
> "I had gone to the audition with the idea of trying out for the Hamilton Burger part," Raymond said.
> "But when I arrived, Erle Stanley Gardner, the author of the Perry Mason books, who was sitting in on the auditions saw me and simply said, 'He's Perry Mason.'"
> Those words were worth a million dollars to Raymond Burr.

Each actor who read for the part of Perry was completely dominated and overshadowed by Burr. No one topped his strong personality. That's why Gardner picked him.

Stanley continued.

At the dinner, our conversation ranged to how someone who up to that time had been in over 82 movies, started his career. Burr explained that as a young man his health had been none too good. As a result, Raymond spent a lot of time trying to build himself up while working in the Forestry Service in the vicinity of Mount Lassen and Mount Shasta, in northern California. He spent much of his time reading Shakespeare, and subsequently went to England, where he studied drama.

My curiosity was, however, that while working in the Forestry Service, Raymond met my great uncle, Charles Love, who had been the fish and game warden in Lassen and Shasta counties for more than four decades.

My recollections are that Raymond performed at about 12 missile sites and antiaircraft gun locations in the Los Angeles area just before Christmas 1956. The most notable of these was at Mount Disappointment Nike Base, located in the mountains north of and overlooking Pasadena. It was here that along with a small four or five piece combo made up of military musicians that a Christmas carol sing-along took place. Given a crystal-clear night, the lights of the city below set an ideal scene for that.

Our conversation then shifted to the subject I was more concerned with at the time. It was a continuance of a tour of the Nike Air Defense Missile Sites surrounding the Los Angeles area.

As a noncommissioned officer in charge of the public information office of the 47th Air Defense Brigade at Fort MacArthur, it was my job to arrange internal publicity to the command units. Raymond Burr did *not* want any public promotion of his trip.

Raymond explained, "I prefer to work the small locations that rarely get the kind of entertainment that big military units get."

Raymond's entertainment at the Nike sites generally consisted of about an hour to an hour and a half of skits worked out with military entertainers—and individual conversations. Often the skits were of the slapstick variety, using two-dozen towels and as many whipped cream pies in the face—Raymond's!

The shows were presented to as many men as possible at each hundred-man site, and the actual job of escorting Burr on his tour of sites around Los Angeles and later Central California fell to Spc-4 James E. Enright of the Brigade's public information office.

Ray presented his show to as few as ten people in the audience at Van Nuys, California. His slapstick performance usually took place in the unit's mess hall, as was normally the case; only in one instance did we have a stage set-up for him.

On another occasion, Jim Enright and I accompanied Raymond to his Malibu home for coffee and refreshments. Burr, an aficionado of many things, particularly liked good coffee and had a blend ground to his own specifications. Spectacular is my reflection of the flavor.

Raymond did everything around the house including keeping the land in tiptop shape.

Raymond's life was about to change in 1957. He had signed a contract with Universal Studios to make three movies. On the strength of that contract, Raymond bought a newly built Malibu house on top of a cliff overlooking the Pacific Ocean. The Hollywood studio was only about an hour's drive away. He rarely got to enjoy his home, however, since he was constantly working or traveling overseas.

Several films he had made were released around the country at about the same time. The first, *Crime of Passion*, costarred Barbara Stanwyck and Sterling Hayden. Raymond is the chief of detectives, and Hayden a lowly detective. Stanwyck plays the ambitious newspaperwoman who marries Hayden and makes up her mind to get him promoted. He, on the other hand, just wants to do his job and stay where he is.

At the chief's house party she meets the Chief of Detectives Pope (Burr) and tries to use her wiles on him, but he is wise to her. Raymond is more worried about his ailing wife, played by Fay Wray, who is in the hospital. In his despair, he visits Stanwyck as a friend he can talk to. She immediately goes to work on him. In a moment of passion, Raymond is caught in her web. Soon Hayden is sent on out-of-town assignments. He becomes aware of what is going on only when a fellow detective starts making remarks about his wife, which result in a fistfight in Pope's office that other detectives witness. Raymond must reprimand both men, knowing full well what the fight is all about.

Stanwyck insists Raymond meet her at a discreet restaurant, where she continues to demand he make Hayden his successor. Raymond tells her he has already decided to pick the detective who fought with Hayden as his successor. He also ends their affair, realizing it was his fault they were caught in this messy business. As soon as he can have his wife released from the hospital, he intends to retire to Hawaii.

Later that evening, Stanwyck is at the police station with Hayden and spies a gun that has been used in a recent robbery lying on the desk and about to be put in the property room and identified and tagged. She pretends to be dizzy, and while the officer fetches a glass of water, she puts the gun under her coat.

Raymond finally arrives home only to discover Stanwyck waiting for him. She creates a scene outside his house, forcing him to bring her inside. He talks to her while mixing drinks. She suddenly appears in the doorway and shoots him in the head with the stolen gun.

Calmly she returns home and goes to bed. In the early hours of the morning, Hayden receives a call and is given the news of the chief's death. Hours later, he returns home to escort Stanwyck back to headquarters, where she is charged with Burr's murder.

Newspapers and fan magazines conjured a romance between Stanwyck and Raymond to further publicize the movie. They did date occasionally,

Crime of Passion, 1957.

but there was no heavy romance, and they remained friends throughout the years.

Raymond made one more feature film in which he is murdered. This one was called *Affair in Havana*, and he played the role entirely from a wheelchair. The film was made in and around Havana, Cuba, before the Castro regime. Raymond portrayed a snarling, cruel, vengeful man, screaming

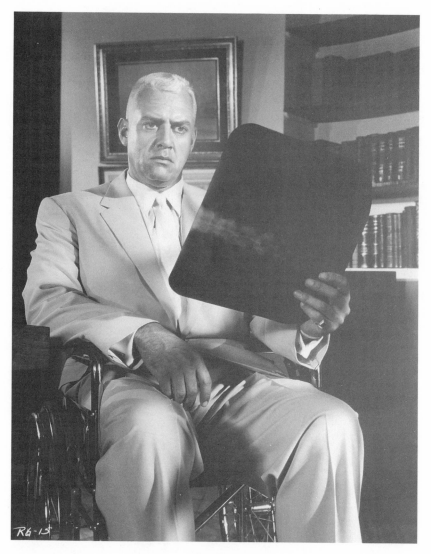

Affair in Havana, 1957. **Burr played the entire role in a wheelchair.**

at anyone and everyone at the top of his lungs. For this role his hair was cropped in a crewcut and bleached white. His wife, played by Sara Shane, had severely injured him in a motorboat accident. Raymond felt she had set out to kill him by deliberately steering the boat onto some rocks. John Cassavetes was billed as the star, but Raymond stole the picture from him with his performance. Cassavetes seemed to walk through the movie in a constant daze while Raymond genuinely portrayed the bitter old man.

He took great pleasure in tormenting Sara Shane, since he suspected she was having an affair with Cassavetes. While arguing by the swimming pool, they were watched by a devoted servant, who could not stand Raymond's treatment of Sara. In a fit of anger, the servant pushed Raymond, wheelchair and all, into the swimming pool. The servant then jumped into the pool and proceeded to drown Raymond while Sara looked on and did nothing to stop him.

The police arrested the servant for Burr's murder. The servant's wife killed Sara. Cassavetes went back to playing the piano in a Havana nightclub as if the entire affair never happened. The scenery and the Latin music were marvelous; the story was not.

This was the last film Raymond made for many years. The pattern of his being killed in movies stopped for the time being. His life was about to change.

IX

Enter "Perry Mason"

Raymond had to curtail many of his various jobs in radio, television, and movies when he entered another phase of his career that was to bring him fame and fortune. Throughout 1956, the producers were looking for the right man to play Perry Mason. A great many actors made tests for the role. Even Fred MacMurray was suggested, although Erle Stanley Gardner, the author of the Perry Mason books, had never seen any of MacMurray's films and did not know who he was. Pierre Salinger suggested Richard Egan for the part. On and on it went until Cornwall Jackson, the producer, remembered seeing Raymond Burr perform in *A Place in the Sun*.

Raymond had read bits and pieces of news about the forthcoming show in *TV Guide*, as well as in newspapers and magazines. He knew they were casting the "Perry Mason" show and went to try out for the Hamilton Burger part. Asked to read and make the test for the district attorney's role, Raymond requested to test for the starring role too. This time Erle Stanley Gardner was sitting in on auditions, and when Raymond appeared, announced firmly, "Raymond Burr *is* Perry Mason." Gail Patrick Jackson and her husband, Cornwall, objected vehemently, but Gardner was adamant.

Raymond was given a contract and a bungalow once occupied by Mae West. Shooting began in early 1956, and 39 episodes were completed and ready to sell to a sponsor. Gail Patrick Jackson had told Raymond and Barbara Hale (Della Street) they would be filming only 18 episodes when they signed their contracts, but as filming progressed, the producers realized they had a good show to offer the sponsors. The Jacksons continued to film another 21 episodes.

Gardner knew what he wanted and threw out many scripts before he was satisfied to film the one finally put on screen. The Jacksons voiced many objections to the great deal of money lost, but Gardner had the final say in most matters. He had seen what the studios did to the movie *The Velvet Claw*, based on his story, and he was not going to let anyone spoil his scripts this time. He allowed the television series to be made only if he gave

Raymond Burr as Perry Mason, 1957.

approval of everything to be filmed. He laid down strict rules and regulations, and the Jacksons finally admitted he knew what he was talking about.

From 1951 until 1956 there were four Perry Masons: radio actors Bartlett Robinson, Santos Ortega, Don Briggs, and John Larkin. Robinson and Larkin appeared in the television version as character actors.

In April 1957, the print media announced that "Perry Mason" would replace the "Jackie Gleason Show." On August 26, 1957, they said it was going to be placed against NBC's "Perry Como Show." On September 3, 1957, Purex and Libby Owens Ford signed on as sponsors. The time slot was set for Saturday nights, from 7:30 to 8:30 P.M. The actual premier date was set for September 21, 1957, with the first episode, "The Case of the Restless Redhead." Whitney Blake portrayed the restless redhead. The first review by Daku for *Variety* said, "Raymond Burr played Perry Mason with finesse, suavity, and conviction. A good choice! He has the ability to stare down a criminal."

Raymond settled down to the problems at hand after "Perry Mason" slowly gained popularity. Between 1956 and April 1957, he worked six days a week filming the episodes and spent the seventh memorizing the next script. He also spent his free time in law courts studying the procedures and poring over lawbooks to absorb the technical language used. He literally became the character, devoting his life to the part. He lived seven days a week in a trailer and later in the bungalow given to him on the set. Occasionally he was able to get a weekend off to spend at his new Malibu home, escaping when the show went on hiatus.

Raymond earned every penny of his salary, sacrificing his personal life for the show. Rarely did he take time off to socialize, attend nightclubs, or premieres, or take a vacation. He played Perry when he suffered from colds, sore throats, high fevers, and exhaustion severe enough to put him in the hospital many times over the years. He got about four or five hours of sleep at night, rising at four in the morning to get ready for the day's work. While Raymond shaved, a man went over and over the script with him, giving him cues and prompting the pages of dialogue he had to memorize each day. He existed on coffee and cigarettes all day and one big meal at night.

The television version initially cost $150,000 per episode and was made in black and white. In the nine years of filming, the cost rose to $300,000 per episode.

Only one episode was made in color, at CBS president William Paley's insistence. If the show had gone to the tenth year, the rest would have been made in color. Paley never saw the color episode, however, Raymond told a reporter. It was shown once, on February 27, 1966, and the series was cancelled in May of that year.

On rare occasions Gardner would turn up at the studio, since he seldom saw the show until it appeared on the television at his ranch. "Erle did read and offer advice on scripts," said Gail Patrick Jackson. "He was wisely constructive and stimulating in his own sympathetic way, and we all called him the Master. He would only suggest, but would not rewrite another's script. Erle was a narration writer, not a scriptwriter. Sometimes there would be 18 scripts in the works, accepted but not good enough to film, according to Erle's standards. All this strict attention to details paid off in the long run."

The "Perry Mason" series won two Emmy Awards for 1959 and 1960, as did Raymond Burr and Barbara Hale. In the ensuing years the show has grossed between $1 million and $5 million and is shown in more than one hundred countries and dubbed in many languages including Malay, Chinese, Yiddish, Arabic, Thai, and Japanese and is subtitled in many more. No matter where you go, even into the jungles of Africa and South America, if a television set is available, you can bet "Perry Mason" will be shown sometime, somewhere.

Raymond went to great lengths never to interrupt the filming of the episodes. He suffered ailments both minor and major, including an accident that happened on one of his many trips to Vietnam to entertain the troops. He went there whenever the show was on hiatus rather than taking a rest or vacation. He was in a helicopter flying to one of the outposts when it crashed. Trying to wrench the door open, he tore the ligaments in his shoulder and had to wear an arm and shoulder cast that also covered his massive chest for three months.

The wardrobe department devised a way to get around the cast by having him wear larger shirts and suit jackets. Viewers thought he was gaining weight again. In "The Case of the Loquacious Liar," which aired December 13, 1960, Raymond's arm is in the cast; at one point he tries to raise it to a more comfortable position and winces with pain. The dialogue refers to it as an old war injury that flared up when Lieutenant Tragg posed the question. The cast was still on when he left for a publicity tour of Australia.

In nine years, 271 episodes were filmed and six were done with guest stars filling in for Raymond when he went into the hospital on December 10, 1962, for major surgery.

Scenes were shot in the hospital room with Raymond either in bed or a chair while talking on the phone to the guest star to give viewers the impression that this was all part of the episode.

He had been diagnosed with potentially cancerous intestinal polyps, which turned out to be benign. A part of his intestines was cut away and a Dacron tube inserted.

During his long recuperative period, the following guest stars came to his rescue: Bill Williams, "The Case of the Bluffing Blast," January 10, 1963; Kent Smith, "The Case of the Prankish Professor," January 17, 1963; Bette Davis, "The Case of the Constant Doyle," January 31, 1963; Michael Rennie, "The Case of the Libelous Locket," February 7, 1963; Hugh O'Brien, "The Case of the Two-Faced Turnabout," February 14, 1963; and Walter Pidgeon, "The Case of the Surplus Suitor," February 28, 1963. Raymond returned for the March 7 episode.

Mike Connors subbed for Raymond in "The Case of the Bullied Bowler," November 5, 1964, when he had infected teeth. Barry Sullivan stood in for Raymond in "The Case of the Thermal Thief," January 14, 1965, when Raymond became ill again. Barbara Hale was out the entire month of March 1964. The scriptwriters got around her absence by saying she was off visiting an aunt. Gertie, the receptionist and telephone operator, became Perry's secretary during that time.

William Talman played his Hamilton Burger role on crutches when his broken leg was in a cast. Later he was arrested on a morals charge, and CBS invoked a standard morals clause and suspended him. He had been at a party that was raided. He was arrested, but the judge threw the case out of court for lack of evidence that there was anything going on except a nude party. Although Talman was proved innocent of anything but being in the wrong place at the wrong time, CBS refused to take him back. Episodes were written with various attorneys taking his place and or Perry going out of town or the country to defend someone.

Raymond was stubborn, too. He sent wires and letters to the officials of the CBS affiliated stations, asking them to bring pressure on the network. He personally answered every letter he got protesting the network's stand in the matter. He refused to let the studio clean out Bill's belongings or remove his parking space sign. His coffee cup stayed in the niche.

In December 1960, Bill was reinstated with a new contract and an increase in salary. Next day a banner with "Welcome Home, Bill" and other messages ordered by Raymond were all over the lot. Gail Patrick Jackson, Raymond Burr, and the cast and crew had successfully pleaded with CBS to bring Talman back.

In later years Talman appeared to have laryngitis. He died of lung cancer in 1968 after filming a passionate plea, on behalf of the American Cancer Society, telling people to stop smoking. The message caused a controversy when it was shown on television before and after his death.

Toward the last years of the show, Ray Collins suffered from emphysema, forcing him to retire from his role as Lieutenant Tragg when it became obvious he was too ill to continue. Collins died in 1963, but his name was left on the credits and his coffee cup was left in the niche until the series ended and the cup was given to his widow.

William Hopper, who played private detective Paul Drake, seemed to be the healthiest one in the group, but he died of a heart condition and pneumonia at age 55, on March 8, 1970. He was followed by Erle Stanley Gardner on March 11, 1970, at the age of 80. Five years after "Perry Mason" had been garnering all kinds of awards and recognition, Gardner told a reporter, "He's granite hard and cow-eyed, but you got to hand it to Raymond, he got to be a damn good lawyer!"

Early in 1963, Wesley Lau replaced Ray Collins in the role of Lieuten-

William Talman, Raymond Burr, and Virginia Field in "The Case of the Prodigal Parent."

ant Anderson. After Collins died, Lau became a regular member of the cast and was replaced by Richard Anderson as Lt. Steve Drumm for the last year of the show. Sergeant Brice was first portrayed by Chuck Webster and was replaced by Lee Miller, Raymond's stand-in and cribbage partner. Miller was also used as a bit player in minor roles until the end of the series.

Barbara Hale portrayed Della Street, the perfect secretary. She was often the butt of Raymond's practical jokes because she could scream so piercingly. To get even with him one day, Barbara took small personal items from Raymond's dressing room. She gift wrapped them, and put them back, one at a time, a few days later. Her attempts were mild compared to Raymond's retaliation. He stripped her dressing room of everything in it—the sofa, chairs, her shoes, clothing, everything down to the smallest item—and crated, boxed, and wrapped each item separately with fancy bows and ribbons, and shipped it all to her home in the valley. The rooms bulged with the packages, and husband Bill Williams and the three children could not even move around. Barbara screamed at Raymond to have everything put back or she was calling *her* lawyer.

The original cast of "Perry Mason" (back row, from left): Ray Collins, William Talman; (front row) Barbara Hale, Raymond Burr, William Hopper, 1957.

"Cost me over a hundred dollars in express charges, but it was worth it," Raymond said, laughing as he recalled the joke.

Another time he had her dressing room filled with all kinds of roses. They overflowed the toilet, bathtub, sink—and he then replaced the roses with huge green plants. Barbara could not get into her dressing room through the potted plant jungle.

Raymond's biggest and best jokes were played with white mice. He put them everywhere. Much to Raymond's delight, Barbara would scream at the top of her lungs every time she opened a drawer, and the cast and crew would know he had got her again in a practical joke.

Years later, Raymond and Barbara were guests on the "Dinah Shore Show." Barbara told the audience how Raymond had filled her dressing room with all kinds of animals—ducks, goats, rabbits, and the like, and had left them there all night. When she opened the door the next morning and let out a piercing scream, a grinning Raymond had them removed. That night when she came home, all the animals were in her front yard and all three children wanted to keep them.

While she was telling this to the audience, Raymond handed out several boxes. He gave one to Shore, who found a beautiful orchid, as did Molly Picon, a friend of his, and Ella Fitzgerald. Barbara, however, was handed a long box containing a dozen red roses. Suddenly she let out a bloodcurdling scream and dropped the box. Two frightened white mice were running around underneath the roses. Raymond shook with laughter, knowing he had not lost his touch. The show went off the screen as a grinning Raymond Burr handed the mice to Shore, who let them run up and down her cupped hands.

All these practical jokes were Raymond's way of releasing the tension on the set of "Perry Mason." Joe Hyams first reported the practical joke about the lime Jell-o in his gossip column. Raymond went to great trouble to make massive batches of the green stuff and fill Barbara's bathtub, sink, ashtrays, glasses, cigarette boxes, pin trays, and any other receptacle he could find.

Raymond started a shelf of coffee mugs with each member of the cast's name on the cups, placed in a niche. If an actor left, his or her cup went too.

During the years of "Perry Mason," script problems never ceased. A representative who wrote for the show stated in *Writer's Digest* in August 1961 that it was the hardest show to work for. Each episode consumed 49 minutes and 51 seconds of air time. The rest of the hour was left either for commercials or trailer scenes of the episode to be seen the following week. Erle Stanley Gardner still refused to budge for poor material and kept those 49 minutes from going stale. Despite his influence, by the spring of 1962 even the actors were adding to the problems.

Raymond criticized the scripts publicly throughout the year, and Bill Talman joined in the criticism in 1963. Gardner felt it was in poor taste and bad public relations to attack one's own show in the press. Gardner's integrity paid off, however; while other top ranking shows faded throughout the years, "Perry Mason" stayed in the top bracket, no doubt partly because Perry never lost a case.

Actually, Perry *did* lose one case at the beginning of "The Case of the Deadly Verdict," shown on October 3, 1963. The jury found Janice Barton, played by Julie Adams, guilty of killing her rich aunt because she refused to defend herself by answering questions. Naturally, Perry proved her not guilty by the end of the hour.

There were two other cases that Perry lost, both in opening scenes of two separate episodes. In one case Perry is told by the judge why he ruled against him and the case is dismissed. Perry spends the next 40 or so minutes proving his client innocent, solving the case out of court anyway.

In the second episode, "The Case of the Dead Ringer," shown April 17, 1966, Raymond played two parts. As Perry, he is charged with trying to buy off a witness in a hearing over a million-dollar dispute. As Grimes

John Larkin, former radio Perry Mason, guest stars in the television episode "Case of the Greek Goddess," April 18, 1963.

he disguises his voice by deepening it and adding a dialect, and wears a thick beard. Perry solved that case too.

Raymond lived on the set in Cottage B at General Service Studios at 1040 Las Palmes Street in Los Angeles from 1957 into the early 1960s. The studio moved to the Red Skelton Studio for the remaining years.

His cottage contained a seven-foot bed and a kitchen with very little food in the refrigerator. He lived mostly on coffee and cigarettes and had perhaps a salad or sandwich for lunch, if he ate at all. Later he managed to sit down to a good dinner and a glass of buttermilk or a nighttime snack before falling exhausted into bed. His schedule seldom varied.

3:30 A.M. Wake-up call. Wash, shave and dress.

4:15 A.M. On set. Coach and Raymond go over lines to be memorized.

5:00 A.M. Rehearsal completed.

6:00 A.M. Scene completed and filmed.

He worked 10- to 12-hour days, filmed scenes, memorized 12–15 pages of dialogue, and rehearsed scenes before filming was completed for the day. This relentless schedule never stopped.

Raymond finally rebelled, threatening to quit at contract renewal time.

Money was not the issue; shorter hours and more time off were, as he was in practically every scene.

At contract time Raymond asked CBS for a loan in order to start his Harbour Production Company. The loan would be paid in full after his projects became a success. He was determined not to make the mistakes he had made when he tried to form Del Mare and later Bursal Production companies. CBS granted the loan, and most of his complaints were resolved to his satisfaction.

Raymond Burr learned a great deal acting the part of Perry Mason. He learned many different ways to get up from his chair, to walk to the witness box while questioning a witness, and to approach the judge's bench. He learned how to get Burger angry enough to provoke a shouting match until the judge rapped his gavel for silence. Most of all, his stock in trade was the ability to stare intently at a witness with his steel blue eyes until the person told the truth—or confessed to the crime.

Perry Mason Day was declared September 9, 1959, in San Antonio, Texas. Raymond got his comeuppance with the help of the San Antonio, Texas, Bar Association and Bill Talman, who had Raymond hauled into court for a mock trial. A real judge almost threw him in jail and later saw to it that Raymond suffered humiliation in a court defeat at the hands of Hamilton Burger. Talman won a guilty verdict against Burr's client, Erle Stanley Gardner.

On hand for the laughs were Barbara Hale, William Hopper, and Ray Collins. The Bar Association held a banquet in their honor, giving the CBS pressmen matchbooks with NBC printed on them—which actually stood for National Bank of Commerce, where the party was held. The Perry Mason Room was dedicated with the help of a couple of lawyer friends of Gardner's.

As Perry Mason, Raymond knew a great deal of law. As Raymond Burr, however, he made big mistakes in several of his own cases and lost. He did not learn the proper procedures in a Phoenix, Arizona, case, when George J. Shaheen finally got around to suing him on September 6, 1962, for a $1,085 debt for food, which Raymond had owed him since 1949. His first mistake was not answering the summons within five days after receiving it on March 2, 1962. He then failed to show up for a court-ordered deposition in June 1962. Mistakenly believing the statute of limitations had expired Raymond lost the case on a default motion and had to pay Shaheen the $1,085 plus $800 more in court costs.

Years later he lost $95,000 in a land deal on bad advice. He turned around and tried to sue the attorneys he had trusted, and lost that case too.

The "Perry Mason" series was critically examined as a sort of documentary on legal procedures. A superior court judge refused to attend a Bar Association convention when he found out Raymond Burr was to be the principal speaker. "I see about as much of Perry Mason as I care to. His program bears *no* semblance of the correct and proper means of administrating justice, or the proper conduct of the lawyer in the trial of a criminal case."

Not being a member of the bar, Raymond refrained from debating the matter. Erle Stanley Gardner's comment was, "He's completely and utterly wrong." Many of Gardner's lawyer friends complimented him on the show's authenticity, which everyone connected with the series went to great pains to ensure.

"The Case of the Final Fadeout," shown May 22, 1966, was the last episode of the nine year series and the end of an era. Everyone got into this one: cast, crew, grips, men on catwalks, cameramen, and stand-ins were all given walk-on parts or lines to say in front of the camera. Erle Stanley Gardner played the part of the judge, loving every minute of his role. Estelle Winwood, the oldest working professional actress in show business at that time, was given a good part. Dick Clark, host of "American Bandstand," played the part of the murderer. Denver Pyle was Jackson Sidemark, a spoof of producer Cornwall Jackson or Jackson Gillis. Others in the cast included Jackie Coogan as the prop man, Marilyn Mason, and James Stacy. The farewell party that followed was not a sad affair.

During the nine years of "Perry Mason," 12 directors were used in order to give each one time to study and prepare the scripts. Even the camera crew was staggered. "Everyone but me," groaned Raymond, but he ended up as one of the highest paid television actors in the business at that time.

An unfair situation occurred relating to the wristwatch Raymond wore throughout the years of "Perry Mason." He took great care of the watch, keeping it in repair at his own expense, and was forced to return the watch to the property department as soon as the last scene of the last episode was completed.

Before Raymond got too involved with the filming of "Perry" for the 1958 season, he appeared on "Mystery Playhouse," which was seen only on the West Coast. The title of the episode was "Face Value," and it starred Gabriel Curtiz and Suzanne Dalbert. For Christmas he filmed a television special, "A Star Shall Rise," playing the part of Balthasar.

Raymond had a brief vacation in New York and went on to Rome, where he had his first audience with Pope John XXIII, which was to have a great influence on his life. The pope told him he seldom got a chance to watch television but he had seen "Perry Mason." They became good friends and Raymond visited him at the summer palace and once in the area near where Pope John was born. He visited the pope many times afterward, until Pope John died. Raymond continued to meet many religious leaders all over the world whenever and wherever he traveled.

Desire in the Dust, 1960.

When "Perry Mason" went on hiatus in 1960, Raymond had a chance to make a movie on location in Louisiana, titled *Desire in the Dust*. The attitudes of the producers and the public had changed drastically by this time. Subjects not allowed on the screen before were now hinted at boldly. In this particular film, the lust of a father for his daughter was the theme. Martha Hyer played Raymond's wicked daughter, and Brett Halsey attempted to rape her. Raymond portrayed a vicious, power lusting politico who let his daughter get away with the murder of her younger brother and paid Halsey to serve the sentence for her. Joan Bennett portrayed his wife, who went insane after witnessing the murder, but it was his daughter he loved in an unnatural way. Character actor Douglas Fowley stole the picture away from the principal players as the drunken, toothless, sharecropping father of Brett.

This film premiered with a big fanfare in Baton Rouge, Louisiana, on September 15, 1960. Governor Jim Davis headed a roster of luminaries from screen, press, and society. The mayor proclaimed *Desire in the Dust* Day. There were 40 simultaneous premieres in and around Baton Rouge, New Orleans, and even Texas, and Governor Davis gave a huge party for the cast, crew and stars. All the events were covered by the news media and television cameras. The next day the critics panned the film: *Desire in the Dust* had laid a giant goose egg. This was the last film Raymond made until 1968.

Several actors and actresses who worked with Raymond on "Perry Mason" recalled him fondly. Virginia Field remembered Raymond as a dedicated and disciplined actor whom she liked and admired enormously. She had been in a number of episodes of "Perry Mason" and "Ironside." Darryl Hickman had first worked with Raymond in 1945 in one of the first films Raymond made, called *Fighting Father Dunne*, where most of his scenes were cut out of the film. In a few "Perry Mason" episodes, Darryl was always accused, and Perry always proved him innocent at the end of the episode. Darryl remembered Raymond as a very warm man, quiet, unassuming, and extremely easy to work with.

Over the years Raymond had been in every facet of show business, and in those years he formed a theory about acting. He told Robert Johnson, who interviewed him for a *Saturday Evening Post* article,

> You use a funnel, and you let in everything that's happening, everything you've read or seen, felt or heard or believed or disbelieved in. The wider you make the funnel, the better off you are. When you get a role, you turn that funnel around, concentrating so hard on the character that the right thing comes out of the funnel.
>
> When I play an already established character—say Henry the Eighth or Perry Mason—I go a step further in order to portray these people properly. I have to delve into their background and the nicest thing about being an actor, you're apt to learn a great deal about history and human beings. You become almost an authority on the subject. In going into those people's lives, you find things that make personalities.
>
> To be a good actor requires knowledge about human nature and I learned a great many things. I know I can't play a 23-year-old anymore, but then I never did anyway. Consequently, I think very much about Perry Mason as an attorney and a human being.

The arguments Raymond got into on the set were over whether Perry would do or say certain things. He developed a language and vocabulary for the Mason character. This attention to minute details no doubt contributed to the show's steady climb in the television ratings. "It got to the point," said Erle Stanley Gardner, "where people don't think they are watching an actor portraying Perry Mason; they think they are looking at a bit of real drama—that the television glass is not a screen, but is a window."

Because of this painstaking attention to details, the series won the Best Mystery Award from the *Motion Picture Daily* television critics and the *Photoplay* Gold Medal Award for the best television mystery adventure series. A national body of lawyers gave Raymond the first Law Day Award and he won the *TV Guide* Award as the most popular male television personality. He also received a Man of the Year award from the Legal Secretary's Club, in Stockton, California, which lay in the trunk of a friend's car for several years. Reminders to pick it up went unheeded until the friend finally caught up with Raymond in order to personally hand it to him.

During the "Perry Mason" years and long after, Raymond was asked to attend many American Bar Association meetings as the guest speaker. Real lawyers were often mighty skeptical about his portrayal of a lawyer who won his cases every week. His stock answer was that he won only on Saturdays—when the show was on television.

Now that he was recognized as Perry Mason, Raymond was asked to appear as a guest on a number of television shows. He appeared on Bob Hope's show, the "Red Skelton Hour," and twice on "The Jack Benny Show." On all three shows he was a comedian, surprising the stars and the audiences with his timing and delivery.

Raymond never became bitter about giving his life to the nine years of "Perry Mason." But he did regret doing the show for so long, because he was denied a social life and a family with children. It is rather ironic that he had a girlfriend in a way in Della Street, but in real life he rarely had time to date anyone.

"It was like being in a plush concentration camp while living on the set. Five years is enough for any series and then bow out gracefully," Raymond said in interviews, although his own series "Ironside" ran for eight years.

X

McGeorge School of Law, University of the Pacific

Due to his fame as "Perry Mason," Raymond Burr received an honorary law doctorate from the McGeorge School of Law, Sacramento, California. The sponsors of the series had commissioned A. Chailbaui to paint an oil portrait of Raymond as Perry Mason in 1965, and the painting was presented to the law library in 1967. A dedication ceremony took place when the portrait was hung over the fireplace. Below the portrait are over a thousand books donated earlier by Raymond.

Erle Stanley Gardner was scheduled to make a speech at the school but appendicitis kept him from keeping the date, and Raymond stood in for him at the commencement, which was held outdoors near a railroad track. All during his part of the address there was a train that came along the track and noisily backed up and switched cars until finally, as Raymond was near the end of his speech, the train pulled out. Afterward Raymond claimed he had given the best commencement address in the whole United States, and no one could prove otherwise. That started a longtime friendship and association between Raymond and Dean Gordon D. Schaber. Raymond supported the McGeorge School of Law in many ways over the years. His original scripts of Perry Mason with notations and bits of business written in the margins by Raymond were bound in leather and are now kept in a dustproof glass bookcase in the law library. Along with the scripts, Raymond donated a hand carved antique bench, a huge globe of the world made in the early 1800s, and a number of rare antique Bibles.

Raymond also helped design the courtroom of the future and took time out to narrate training films for use in the classrooms. The use of television in courtroom trials originated in the McGeorge School of Law, and the sometimes controversial idea has spread slowly throughout the country.

In order to help with the expansion of the law library and other building projects, Raymond decided to auction off some of his art collection.

Every painting or article had his autograph attached to the back of it. A great deal of publicity helped make the art sale a huge success and netted the school several hundred thousand dollars. The antique Bible collection was also sold. Raymond also tried to sell his "Perry Mason" scripts, but when no one could meet his price, he bought them back himself and redonated them to the law library. Enough money was raised to complete many building projects, and the campus is now spread out over 20 acres.

Raymond was invited to speak before many bar associations and addressed the Sydney, Australia, Bar Association on June 10, 1961. In Melbourne he met head on with the Australian version of "Meet the Press." The panelists rudely questioned him about his personal life and the "Perry Mason" show. Raymond managed to keep his Irish temper in check, however. The Australian people who saw this outrageous display of their reporters swamped the television station with telephone calls and wrote to the newspapers, condemning the heartless questioning and apologizing for the bad manners of the press. While in Melbourne, Raymond spoke to the law students at Melbourne University.

In Sydney, Raymond was given a warmer welcome. He composed and directed a variety show using local talent. Later in the evening he appeared on television again to introduce a "Perry Mason" episode.

Another school needing help was the Ramona School in Los Angeles, California. During filming of a "Perry Mason" episode, Raymond heard about the school needing money for repairs. He recruited the rest of the cast in order to do a play to raise funds. The cast rehearsed *The Happiest Millionaire* between filming their scenes. The play was put on for two nights, netting $17,000 for the group of nuns. The cast worked for free. The only money used was for the expenses of putting on the show.

His strong interest in art and collecting paintings from all over the world led Raymond to open an art gallery. Hilda Swarthe became his partner, and eventually they had branches in Beverly Hills, Phoenix, and New Mexico. The galleries became a huge success. Raymond finally bought out the partnership and opened a gallery on La Cienega Boulevard in Los Angeles that displayed the art of undiscovered painters. Actor David Whorf had an exhibit, and a painter who did his work while in prison was given a chance to display his work after he was released.

Unfortunately Raymond was expected to be at the gallery to sell art and mingle with the customers, an impossibility while he was filming episodes of "Perry Mason" or performing onstage. Raymond had to rely on other people to run the galleries. The gallery at 456 North Rodeo Drive in Beverly Hills was doing excellent business, but eventually he had to give up all the galleries due to other commitments.

Raymond made a "Favorite Story" drama for television when "Perry Mason" went on hiatus. The title was, "How Much Land Does a Man

Need?" Next, he appeared on the panel show "Meet the Stars," and was the first guest on KLAC's "*TV Guide* Show." The polls had voted him the best liked performer. For the second time he won the *TV Guide* Award.

When he won his second Emmy Award in 1960, Raymond's date was his longtime friend Barbara Stanwyck. She cried on his shoulder when it was announced she had won an Emmy for her show "Big Valley." Raymond calmed her down in time for Barbara to go onstage, make her speech, and claim her award. Later in the evening her gown caught in the chair just as she went to stand up. The dress ripped and Helen Ferguson, her friend, summoned someone to get a needle and thread. Helen repaired the gown in time for Barbara to join Raymond at the party after the awards.

Raymond was the grand marshal for the Seafair Parade in Seattle. When he landed at the airport, fans mobbed him and the police had to come to his rescue in order to get him safely into the car. Shortly afterward, a severe throat problem from a viral infection put Raymond in the hospital. This was complicated by a painful back problem.

When he was released from the hospital, he flew to Japan, Rome, Frankfurt, and Stockholm. In Rome Raymond had an audience with the Pope. After this whirlwind trip he returned to the States supposedly to vacation. His idea of a rest was to go on the road with the stage play *Critic's Choice*. The two week engagement at the Northland Playhouse in Detroit set house records, as it did in Highland Park, Illinois.

Raymond spoke to the graduating class of the Pasadena Playhouse when he was awarded the Gilmor Brown Award for his outstanding work in a specialized theatrical field. While there, Raymond was able to renew old friendships with the faculty members and alumni. Since the death of Gilmor Brown rumors had spread that the school was not doing well financially and might eventually have to close.

He returned to the Northland Playhouse in Detroit, Michigan, the following summer. This time the play was *Anniversary Waltz*. The production was billed for two weeks and played to capacity audiences, netting Raymond $20,000.

The Kenley Players, a stock company, joined forces with Raymond to present the comedy *O Men, O Women* at the Veterans Memorial Theatre. The same play was performed in Totowa, New Jersey, at the Gladiator Music Arena and in St. Catharines, Ontario, Canada, always breaking house records with standing-room-only signs in front of the theaters.

On his way back to California, Raymond spent three days in Louisville, Kentucky, enjoying the Derby Festival Fair and doing a two-hour radio show. Later, in Phoenix, Raymond attended a Bar Association Breakfast. Raymond met with a group of legal secretaries and took time to appear on a local Cerebral Palsy Telethon Fund Drive. Then it was back to Los Angeles and to work.

XI

Harbour Productions and Universal Studios

In May 1966 Raymond signed a long term contract with Universal Studios. For the next seven years he would make films for television and theaters. That same month he signed a contract with the NBC network.

Lester Salkow, his former agent, became president of Raymond's Harbour Productions, and Leonard White was made vice-president. Three projects had been planned, and Seeleg Lester was to produce one. Writer Sy Salkowitz would produce a half hour sitcom. The third venture, still taking shape, was based on an idea by Collier Young. With these things taken care of, Raymond took part in another important event.

The city of Los Angeles celebrated the 170th anniversary of the Bill of Rights with a parade and a ceremony. Raymond was invited to dramatically read the Bill of Rights. Immediately afterward, he went on his way to Vietnam.

This time he came back home with an injury to his right hand from rusty machinery. The medics had taken care of the hand, and Raymond had kept on with his tour of the Far East and Southeast Asia. As soon as he returned home, he narrated a special for a "Big Picture" television show titled "Why Vietnam?"

Raymond's own television special, "This Is Canada," made by his Harbour Production Company, was shown on August 25, 1965, for CBS. Narrated by Raymond, it was quite successful and well reviewed in most of the U.S and Canadian newspapers.

Now that "Perry Mason" was no more, Raymond had time to go back to filmmaking. He wanted to change his image and hoped that a film he was making would help people forget he had been Perry Mason. Needless to say, everywhere he went people called him Perry Mason.

He signed for a guest role in the television show "The Road West," to be shown in October 1966, but was forced to give it up when the horse he was riding in the show spooked and threw him. Victor Jory replaced him.

Raymond Burr enters a South Vietnamese Army Compound in August 1965 on his way to talk to American troops fighting in the Qui Nonh Sector. Raymond made many trips abroad to visit U.S. servicemen.

While he recuperated he was named Man of the Year by the California Men's Apparel Manufacturers. Rather than give him their usual award, they donated clothes to South Vietnamese refugees in his name, which pleased him very much.

Raymond completed a film in 1968 for Universal Studios called *New Faces in Hell*. Afraid the title would offend some people, the studio changed

Gayle Hunnicutt, Jason Evers, and Raymond Burr in *P. J.*, 1968.

it to *Criss Cross*, which did not fit the theme of the film, either, and had been
the title of an old Burt Lancaster film in which Raymond had had a bit part.
A relative newcomer, George Peppard, was playing the part of the main
character, Peter John Detweiler, so the studio came up with the title *P. J.*
George was given star status, with Raymond as the costar.

Raymond had gained considerable weight again. His hair was bleached
white and cut so short he looked nearly bald in the studio's idea of a middle-

Jimmy Durante and Raymond Burr in a comedy sketch from "The Jimmy Durante Show," 1975.

aged tycoon. Gayle Hunnicutt was cast as his mistress, and Coleen Gray played his long suffering wife.

To his delight, Raymond played the role of a cruel, tightwad tycoon. He tormented his staff, his relatives, his wife, and his mistress; he knew they were all after his money. Raymond was back in the type of role he had played so well when he first started in movies, but films had come a long way in the permissive use of themes and dialogue.

The basis of this movie was Raymond's hiring Peppard to protect his mistress. Later, Raymond went gunning for Peppard with a hunting rifle. Peppard thought he had killed Raymond in self-defense, only to turn around and discover the mistress standing behind him with a smoking gun poised to kill him too. As usual, Raymond was killed in the final scenes. The reviews of *P. J.* were mixed. In the years since it was released *P. J.* frequently turns up on television and cable at any hour of the day or night.

Raymond was involved in an automobile accident with Arthur Rossen and Joy Moran. They sued him for $20,000 in the traffic suit, but the case was settled out of court.

Then with a group of others, Raymond arranged for a train to tour from Washington, D.C., to San Francisco, collecting tools, soap, clothing, and the like, to be given to the Vietnam villagers as Christmas gifts. Appearing on Art Linkletter's "House Party" show, Raymond spoke about Vietnam. He then showed up on Johnny Grant's show for KTLA, "Standby Stage 5."

He appeared on the "Jack Benny Show" in comedy sketches, something he wanted to do more of. He appeared on "The Beautiful Phyllis Diller Show," as well as on the "Don Knotts," "Flip Wilson," "Red Skelton," "Dean Martin," and "Jimmy Durante" shows. Raymond sang "Ink-a-Dink-a-Doo" with Jimmy and ended with an imitation of him.

Other shows followed, such as "The Andy Williams Show" and "The Glen Campbell Show," where he again enjoyed doing comedy sketches, which the audience was not expecting from this dramatic actor. On "The Dean Martin Show," Raymond said, "when I watch 'Perry Mason' reruns and see people I defended, they are the same people I put in jail on 'Ironside.'" For the "Dick Van Dyke Show," Raymond whistled the "Colonel Bogey March," then acted in some comedy sketches with Van Dyke.

He hated to appear on interview shows, but from time to time he had to plug his new series or a special movie. He appeared on the talk shows with Johnny Carson, Merv Griffin, Dinah Shore, and many others.

Between appearances, Raymond was cited by the Freedom Foundation at Valley Forge for his many tours of Vietnam. He was given the Human Relations Award of the Anti-Defamation League of B'nai B'rith.

His television film, called "Ironside," was scheduled to be shown on March 28, 1967, but Raymond was overseas when it premiered.

XII

"Ironside"

Just before work on the pilot film of "Ironside" was started, Raymond left to fulfill his obligation to be the grand marshal of the centennial parade in his hometown of New Westminster, British Columbia. Raymond went in November 1966 to take part in the ceremonies and a family reunion of over 70 Burr relatives. Dignitaries came aboard to greet him as he boarded a replica of the first steam powered, paddle wheel boat, called *Beaver*, then led the motorcade to the City Hall, where he stood on the steps and read a copy of an old proclamation.

His right hand was swollen and in pain, but he kept his discomfort to himself, except to say he could not shake hands with his bandaged hand. The hand he had injured on rusty machinery on his last trip to Vietnam was not healing properly. After the festivities of the weekend were over he was to have the hand operated on. He was also scheduled to make a movie about a cop who becomes a paraplegic.

He also had to face a lawsuit for a deal his Burr Galleries had made in 1963. The painter took Raymond to court, claiming he had made an agreement to sell nine paintings but had received payment for only seven. The case was finally settled out of court.

The hand was successfully operated on, Raymond made the film, and he flew off to his newly acquired Fiji Island. As soon as he got back to the States, Raymond found out the movie was a success, and he started filming episodes for the fall season and beyond.

The original title of the two hour special was to be "Old Ironsides," based on an idea Collier Young had wanted to produce. The film was made by Raymond's newly formed Harbour Production Company. Quite a few actors tested to play the leading role, but none seemed to fit the character. Finally, the producers asked Raymond to play the part—Collier Young had had him in mind for the role all the time. "Ironside" made its debut on NBC on March 28, 1967. In the pilot, Commissioner Randall has loaned Ironside his house, thereby forcing his chief of detectives to take a vacation he does not want. The opening scene shows Raymond trying to quiet some chickens in a coop. He turns out the light, shouting to the chickens to shut up and go to sleep. Then he walks back to the house, talking to himself in the crisp night air.

Suddenly, as he fixes himself a drink and reaches for the telephone, shots ring out and Ironside falls to the porch floor. Six bullets pierce the night air. The audience assumes his hand has been hit by one of those bullets.

The reviews were mixed but generally positive, and work on the new series began. It was filmed by Harbour Productions, Raymond's company, which had produced episodes of "The Bold Ones," "Medical Center," "The Robert Stack Series," and a few of the early "Name of the Game" series, among others. He demanded good scripts, quality acting, and opportunities for him to direct and write dialogue.

Raymond came back from Fiji in May 1967 to start filming episodes of "Ironside" for the 1967-68 season. The first episode was shown on September 4, 1967. Raymond hoped to arrange his schedule to film the series for eight months and take off for the other four months. During this hiatus, he did guest shots on other television shows, if for no other reason than to prove to the public he really could walk; he was so convincing in his role as the wheelchair bound detective, his audience was beginning to believe he was a paraplegic. Visitors to the set were shocked whenever he got up from the wheelchair and walked away.

Raymond's character was difficult to mold in the beginning. At first he was portrayed as a bourbon drinking, hard-nosed cop who had been shot in the back. Paralyzed from the waist down, he had to prove he could still use his brain to solve cases. The first case was finding out who had shot him and why. He bullied his coworkers into putting the pieces of the puzzle together to solve the case.

Gene Lyons played Commissioner Randall, Ironside's boss. They were old friends from radio and film days as well as from episodes of "Perry Mason." In "Ironside," Lyons was excellent as the pertinacious head of the Police Department who clashed many times with Ironside over procedures. Sometimes he let Ironside have his way, while other times Ironside schemed to circumvent the Commissioner.

Don Galloway was chosen to play Detective Ed Brown. He had been a page at NBC while trying to get acting jobs and had played Kip Reisdale for a year in the soap opera "The Secret Storm." An excellent poker player, Don got along quite well portraying Ironside's assistant. He and Raymond became good friends, eventually traveling to foreign countries to promote the series.

Barbara Anderson was the young blonde actress chosen to play aristocrat Eve Whitfield. Eve had decided to join the police force and was assigned to do the office work for "The Chief" and run down clues as part of the team.

Raymond Burr as the wheelchair bound Ironside.

Don Mitchell was introduced as an angry young black man who had had a run-in with the law, that is, with Ironside. Ironside hired him to drive his refurbished paddy wagon and be the legs he no longer had. Through the series, Mitchell's character turned from an angry young man into a damn good policeman and, finally, a lawyer. As Ironside put it, "I don't want any dumb people around me," and Ironside made Mark Sanger, Mitchell's

Don Mitchell and Raymond Burr in "Ironside."

character, go back to school while still helping him on cases. Mitchell learned a great deal about acting from Raymond, and they too became good friends.

An episode took six days to complete. In the beginning, cast and crew would film for ten months to keep up with the demand for the series. Sitting in the wheelchair, Raymond had to look up at the other actors who were

The cast of "Ironside": Don Mitchell, Raymond Burr, Don Galloway, and Barbara Anderson.

standing, and the strong soundstage lights permanently damaged his eyes. The wheelchair became agony for him as the long hours of filming gave him back trouble. No wonder he got to the point where he hated that wheelchair.

Raymond also found he had to be careful not to drive after he had had a drink or two. This was a carryover from the "Perry Mason" days, when he tried not to break any laws.

After the first year of "Ironside," Raymond was nominated for two Emmy Awards, for best single performance as an actor in the show's premiere and for best actor in a dramatic series. He won neither award, however.

He subsequently flew to Madrid, Spain, to receive the Foreign Actor's Award. "Ironside" became a popular series in Spain. Next stop on the promotional tour was London, then 12 other cities in 10 countries in 14 days. He then flew on to Hong Kong, China, Taipan, and Japan. In Australia and New Zealand background shots were filmed for possible future episodes of "Ironside." In all, Raymond visited 58 cities on this trip, which included a goodwill tour for Universal Studios and his Harbour Production Company.

E. G. Marshall in the "Seven Days in the Life of Ed Brown" episode of "Ironside."

Resting on his Fiji Island, Naitamba, Raymond caught the flu, which turned into pneumonia, delaying his return to the States to film the third season's episodes. Once back in California, Raymond attended a Paralyzed Veterans Association convention.

At the convention, a paraplegic named Chrysler met him in the office building and told him it was possible to go down the escalator in a wheel-

Burr posing as an artist in an episode of "Ironside."

chair. Chrysler was referring to a scene in the pilot film of "Ironside" where Raymond rolls his wheelchair up to the escalator and grabs the moving rails, forcing him to stand in a bent over position with his feet turned inward. When Raymond reaches the bottom, he is thrown flat onto the stone floor.

Chrysler rolled over to the escalator in his wheelchair and, while an

Chief Ironside "resigns" from the police force and poses as a wino to trap a murderer in "Downhill All the Way."

amazed Raymond Burr watched, took off his pants belt and strapped himself to the chair. He got as close to the moving stairs as he could and locked the wheels. With his hands he grabbed the moving rails, using the force of gravity to propel him onto the step. Chrysler used his feet and legs as a brake, since he had already pushed the pedals up and out of his way before starting down the escalator. As he neared the bottom, he let go with one hand just for a second in order to release the brakes. Reaching the bottom, he rolled clear of the last step just as the step disappeared into the escalator. "It was all a matter of timing," he said as he grinned at Burr. Then he proceeded to show Raymond how to get back up the escalator by rolling onto the step backward and holding on to the rails with his strong hands and arms. Raymond was astonished, and told him so.

When things went wrong and pieces of the puzzle would not come together, Ironside sometimes went too far in his criticism of his team. In one emotional scene Ed Brown told him off, reminding Ironside that he never let Ed forget he was disabled. "You're the one who seems to forget it. You weren't all that good even when you had legs!"

Ed stormed out the door with a regretful Ironside calling after him. Gradually, the format changed as the characters were molded into a mature family group.

Reporter Martin Williams commented on an episode titled "Too Many Victims" in an article, "Move over Hamlet, Here's Ironside."

> Burr did a truly remarkable job on that show. The situation was unremarkable to be sure; but Burr as Chief Ironside, had to turn in another policeman, a lifelong and respected friend. The policeman, played by Forrest Tucker, had deliberately framed a dope pusher they both knew was guilty. Using nothing but his face, arms and voice, Burr offered, in several scenes, a rare insight into the nature of human feelings and sensitivity at war with human reason.
>
> Burr is often superb in this series.
>
> Once handed the probably inevitable script in which a surgeon raised the possibility that the use of Ironside's legs might be restored by an operation, Burr had a superb actor's comment.
>
> It is possible to describe his reaction only by saying that he actually once *was* an active man who had lost the use of his legs years before. Now Ironside was given a torturous moment of hope as he felt a faint sensation in one of them.
>
> If anyone wishes to describe what Burr shows us so often on this program — the fundamental conflict between emotion and reason in a man of intelligence and sensitivity — if anyone wants to describe this as merely "escapist entertainment," he is welcome to, but I think he will be very wrong to do so.

"Ironside" filming was rearranged so Raymond could go to New Orleans for Mardi Gras, February 7 and 8, 1970. He had been invited to be honored as King Bacchus II, the god of wine. Later that month, Raymond received an honorary Doctor of Theatre Arts degree at the Pasadena Playhouse, where he addressed the graduating class. The faculty, graduating class, and students gave him a standing ovation. A sense of sadness pervaded the ceremony, since the school was in financial trouble and was soon to be taken over by the Bank of America.

Between episodes of "Ironside," Raymond appeared on the "Don Adams Show" in an ad-libbed takeoff on detective shows that included a corpse shaking with laughter on the floor. When he raised his head to see what was going on, one of the actors would casually stroll over and push him down with his foot.

With "Ironside" on hiatus, Raymond flew to Auckland, New Zealand, arriving on his birthday, May 21, 1970. The Hotel Intercontinental gave him a birthday party, which was televised. He then went on to Sydney, Australia, where he had a film crew make background scenes on the docks in sight of the Sydney Harbour Bridge. Later, these scenes would be incorporated in an "Ironside" episode. Raymond's business manager, Robert Benevides, came along on this trip, which included a stop in Naitamba, Fiji. Raymond's island home was being destroyed by giant termites.

Under doctor's orders, Raymond was supposed to relax on his island for two weeks. Instead of resting, he filmed scenes in various locations of the Fiji Islands to be used in an "Ironside" episode first titled "Return to Fiji" but later retitled "Vacation in Fiji." Some scenes were shot on the main island's capital city of Suva in order to capture local customs, areas of interest, and the beauty of the island. Benevides and Raymond left Fiji for London in July. A few days later they were in Madrid, where Raymond accepted the Golden Quixote Award. "Ironside" was still popular all over Spain. They flew on to Frankfurt, Germany, where "Man of Iron" had gained popularity. In August, Raymond was in Vancouver as the grand marshal in their parade for the Town and Country Fair.

Raymond received the news that the Pasadena Playhouse had closed after 50 years of teaching acting, putting on excellent plays, and graduating famous students. The Bank of America took over the Playhouse for delinquent payments of $284,675 owed on the outstanding mortgage. The property deteriorated over the next few years and, despite a variety of efforts, the theater could not be saved.

During the year, Raymond filmed the opening and closing sequences of a series titled "You and the Law." He was the host of these half hours of intense discussions by law experts meant to alert viewers to their rights under the law. Unfortunately, the episodes were shown late at night. Interested in the future of several small colleges, especially for minority groups, he joined Florida's Memorial College in Miami as chairman of the National Advisory Board.

After completing the fourth season's "Ironside," Raymond took time out to film a "Dean Martin Show," donning a wig to play Harpo Marx. Just before the start of filming the fifth season's episodes, Raymond rushed up to Canada to visit his parents. Minerva had to have several operations on her legs, and he was worried about her and whether his father would cope while she was in the hospital.

Convinced they were both all right and able to handle their problems, Raymond returned to start filming and directing several episodes of "Ironside." After these were completed, Raymond decided to film some of the episodes ahead of time for the sixth season. The producers had perfected a way to have him do all his scenes within a short time period. These were then incorporated into his scenes with the other players. Although Raymond appeared to be talking and looking at Don Galloway, Barbara Anderson or Don Mitchell, he was actually speaking to the wall or to someone feeding him cue lines off camera. Sometimes a double was used, wearing a wig to look like the back of his head and neck. Lee Miller usually was given this job, since he was the same build and height. This way, Raymond was able to film all of his scenes in a few months and be off traveling or filming guest appearances on other television shows, with the audience none the wiser.

May 1971 found Raymond on his island, Naitamba, walking among the people who worked for him. They gathered the crops, tended the cattle, and took care of his orchid farms. A film crew joined him in Fiji on this island hopping work tour. The first stop was the Tonga Islands, where they filmed a documentary intended for 1972 release. Raymond met the King of Tonga, who weighed 400 pounds—in comparison, Raymond looked thin.

An Australian company joined them to make a documentary about Polynesia. Raymond appeared in this film and did the voiceover narration. A two hour version was shown in schools and colleges, while a one hour version was made for television.

Tahiti was the next island where filming took place before the crew moved on to Samoa, Easter Island, Hawaii, Peru, and Mexico. Filming for "Ironside" resumed in late August. The other actors were required to be in the scenes with Raymond that could not be done any other way.

One day during filming, Raymond suddenly stopped speaking in the middle of a sentence. He tried again and was surprised, then shocked, as his mouth filled with blood that gushed out of his throat and onto his clothes. Holding towels to his mouth, Raymond was rushed to a throat specialist. The doctor discovered a blood blister on his vocal chords that had burst. After he removed the blister and treated his throat, the doctor sent Raymond home and ordered him not to speak for over a week, until his throat healed.

Of course the fan magazines had a field day turning out stories with screaming headlines such as "Raymond Burr Almost Bleeds to Death," "Will Raymond Burr's Career End?" and "Raymond Burr's Life in Danger from Throat Surgery!" Rumors ran rampant until he returned to the set and resumed filming the scenes he had missed. Meanwhile, everyone worked around him, as they had done before.

Burr and George Kennedy in "The Priest Killer."

"Ironside" introduced a gimmick to television that was later copied by other shows. Two popular series were combined into one two-hour episode. "Sarge," a show featuring George Kennedy as a detective who became a priest, was merged with "Ironside" for an excellent drama titled "The Priest Killer." The idea worked so well it was repeated a few seasons later.

Raymond was invited to Washington, D.C., to take part in a special television show from the refurbished Ford Theatre with President Gerald and Betty Ford. The event was televised November 15, 1971, with Bob Hope as the master of ceremonies. Raymond along with other celebrities danced and sang "Hello Dolly" to Carol Channing. He also did a dramatic reading and joked with Hope.

Immediately afterward, Raymond left for the Azores, France, England, and Denmark. While in London, he visited Lord Snowdon, who demonstrated his newly designed wheelchair invention. An ordinary kitchen chair was put on a wheeled platform and an attached motorized battery operated the chair in any direction. Raymond helped Lord Snowdon arrange financing for the manufacture of the chair. Since then, many improvements have been made on this mechanized wheelchair.

In a London television studio, Raymond took time to film the "Kopy-kat" television show with Rich Little. Little's impression of Raymond amused him, and he gave Little permission to use the impression in his nightclub act or onstage. Little asked Raymond why he took deep breaths before starting a sentence. "To stay alive," Raymond replied.

He then went to Yorkshire, England, to read Bible verses on television. France was the next stop, then Raymond appeared as a U.S. juror at the 12th Annual International TV Festival of Monte Carlo. He continued this role for many years after. While in Monte Carlo, he visited Grace Kelly and Prince Rainier. Kelly and Raymond had been friends for years before they appeared together in *Rear Window*. Denmark proved a big disappointment. Raymond had gone there primarily to arrange filming of new projects for his international production company but could interest no one in either the project itself or the investment in it.

Returning to the States, Raymond went to Washington, D.C., to speak to the President's Committee for Employing the Handicapped about the problems disabled people face in everyday life. He stressed the difficulty a person in a wheelchair faces trying to enter a public building with stairs but no incline or to use a public restroom with doors too narrow to enter or toilets the wrong height to be used by a person wearing braces. Airplanes, trains, and buses refused to take aboard a person in a wheelchair or with a seeing eye dog. Raymond spoke all over the country on this issue. With his help, laws now have been changed. Public restrooms must have at least one booth with wide doors, hand rails, and higher toilets. The handicapped symbol is recognized worldwide. Parking lots must have spaces set aside so the handicapped can shop for groceries, clothing, and other essentials. All new buildings must have ramps and elevators level with the floor so a wheelchair can roll in without being caught on a metal sill. Special buses and airplanes are equipped to take people in wheelchairs. Travel agencies now specialize in tours all over the world for those who are blind, hearing impaired, or have some other handicap. "Ironside" was no doubt an inspiration to those fighting for the rights of the disabled.

Nominated in 1972 for an Emmy Award for "Ironside," Raymond did not win this time, either. Meanwhile, he decided to sell the syndication rights to all episodes for $1.5 million. He owned 50 percent of the show, so his share was substantial. Starting in 1974, when Raymond planned to retire from the show, over 175 episodes would be shown at least five times. "Ironside" is now being shown in more than 80 or 90 countries.

Raymond continued with other projects during the "Ironside" years, including a celebrity tribute to Alfred Lunt and Lynn Fontaine. Joining Broadcaster Hugh Downs, he narrated a documentary titled "Survival of Spaceship Earth." Made for the Atlantic Richfield Oil Company, the controversial film was quickly withdrawn from theaters and television.

Betty White and Raymond Burr narrated the Pasadena Rose Parade for the fifth and final year together in 1972. White said of Raymond,

It was my delightful pleasure to work with Raymond. We had a great time teasing each other and there were several "family" jokes. One was a running gag about dragons which started on the air during one of our broadcasts. I couldn't rest until I found a dragon to give to Ray and I searched all over town for days. Dragons, it seems, were as rare as hen's teeth, or is it the other way around? Finally found one and paid far too much for it, and by that time the joke was a little stale, but nonetheless shared. Since then, wherever I go, every counter seems to be overflowing with dragons of all kinds and descriptions. I never see one without thinking of him.

He is a man of great passions, grandiose plans, and innate sweetness. Among his passions are his passion for Beatrix Potter, orchids, and for a long time, being King of his Fiji Island.

Other actors and actresses who worked with him in "Ironside" had kind words. Character actor Alan Napier says he was on friendly but distant terms while working with Raymond. Joyce Van Patten found him a charming and talented man. Anne Francis considered him delightful; he had a good sense of humor and was most professional at all times.

Raymond played Caesar in a sketch on the "Beautiful Phyllis Diller TV Show." Diller recalled,

We ate at a Mexican restaurant and I remember pointing out that our waitress looked fat in her dumb dirndl. He gave me such a look! He has always fought fat. He regaled me with stories about an island he owns and how he makes his own champagne. He is a connoisseur of fine wines. I was surprised to hear he hailed from Berkeley, California, and he spoke mostly about his mother and never mentioned his father.

Phyllis knew Raymond from early days in San Francisco when she was starting out in comedy. Raymond would come to whatever club she was playing in to enjoy her act.

Kim Hunter could not recall any practical jokes being played on her by Raymond, but Johnny Seven, who played Lt. Carl Reese on "Ironside" for seven years, recalled a practical joke Raymond played on him that backfired.

Whenever the powers that be want to rid themselves of a running character, they will kill the character off. If an actor is enjoying his work and making a good living, being killed off could be a really traumatic experience.

We were shooting a segment of "Ironside" involving a credit card scam. In this seg, the heavy was portrayed by James Drury ("The Virginian" of yesteryear) and the heavies capture Lieutenant Reese (me). They beat up and torture Lieutenant Reese, trying to get him to talk. Just before the

Raymond Burr as Edgar Bergen and Sonny Bono as Charlie McCarthy on the "Sonny & Cher Show," 1974.

heavies kill Reese, like the cavalry, Ironside, Ed, and Mark come to my rescue and save my life.

About 2 P.M., the day we were shooting the rescue scene, the assistant director handed me some revisions. We continued shooting, but all afternoon everyone was looking at me strangely—especially Raymond—almost as if they were expecting me to do or say something unusual. Nevertheless, we completed shooting the rescue scene and I left for home.

After dinner, I decided to look over the revisions that were handed to me that afternoon, assuming it would contain new scenes for the following day's filming. Strangely, one of the scenes had the same number as the rescue scene we had already completed! It took just a minute to realize why I was the focal point that day. The scene was bogus and someone was trying to get a rise out of me! It went something like this:

[The heavy undoes his tie and wraps it around Lieutenant Reese's neck and begins to twist it. Reese begins to gag, turn blue, then purple, and then with a loud gurgle, falls to the floor just as Ironside, Ed, and Mark rush into the room. Ed kneels over Reese.]

IRONSIDE (worried): How is he?

ED (sadly): He's dead, Chief.

IRONSIDE (as a tear rolls down his cheek): Call the meat wagon.

I later found out, the producer and Raymond had conspired to shake me up, to see my reaction by getting me to believe that they were writing me out of the series! I imagine the anticipation Raymond must have been experiencing and the frustration when I behaved as if it didn't matter, or I didn't care. I also found out later that everyone involved thought I was the "coolest cat," for not being ruffled by being written out of the series.

Am I glad I put those revisions in my suitcase *without* reading them! It did matter, though, and I did care.

We went on for three more successful and happy years together, but every once in a while I reflect and wonder what my reaction would have been if I *had* read those revisions while we were shooting the rescue scene. I guess I'll never know, but, I can smile when I think, neither will the Chief—Raymond Burr. Good luck, Big Fella.

Don Galloway tells about one of his favorite moments:

We were filming "Ironside" under the direction of Don McDougall. Mr. McDougall had the unnerving habit of neglecting to say "Cut!" at the end of a scene, thus leaving the actors rather in limbo.

This particular scene consisted of a long move down a hallway, and an exit through double doors at the end. Don Mitchell and I were escorting Ray in his wheelchair, and also in attendance was Roman Gabriel, at that time quarterback of the Los Angeles Rams, who was playing a policeman in this episode.

We moved down the hall and went through the doors. The scene was over, but—sure enough—no reassuring "Cut!" from the director.

We found ourselves immediately adjacent to the exterior door of the soundstage, and Ray simply kept on going, the rest of us following. We left the soundstage and ventured into the bright sunlight, heading for the main street of Universal Studios. Arriving there, we made for the main gate, and waved at Scotty, the guard, as we left the lot. A right turn onto Lankershim Boulevard put us within three hundred yards of a saloon called the Left Bank. I perceived correctly that that might be our destination. Gabe, somewhat more accustomed to dodging defensive linemen than to figuring out the quirks of the film business, didn't quite understand what was happening, but he was glad to be off the stuffy soundstage and out in the open air, so he was happy.

So were we all, in fact, having quite a good time, and incidentally causing some disruption of traffic flow along Lankershim in the bargain.

We almost made it! I was literally reaching for the door of the Left Bank,
my mind joyful at the thought of the delights awaiting us therein, when
an assistant director caught up with us on a dead run. A moment passed,
as the assistant seemed to be considering joining us in our outing. But
then, alas, the intensive training beaten into the man by the Universal Production Office took over, and his eyes snapped into focus.

"Mr. McDougall says 'Cut,'" he reported sadly.

We considered this news for only a second, then Ray said, "I feared as
much," and we turned back, thirsty but unbowed, as we returned to work.
And that is how Raymond Burr taught Don McDougall that "Cut!"
follows "Action!" as surely as night does day.

Mitchell recalls his first episode of "Ironside":

When I was chosen to play Mark Sanger, I was petrified. Petrified of
working in television and with Raymond Burr. He had been a big star, a
huge man, stern and strong on the television screen during my lifetime.

I'll never forget that first day on the set because I kept flubbing my lines.
I didn't know why I was doing that. The lights were hot and getting hotter,
it seemed to me. I kept thinking, I'll get fired before I can do anything on
the series.

About 11 A.M., Mr. Burr called a halt, looking at me for what seemed
a long minute. Then he quietly said, "Let's do it again." We began again
and this time Mr. Burr muffed all of his lines, deliberately.

I looked at him and he looked at me, not saying a word to each other.
I got the message loud and clear that a major star can make mistakes too.
We tried the scene again. This time everything went perfectly.

Today, Raymond and I work on the same wavelength. We seem to
know what the other one is thinking. We seem to read each other's mind.

Raymond has helped me develop as an actor and as an individual in
areas I never thought possible to enter.

Millions of people watch a black man doing something important in
"Ironside." Mark is not a token Negro in Ironside's world. He is an important, needed, human being with emotions inside of him and being given
a chance to express them. He's a man who sometimes gets on your nerves
and sometimes makes you sympathetic toward him.

In a large sense, I feel Raymond has been almost like a father to me. He
may be a figure of authority, but he's also a person who is ready to lend
a helping hand. He is concerned, never hesitates to show his concern and
does something about it. I would do anything for him.

Raymond encouraged me to keep on learning my craft. There is no such
thing as a good performance, since there is always a better one inside of
you. I work hard to get the best performance out of myself. I work even
harder the next time to improve what I have already done. Raymond
believed in me while giving me a chance to show him what I could do. He
continues to believe in me, and I hope to continue to earn that faith.

An interesting prop in the series was the van Mark or Ed drove whenever Robert T. Ironside wanted to get somewhere. Ironside eventually learned to drive the van himself using hand controls attached to the steering wheel.

The van was custom built at a cost to Universal Studios of $47,000. The old paddy wagon had gone over a cliff in one episode to justify the people of San Francisco donating a new van to their Chief. The van had a hydraulic lift that lowered from the side door and was the costliest part. This enabled Raymond to roll his wheelchair in and out, up or down, just by pushing a button. Special items, such as a small refrigerator, a shortwave radio, a telephone, and storage cabinets with all sides within reach of the chair, were installed. One cabinet held bottles of his favorite bourbon, another a tape recorder. Various parts of the roof were removable to allow filming inside from any angle or side. Soon after the van appeared in the series, custom built vans began appearing on the roads.

Not long after the series started, a paraplegic veteran was hired as a stuntman. He had to be about Raymond's size and build to act out the stunts dreamed up by the scriptwriters. If the paraplegic could do them, then Raymond acted them out. If some of them were too difficult or could not possibly be done without injury to either man, the script was rewritten.

Raymond broke from his "Ironside" schedule to make a project dear to his heart.

XIII

Pope John XXIII

Raymond Burr had dreamed for over twenty years of making a feature film about the life of Pope John XXIII. He spent over ten years researching the life and career of this remarkable holy man.

Raymond was captivated by him when they first met in a private audience. The Pope whispered to him that he had seen a few episodes of "Perry Mason" and had enjoyed them very much. He explained that his duties did not permit him to watch much television. Afterward, whenever Raymond was in Italy he would request an audience with him, until the Pope's untimely death. Through the years he visited every Pope, but none left as great an impression on him as did Pope John XXIII.

His desire to star as the Pope in a full length movie grew stronger over the years. He hired researchers to find material as well as doing research and keeping notes of his own. He was torn between waiting to make his film later and doing a television version right away. Universal Studios had approached Raymond about starring in a television play about Pope John. The studio won out, for a number of reasons. Raymond was already under contract to them, and he would be allowed to produce the film under his Harbour Production Company banner. The story would deal with only one important dramatic incident in the Pope's life. He would have the best writers, director, and actors to work with and could do the television play between filming episodes of "Ironside."

When everything was agreed upon, Raymond and Don Galloway flew to Ireland to meet Monsignor Thomas Ryan. Monsignor Ryan had a thick Irish brogue and, in due time, Pope John's speech had taken on a combination of accents—Irish, Italian, and English. Don Galloway had to try to acquire an Irish brogue in order to play the part of Monsignor Ryan.

After the visit, the two men flew to Rome and filmed scenes at the Vatican and St. Peter's Square. The rest of the film was made at Universal Studios and on location at a Los Angeles pier. An old freighter was to be used for scenes requiring a dilapidated ship. Just such a ship had docked at a pier a few days prior to the shooting date.

Suddenly, filming was delayed when the FBI acted on a tip and seized the ship. A search of the old tub revealed a cache of dope. No one in the cast or crew was involved, but Raymond, being a well known celebrity, was the subject of huge headlines and fan magazine stories about the raid. Sensational stories succeeded only in gaining publicity for the film, however, and filming was resumed after a delay of a few days.

On Easter Sunday, April 22, 1973, "A Man Whose Name Was John" was shown on television and received excellent reviews. "The makeup job on Raymond Burr was astonishingly close to the real Pope," the critics exclaimed. His amazing portrayal earned accolades for Raymond. The Pope was not a tall man, and in order to make the 6-foot-2 Burr appear shorter, a special pair of shoes had to be made for him. Although they looked ordinary, Raymond's feet were actually flat on the ground. Galloway's shoes were built up to make him tower over Burr, and Raymond walked slightly stooped, since the Pope had walked that way. Galloway's hair was reddened to make him look like Monsignor Ryan.

Raymond tried to talk with an accent as close to the way the Pope talked and recited the Latin phrases over and over again from recordings made by Father Moretti, who acted as technical adviser, until they sounded natural. He cut his hair short and bleached it to simulate the Pope's white hair. His eyebrows were shaved, thinned out, and reshaped. The putty false nose was styled to look more Roman. When photos of Angelo Roncalli were placed beside Raymond Burr's, they looked almost like twins.

"Pope John had a marvelous sense of humor, which we used to great advantage. He was a man, gentle, but with great strength. His influence was really felt far and away beyond the confines of the Catholic Church," Raymond said.

The events of the film take place for the most part during World War II, when Angelo Roncalli was Archbishop and papal nuncio to Turkey. The Archbishop was instrumental in saving the lives of 647 displaced Jewish children from Nazi persecution by issuing baptismal papers in Christian names for each child. Pope John also persuaded Turkish officials to give sanctuary to these children until they could be sent to Israel, where they would be safe.

The children in the film were selected from various yeshivas in and around Los Angeles. They were supplied with ragged clothing and dirtied to look like forlorn, abandoned waifs. The film's remarkable crew, actors, and directors came from every religious and ethnic background.

"A Man Whose Name Was John" was shown worldwide. Although Raymond did not win any awards for his acting, the film itself garnered a great many prizes, especially from religious groups.

After completing the Pope John special, Raymond signed on as master of ceremonies for "Keep America Beautiful," a musical comedy television

Raymond Burr as Archbishop Angelo Roncalli in a scene from "Portrait: A Man Whose Name Was John."

film about ecology. He sang and danced and performed comic sketches with Lena Horne, Ruth Buzzi, and Don Knotts.

He then flew to Copenhagen, Denmark, to arrange filming for his Raymond Burr International Production Company. From there he went on to Portugal and the Azores to arrange filming for a project, "Henry the Navigator," which he had been working on for some time.

By June 1973 Raymond was back filming the seventh season of "Ironside." After several episodes had been completed, he suddenly flew back to the Azores on business. Perhaps it was the disappointment in his business ventures that fell through or worry, stress, and overwork that contributed to a major health problem just as he was leaving the Azores. There are conflicting reports as to whether the Portuguese airliner Raymond was on had taken off or was still on the ground. In any case, Raymond started to experience chest pains that progressively worsened. Signs of panic appeared on his face as he broke into a cold sweat. He let the friend sitting beside him know he was in distress. Immediately his friend notified the flight attendant, who in turn notified the pilot. The pilot called Azores flight control to get an ambulance to come to the plane.

Raymond was taken to the Azores Army Hospital. Fortunately, the hospital was close to the airfield and had all the latest up-to-date equipment, as a summit meeting had recently been held in the Azores and the equipment that had been brought in had been left behind.

Universal Studios, upon getting the message, contacted a heart specialist in London, requesting he fly to the Azores. Raymond was in the intensive care unit for almost two weeks before he was out of danger. When the British specialist decided he could be flown to the States, a private plane and ambulance brought him to the UCLA Medical Center. This transfer was done so quietly the press was not aware he was in the Medical Center until days afterward. He spent another week going through a battery of tests before he was allowed to go home under strict orders to rest.

Worry over six bad "Ironside" scripts for the 1973 season undoubtedly contributed to the August 10, 1973, heart attack. Raymond had been complaining steadily but getting nowhere with the producer and was fed up. He was also concerned about what would happen to the players and technicians on the set if he decided to end the series sooner than he planned. Trouble with his orchid farms in the Azores added to these problems.

Meanwhile the "Ironside" set had to shut down pending Raymond's return. Every scene that could be done using Lee Miller, his stand-in, had already been filmed.

Finally, the day came when Raymond was allowed to return to work on a limited basis. He had not come in the usual way and had missed the banner stretched across the road that read WELCOME BACK RAYMOND. He had gone directly to his bungalow, but when he heard what they had done for him, Raymond came out and instructed his driver to go around to the other entrance to Universal Studios. There he made the grand entrance the people on the lot had been waiting for.

Raymond resumed work but was ordered to work only until lunchtime and to rest at home the remainder of the day. The studio doctor and his personal physician stood by to make sure he followed orders.

The cast of "Ironside" late in the show's eight season run.

By October Raymond was well enough to fly to Sydney, Australia, to take part in a ceremony on October 19, 1973, for the brand new Sydney Opera House. He brought his parents, who had never been out of the United States or Canada, to Sydney. Minerva Burr walked with great difficulty, using two canes. She was keeping a secret from her husband and Raymond in order not to spoil the trip: She never let them know that she was slowly dying of cancer.

Raymond and his parents came back to the United States and his Hollywood Hills home. He had persuaded them to stay with him for a while and hired someone to care for them while he was away at the studio.

December 1973 brought more problems for Raymond. His mother's health was deteriorating. He had been given bad advice in a land deal in which he had invested $95,000. Because the bad advice was given by a group of lawyers he had trusted, Raymond brought suit against attorney Donald Leon for breach of oral contract. Raymond asked for damages, citing legal fees to Leon and the other attorneys and the embarrassment of a wage garnishment that took place in 1967. Superior Court Judge Norman R. Dowds dismissed the suit because Raymond failed to appear in court and had failed to prosecute within the five year limit.

Problems on the "Ironside" set culminated in Raymond's dramatic firing of director Barry Shear in the middle of filming an episode. Shear had been given conflicting orders about how long Raymond was to work. Raymond was also extremely worried about his mother and sensed something was radically wrong with her.

Problems mushroomed, and Raymond let Shear go. The reason given was artistic differences.

Headlines blared Shear's accusation that everyone was afraid of Raymond Burr—when Raymond laughed, everyone laughed, but if Raymond let his Irish temper get the best of him, everyone walked softly and kept their distance until the situation passed.

Don Weis, who had worked with Raymond for many years on "Perry Mason," defended Raymond against Barry. So did others, who disclaimed Shear's angry statements to the media. Frustrated, Raymond began to smoke again, a habit he had given up on doctor's orders following his heart attack.

He grew increasingly concerned about his mother, who was in the hospital in critical condition. He would rush to her side whenever possible. Minerva Smith Burr died of cancer at the age of 81 in January 1974, and was buried in Canada.

Not long afterward William Burr decided to go back to his beloved Canada to live, despite pleas from his son to continue to live with him. William entered a Vancouver nursing home for a short while. Later he moved to Delta, a few miles from Vancouver. A long time passed before Raymond saw his father again.

Barry Shear died of cancer about a year later.

Raymond also lost a boyhood friend. Daryl Davy's father had worked in the same hardware store with William Burr, and the two families had been friends since 1923. Daryl Davy died from injuries he received in an automobile accident in Canada.

When "Ironside" went on hiatus during February and March of 1974,

Raymond Burr in 1974.

Raymond put all this sadness behind him and went to Rome and then on to tour southern Europe. The series was expected to resume in April.

Raymond had been enthusiastic about filming episodes in Fiji ever since he did the "Vacation in Fiji" episode. All plans of filming out of the country had to be canceled. The logistics of sending cameras and a crew to the islands proved too costly, there were problems with the unions, and the Screen Actors Guild was threatening a strike. Disappointed, Raymond turned his concentration toward completing the last 12 segments of "Ironside," beginning late in October of 1974. Filming had to stop when Raymond became ill and entered Century City Hospital for removal of his gall bladder. His weight made this a dangerous procedure.

News had been leaked to the press that he was filming the eighth and last season of "Ironside" as soon as he recovered and could go back to work full time. Bad scripts, arguments with the top brass of Universal Studios, and his health problems had taken their toll on him. The ratings were slipping, too, as the series went up against other new and outstanding programs.

By mutual agreement among Raymond, NBC, and Universal Studios, "Ironside" was canceled and some of the last episodes were made part of the syndication package. Since he had already sold his syndication rights for a good deal of money, he could bow out while still on top and go on to new adventures.

On December 10, 1974, production ended after eight seasons. The last episode, titled "The Faded Image," was shown on January 16, 1975. The "Raymond Burr Show" reruns reverted to the "Ironside" title and, over twenty years later, are still being seen in various countries and at various times in the United States.

A few years later Raymond again signed a long term contract with Universal Studios. This contract called for him to make series, specials, and movies for television and gave him the opportunity to direct, develop story ideas, and write scripts. Meanwhile, it did not take long to dismantle the "Ironside" set, but the Chief did not give up his bungalow office. Many years after Raymond ceased filming the series, he continued to make speeches on behalf of the handicapped.

XIV

"Mallory,"
"Kingston Confidential,"
More Television Shows

Raymond left for England to film scenes for "The Inventing of America." Britain's James Burke and Burr joined forces in a documentary about how one invention led to another, and to another, and so on.

Raymond was portraying a frontiersman of the early West in a scene filmed in a wooded area outside London. The leather fringe on his jacket was too long and kept getting in his way as he moved about. The fringe had to be cut off periodically. He knelt to demonstrate the invention of the flint rifle. Suddenly he jumped and frantically brushed himself off. He had been kneeling in a large ant hill, and the ants had climbed up the dangling fringe and were crawling all over the leather suit. There was a long delay in shooting while Raymond and his costume were de-anted.

During his stay in London, Raymond was given a party on a riverboat moored in the Thames River. Much to his delight, there were several children on board who shared the celebration with him. Filming was finally completed in and around England and the two men flew to Rome for scenes to be made there, then on to Wellington and Auckland, New Zealand, for more filming. Other scenes were completed in and around several parts of the United States. Thomas A. Edison's laboratories in Menlo Park and West Orange, New Jersey, were used extensively. The special was scheduled to be shown on July 4, 1976, to be tied into the celebration of the American Bicentennial.

Prior to his trip to England, Raymond went to Portugal to complete transactions to purchase a seaside inn on the island of Fayal. He also bought property to raise acres of orchids for export. In Singapore, Raymond spent two days buying a consignment of orchids that he intended to grow on his Fiji Island, Naitamba. He also completed a deal to send 1.5 tons of orchid blooms to his farm near Nandi, on the largest of the Fiji

Islands. They would be field grown, and some rare orchids would be culti-vated in huge, special greenhouses. All would eventually be exported for sale. Raymond had to face the ever changing market for orchids and the fluctuating wholesale prices.

From Singapore, Raymond flew to Israel to spend a week visiting wounded men and women and the disabled. An Israeli paraplegic grabbed Raymond around the neck and pulled him down in a big hug in gratitude for coming. Next stop was Auckland and Wellington, New Zealand, for the Handicapped Olympics. At a luncheon for five hundred he paid tribute to Eve Rimmer, New Zealand's paraplegic Olympic gold medalist, and to those working in the field of rehabilitation for the handicapped. He told his audience that his interest went way back to the end of World War II. "I've been striving ever since to call attention to the wheelchair bound people who needed help and needed ways to help themselves," Raymond stated during his speech.

Don Galloway and his family went on this world tour with Raymond. While they were in Sydney, Australia, the Galloways came down with the flu, so Raymond went to New Zealand alone. During his tour he visited the Laura Fergusson Home for Disabled Persons and the Wilson Home for Crippled Children, where he autographed the plaster cast of a 14 year old boy. Raymond managed to raise $2,500 in the few days he was there and was told he resembled the late prime minister, Norman Kirk.

Raymond talked about making a film about Kirk, and of writing the script and narrating the documentary himself. Kirk had met Raymond once, and they had continued the friendship via letters and phone calls. Kirk gave Raymond a walking stick and extracted a promise that Raymond would come back to his country to help the Fergusson Trust and aid the handicapped. Raymond kept his end of the bargain and was wined, dined, and honored in a traditional Maori festival greeting. The film about Kirk never materialized.

Returning to Sydney, Raymond found the Galloways had recovered enough to travel. He and Don flew to Melbourne and were guests of honor at Dallas Brooks Hall and appeared on the "Night of Stars, Freedom from Hunger" television show. Picking up Linda and the children, they flew to Fiji and sailed to Naitamba, where they all relaxed on Raymond's island.

Raymond was back on the Universal lot in October 1975. He filmed his own production of *Mallory*. To publicize the film, Raymond appeared as a guest on the "Tonight Show." Film clips of *Mallory* were shown, but Raymond would not look at them. When Johnny Carson asked why, he replied, "I made them, I enjoyed making them, I got paid for doing them, but I don't get paid for watching them! Oh, I do look at the daily rushes if there is a problem that has to be solved, but I don't look at the completed versions."

Raymond Burr and Robert Loggia star in *Mallory*.

A shock wave rippled through the audience when they saw the curly, unattractive wig Raymond wore as Mallory, and they laughed during a serious scene shown on the monitor. He got the same reaction from a "Merv Griffin" audience. The television critics were not kind either. No one could believe Raymond as a shady, crooked lawyer — not after so many years as Perry Mason. Only a few mentioned the wig or criticized it, though.

In December, Raymond was a presenter for the ninth annual Image Awards and then rushed through nine cities in three days, talking about a film documentary of "The Last Supper" that he had narrated. He flew on to Toronto for the Flowers Canada Convention. This led to a promise to appear on a Canadian garden television show.

After the show, Raymond invited the woman who produced the show to come down to his home in California and bring a crew to film the rare orchid plants inside his greenhouses. When she came down to do the show, she proceeded to boss Raymond around, despite admonitions from the crew not to treat her host that way. Raymond politely but firmly put her in her place, and the filming went smoothly from there.

In 1976 1,500 top television executives selected "Perry Mason" as the top show and their favorite in the years 1950 to 1976. Filming started in the spring of that year for a new series Raymond was gambling on. The pilot film of "Kingston Confidential" opened the new season in September. The series was sold on the strength of it and began in January 1977. Raymond played an investigative reporter; Nancy Olsen, the owner of a chain of world famous newspapers, was his boss.

When he had a day off from filming this show, he flew up to Sacramento, California, to narrate training films for classroom use at the McGeorge School of Law. He had narrated many such films and many students often did not recognize him as the voice behind the film.

For Guenette-Asselin Productions, Raymond signed to do special films to be distributed under the name Sunn Classics. On July 3, 1976, "The Inventing of America" was shown nationwide and later worldwide to excellent reviews.

During July and August, "Kingston" was on hiatus. Raymond took Don Galloway with him to do a stage play, *The Good Doctor*, which opened in Chicago on July 12, 1976, at the newly built Drury Lane Theatre at Watertown Plaza. The reviews of this Neil Simon play were not good. To bolster attendance, Galloway and Raymond appeared on the "Phil Donahue Show" when he was still broadcasting from Chicago. Answering a lot of personal questions from the audience, Raymond admitted he smoked too many Salem cigarettes, talked about life on his Fiji Island, and plugged his new series, "Kingston."

After about two weeks of performing in *The Good Doctor*, Raymond developed severe dental problems. He tried to go on with the show but finally gave in to the excruciating pain, and at his request, the play folded on August 8. Galloway and Raymond flew back to California, where Raymond went directly to his dentist. There were rumors he quit the play because of the bad reviews, but the agonizing dental problems had simply hit him at the wrong time.

Back in California, Raymond appeared on "The Captain and Tennille

Show" and completed 13 episodes of "Kingston Confidential." He went to Kitchener-Waterloo, Canada, in the fall of 1977 to be the grand marshal for their parade and came back to film a week's supply of the "Hollywood Squares."

He then signed for a part in an epic to be shown over 26 hours of television. "Centennial" was based on James Michener's book about the generations who settled in and built part of Colorado. Raymond's part was five hours within the saga and required him to grow a beard and dress in 1860s costumes. Robert Easton, an actor and dialect coach, was hired to coach Raymond in a German accent for his role as Hermann Bochweiss, the silversmith. He played Sally Kellerman's father in the film.

There were a great many stars in this opus, which was filmed for the most part in and around Colorado. The episodes took almost a year to complete and were then shown on telvision in one, two, or three hour segments; sometimes weeks would go by before the next episode was shown. In the reruns years later, all episodes ran in sequence over a number of days until all 26 hours were shown.

Since Raymond's part was filmed over a period of time, he was able to do the narration for another epic television miniseries, "The Bastards/ Kent Family Chronicles." Hoping to try another series, Raymond started his own film for television under his RBI Production Company. "The Jordon Chance" turned out to be a movie of the week for CBS-TV and was never made into a series, although he made the rounds of talk shows to advertise it.

In New York and Boston for the flower conventions in December 1977, Raymond appeared on Boston television to talk about a special he was making for the Public Broadcasting System (PBS), "Christmas Around the World." He also was a guest on "Good Morning, America," with his friend David Hartman. Hartman had appeared in an early episode of "Ironside" and played the doctor in "The Bold Ones," a series Raymond produced. One episode combined the "Ironside" and "The Bold Ones" teams. Hartman had starred in "Lucas Tanner," also produced by Raymond's company. Raymond mentioned in the interview that he had lost his only son, which had sparked his interest in education.

"Christmas Around the World" was shown live on the PBS networks on Christmas Eve afternoon, December 24, 1977, and again Christmas Day on film. For the first time, satellites were used to show how Christmas was celebrated in other countries. Raymond narrated the entire event, and the program turned out to be a huge success.

When he returned to California he received the disappointing news that "Kingston Confidential" was canceled after 13 episodes had been shown. Raymond complained, "It was poor scripts, and the show should have been canceled after we filmed four episodes." Evidently, the public did not take to his portrayal as a newspaperman. Also, both "Perry Mason" and "Ironside" were still being shown in reruns all over America and the world. A few months later, Ed Asner debuted as a tough newspaperman in "Lou Grant" and that show was a hit.

An article appeared in the *Los Angeles Times* announcing the Pasadena Playhouse would open again. The city of Pasadena had received a $1.3 million grant to restore the Playhouse, Raymond's alma mater. Since that time, however, the school has not been revived to its former status.

Raymond was the guest speaker at the commencement exercises for the graduating class of 1978 at McGeorge School of Law. A few days later he was back in New York City to join Walter Avis in a new adventure. The Avis-Rent-a-Car associate invited a group of people to a party to introduce the concept of selling cut flowers by wire. Teleflora has became a successful enterprise. Raymond traveled to Toronto, Montreal, Indianapolis, and back to New York City to promote the venture. While he was in New York City he worked with a chemist to develop a line of soaps and cosmetics using the products from the Fiji Islands.

XV

Naitamba, Fiji Islands

The first chance Raymond got after launching the Teleflora venture, he flew to his Fiji Island, Naitamba, for a rest and to enjoy a swimming and fishing vacation. During World War II, Raymond had become familiar with the various islands in the Pacific Ocean. After the war, he spent a great deal of time sailing on the high seas in the Pacific area. When he started making a name for himself in films, Raymond decided to invest in a home and land. He bought property and a house in the Caribbean area to which he could escape, but property developers drove him out. The same thing happened in the Bahamas, so he tried Hawaii, where it was not long before a hotel was being built alongside his house.

In 1965, between episodes of "Perry Mason," Raymond was on a ship bound for the Fiji Islands. He had left Australia and New Zealand, where he had been promoting the series, and the ship had slowed due to fog. When the fog lifted, Raymond saw an island in the far distance. The island stood out by itself. After the ship docked in Suva, the capital city on the main island of Fiji, Raymond searched the real estate offices to find out who owned the island and if it was for sale.

The island was owned by an 83 year old woman. She had been brought to the island as a bride over 62 years before. Her husband, Gustave Mara Henning, head of an old Fijian family, had been a German planter, and they were the only nonnatives on this particular island. Elizabeth Henning had been a widow for at least 12 years, and her children were all grown, living on other islands or in various parts of the world. She was willing to sell for the right price and to the right person.

Raymond flew over the island in a Fiji Airways Dakota plane and dropped a tube containing a message with his offer to Mrs. Henning. If he had used the shortwave radio, the party line might have spread the news all over the South Pacific. Mrs. Henning got on the radio long enough to accept his offer and arrange their meeting.

The June 1965 contract called for a special clause Raymond insisted on when he bought the island from her. Mrs. Henning was to remain on the island as long as she wished, and she would be buried beside her husband in the little cemetery Raymond had set aside for her. A few years later, Mrs. Henning was killed by an automobile while she was visiting the main island of Viti Levu. Raymond kept his promise and buried her beside her husband and hired someone to take care of the cemetery.

The island is in the Lau group of the Fiji Islands. There are a total of about five hundred islands, both large and small, although the entire Fijis are about the size of the state of New Jersey. The island paradise lies 330 miles under the Southern Cross in the South Pacific. Latitude is about 17.01 south and longitude about 179.19 west. The rest of the Lau group of islands are spread over 280 miles north and south. Some of the islands are inhabited, but many are too small to be anything but bird sanctuaries. The islands once belonged to Tonga but were annexed as a British Crown Colony on October 10, 1874.

The Fijian people intermarried with the people of Tonga and take exceptional pride in being a blend of many cultures and enjoying a life-style both simple and contemporary. The main islands are very modern, with many fine hotels that cater to tourists. The nearest island is Taveumi Island, over 54 miles away. The name of the island has been spelled in various ways as Naitaumba, Naitauba, or Naitaba. The *National Geographic* magazine has it spelled as Naitamba.

Naitamba is a volcanic atoll that in some places rises 650 feet above sea level. Raymond purchased over four thousand acres for about $200,000. There are about 180 inhabitants on the island. The population size changes periodically as the children grow up and go to the other islands for schooling. The island has a copra plantation, gold mine, and acres of trees bearing macadamia nuts, passion fruit, and breadfruit.

Although the island is protected by a refreshing lagoon and there is perfect weather all year round, occasional cyclones, typhoons, and hurricanes do strike the area. One year a cyclone struck and destroyed Raymond's plantation and some homes in the village. Luckily, no one was hurt. He subsequently rebuilt everything using better materials to withstand the elements.

On October 11, 1970, the Fiji Islands became independent of Great Britain. Raymond took time off from filming "Ironside" to be there and watched Prince Charles, representing Queen Elizabeth, turn over the islands to the Fijian people. The colorful ceremony was very impressive, and Fiji also joined the United Nations as member 127. After the ceremony, Prince Charles told him the entire Royal Family enjoyed his "Ironside" episodes.

Anytime Raymond decided to visit his island, he had to arrange connecting flights ahead of time. The first flight started from Los Angeles to Hawaii. The second flight was to Nadi Airport, Fiji. Upon arriving at the airport, Raymond either went overland by car to the other side of the main island or rented a helicopter. At the harbor, the island ferryboat was his next mode of travel and brought him 54 miles to Taveumi Island. Here he had another six hour journey by boat, through riptides, coral reefs, and wrecks in order to reach his own island.

The last part of the trip is what Raymond loved the best. He clung to the rigging, enjoying the salt spray as the ship glided through the blue Pacific Ocean, closer to his home away from home. At first sight of land, Raymond looked for the friendly Fijians who came out in canoes to greet him. Next came the smell of copra drying in the sun. The scent of citrus also assailed his senses. He heard the surf breaking upon the sandy beach and the reef. Long before this, Raymond had heard the sound of drums announcing "company is coming." The weight of his California world drifted away as he relaxed in his plantation home with a cool Fijian beer. If all connections were met, it took him a little over 48 hours to get to Naitamba.

At first, Raymond lived in the hundred year old plantation home where Mrs. Henning had lived. One year he discovered termites (large white ants) had taken control of his house, and it had to be torn down. A new house was built on a hilltop overlooking the sandy beach. The windows were open on all four sides so Raymond could see and hear the ocean from any direction. Here Raymond found peace and tranquility and was surrounded by antiques, curios, and his art collection. He had collected art on his many trips around the world. Some of the art work he had shipped from his Hollywood home.

Even on Naitamba, Raymond could not seem to sleep beyond four-thirty or five o'clock in the morning. Donning a pair of washed-out blue jeans cut off at the knees, a thin shirt, and a pair of sneakers, he set off to mingle with the people, walking all over the island. About four in the afternoon he returned to relax until dinnertime, between six and seven; then he fell into bed around nine or ten o'clock. From his window Raymond looked out onto a phosphorescent sea. The sky was filled with millions of stars, sometimes twinkling, and he occasionally glimpsed a falling star.

One of the things Raymond discovered on Naitamba was a rain forest. Since he knew this area was a taboo, he respected the Naitambans' wishes and left it alone.

A gourmet cook, he soon discovered the joy of learning to cook Fijian style. He already knew how to cook Spanish, French, and Italian dishes. Raymond said, "Chinese cuisine by far is the most sophisticated and there are 80,000 recipes in Chinese cooking. In France there are maybe 83 ways of cooking beef."

About 30 or more children of various ages attend a school he had built near his home. Sometimes Raymond became the teacher to find out what the children had learned. At night the adults were encouraged to come and learn many things they had never had a chance to. English is spoken, and so are Fijian and Hindustani. Raymond learned the languages enough to converse with the elders, but was never able to be there long enough to carry on a fluent conversation.

The school was used as a church until he had a church built to accommodate six different services. Most of the Fijian people are Methodists, dating back to missionary days of the 1800s. Hindu is the other religion that uses the church. All religions are respected with dignity on Naitamba. Sometimes Raymond sat on his veranda listening to the singing and the bells that rang between services. He also preached the sermon or read passages from the Bible when he got the chance.

To keep disease from getting out of control, he hired a firm from New Zealand to fly over the island and spray insecticide and instructed the people how to keep insects under control at all times. Through the ensuing years, Raymond improved housing, water, and sanitation facilities. He added electricity, indoor plumbing, and many other modern conveniences. He provided and accumulated books for the school and library. Along the way, he discovered there was no dictionary of the Fijian language with English translations, so Raymond encouraged several academies and universities to come and work on the project.

Raymond imported livestock and poultry to increase the food supply. Over the years he experimented with cash crops that would adapt to the tropical climate and succeeded beyond expectations.

He sponsored a student-teacher exchange program between the universities of the South Pacific and Hawaii. A secondary school on the small, isolated island of Vanua Mbalavu received thousands of dollars in donations from Raymond, and he paid the expenses for six young Fijians to come each year to complete their education in the United States. The children lived in his California home with Robert Benevides's aunt as their guardian.

He built a hospital and staffed it with doctors and nurses recruited from the big islands. They in turn trained some of the island people. There was a flu epidemic on the island one year. Raymond radioed for medical supplies to be flown over the island and dropped near the hospital. Some of the supplies, like thermometers, landed in the coconut trees, and the people were too sick to climb up and get them. Raymond also caught the flu, which turned into pneumonia, delaying his return to the States until he was well enough to travel the distance to California.

To show their love and gratitude for him, the people made him an outrigger canoe and a mat woven with many fringes to denote his noble status. Raymond proudly sat cross-legged on the mat, which became a little difficult at times for a very big man.

Raymond decided to start a profit sharing plan for the people who worked for him, giving the workers paid vacations and a type of social security. No management-labor problems occurred. The island workers collected the coconuts, from which they extracted fats, oils, meat, and milk. From candlenuts they extracted the oil, also. Lemon grass was pressed to extract a perfumed citronella oil and was mixed with coconut oil. The islanders used this oil mixture as a body lotion. What they did not use on the island, Raymond exported to be used in medicines and other products; 50 percent of the coconut oil was used to make four different soaps and six different men's colognes. The soap works even in salt water, and it is excellent for the skin. A mixture of lemon grass and lemon leaves makes a fragrant tea. Paper mulberry trees are used for the inner bark to make bark cloth and mixed with tapioca starch. This is then stenciled with brown or black dye. Kava, another product, is a diuretic drink but nonintoxicating.

Most of his activities regarding these products led to Ventures of Fiji and to the Ventures of Fiji, Canada, Ltd., which had an office based in New Westminster, British Columbia. The new company started January 22, 1968.

Raymond bought land in the Azores for orchid farms. Over ten thousand orchid plants grew on his plantation in Fiji. The orchids from Fiji and the Azores were shipped all over the world.

Added to these investments were a copper mine and a cement works. Then Raymond joined New Zealand's Phillip Harkness and Hong Kong newspaper owner A. W. Sian in publishing the *Fiji Sun*, making the newspaper the second largest paper in the South Pacific area. Raymond also added a hotel to his enterprises.

In the first few years he owned Naitamba, Raymond was not able to spend more than a few weeks on the island. Over the years he arranged to spend more time there to enjoy fishing, sailing, swimming, and walking for the exercise, while checking on everything else. The shortwave radio was his contact with the outside world since there were no phones, television, or airstrip on the island.

Twenty years later, when time and traveling became too difficult for him, Raymond decided to sell Naitamba. The Fijian government tried to raise the money to meet Raymond's $2.5 million price but failed to do so. Naitamba was finally sold to a group of American investors who agreed to the contract Raymond had written. He still wanted a part of the island to return to when he could come back. The graves of the Hennings in the little cemetery were to be left undisturbed and receive perpetual care. The American investors had to continue to improve the island and treat the Fijian people with dignity and respect. He did open an orchid farm for tourists to admire and to visit to buy his rare orchids.

Raymond's reason for selling the island was to settle his estate. Plans for the island could not be carried out unless he was there all year round. He also wanted to get back to doing stage plays, television, films, and other projects.

All clauses had to be agreed to before he signed over the island.

On May 14, 1987, a coup put the Fiji Islands under the control of Ratu Sir Penaia Granilau. Raymond lost a great deal of money he had invested in the orchid farms. He never dreamed such an event could happen.

XVI

Raymond Burr's Children

Raymond Burr's interest in children can be traced to a special holiday celebration he arranged one year at Christmastime. He came home one day near December 25 to inform his mother he was bringing home some children to celebrate the holiday with them. He forgot to mention just how many he had invited or how many of their counselors were coming along. He bought and dragged home a tall Christmas tree that he and brother James Edmond set up in front of the old fashioned high windows and trimmed like two mischievous little boys. Raymond arranged and cooked the dinner and left the rest of the last minute details to his mother and grandmother.

A dozen or so children of all age groups and three counselors arrived on time. Hours went by before Raymond showed up. The children were getting restless when a car screeched suddenly to a halt outside the house. A grinning Raymond, arms loaded with gaily wrapped parcels, came bounding up the steps. The children jumped up and down with joy and excitement when they saw the packages. Dinner came first, however, and the packages were put under the tree. Edmond and Raymond played Santa Claus, handing each child two gifts—a sweater and a game or toy—as his name was called. They then sang Christmas carols and left the house, happily carrying their gifts.

Raymond and his family were left with fond memories of that particular Christmas. Once, years later, Raymond mentioned to an interviewer that when he was a child he had never received a train set for Christmas. When he was about 27 years old and could afford it, he bought his first train set. He loved trains and ferryboats. He used to travel across San Francisco Bay on the ferry and had fond memories of the time. Raymond continued to add to his train set over the years and had an elaborate setup in his home. The trains ran not just at Christmastime but whenever he had a houseful of children. Raymond was also helpful in getting a passenger train running across northern California.

Raymond's interest in children continued when he was a struggling young actor in films. He became a volunteer father in the Mickey Finn's Boys Club. The children were between the ages of nine and 12. Most were orphans, abused or from broken homes. His heart went out to these unfortunate ones, and he kept up with the club for many years until the pressure of his work pulled him away.

When Raymond lost his only son, Michael Evan, to leukemia in 1953, he longed to fill the emotional void that was left. He began to notice the waifs in the streets of the cities he visited on his travels around the world. Some were ragamuffins, some had no shoes, and others shivered in the cold for lack of adequate clothing.

One day a friend told him about the Foster Parents Plan. At that time, the cost to clothe and feed a child was ten dollars a month. Raymond was given a picture and information about each child he adopted. The letters he sent were translated into the child's language and if the child could not read, the letters were read to her or him.

This was the beginning of a love affair between Raymond and 27 children from all parts of the world. In his world travels, he would visit the children, taking them shopping for new clothes, toys, books, and games.

He requested foster children that needed the most medical care. The children themselves often worried about their unadopted sisters and brothers. Explaining his interest in the program to a reporter, he said, "If I send money to them, they don't spend it on themselves. They share it with other children and parents, if they have any. They don't know the meaning of the word greed or hoarding. Their way is to keep the family together no matter what is given to the fortunate one."

Raymond's first foster child was an Italian boy named Francisco Corvino, who was born in 1954 and was assigned to him in 1959. This child's father had died of peritonitis at age 32 and the mother earned ten dollars a month doing laundry. The family existed on occasional food packages and free medical aid. Raymond saw him each time he came to Italy, especially when he traveled on behalf of the "Perry Mason" series. In 1963, Christano T. David came from a Filipino orphanage. He too had been born in 1954. Ciro Onza, another of Raymond's six Italian children, was adopted in 1964.

On one trip to Korea, Raymond met Lincoln White, a Korean child whom he adopted in 1964. Years later, grown up and an officer in the Korean Army, Lincoln was on his way to West Germany and stopped over for a few hours in Los Angeles. Lincoln was at the airport when he called Raymond at Universal Studios. An excited Raymond told him to get a cab and come directly to the studio. The two men spent a few hours together. Both took pride in the father-son relationship.

Raymond acquired four children on his many trips to Vietnam, starting in 1967. Phan Lee, Maria Rorano, Cong Lee, and David were brought to Saigon, and Raymond took them on a shopping spree. He spent two days with them and the interpreter. Their love and respect did not need interpretation, however. Even when there were five or six children and the parents, he gave money to support them all. He wrote to them and sent seasonal gifts. On his trips to Vietnam, he always made sure there was enough time to visit all the children. They would all chatter away in Vietnamese and English. Raymond had learned enough Vietnamese to ask questions and he would be answered with a torrent of words mixed with giggles, which the interpreter would try to translate. He also supported an orphanage in Vietnam for many years.

In 1960 Raymond adopted Duk Hwa Lee, a Korean boy whose father had lost both legs in the Korean War. Raymond gave him $132.41 to help get him started in the poultry business. Raymond said, "He was worth every single penny of it. They all want to be self sufficient, not lean on charity. They all have pride in helping themselves achieve." Raymond learned to speak enough Italian, Greek, Korean, Vietnamese, Filipino, Fijian, and Hindustani to communicate with all of the children and tried to teach them some English.

Leper children from Paengyong Island in the Yellow Sea, near Korea, were added to his family and supported for many years. He also adopted a Filipino girl, Rosaria R. Palcotelo, in 1963. Both her parents had died of tuberculosis and Raymond helped with her medical care. In December 1963, Raymond added a Greek girl, Maria Kurayanni, to his adopted family. She came from Stylis, near Lamia, in central Greece. When he went to Athens in 1980 to film his part in "The Acts of Peter and Paul," he made sure he found time to visit Maria and her family.

Through the Save the Children Plan, Raymond adopted three girls from Messina, Italy. Andrea Di Biase was born July 7, 1954; Elvira Palastro, December 18, 1950; and Carmelo Peditto, January 25, 1955. Elvira had had polio at the age of three, and he helped with her medical bills.

Letters from his children, once grown, still came to him. They told him how well they were doing and about their family life. They continued to thank him for the love and affection he had given them. As children, their letters had been filled with news about school and home activities and holiday festivities. They would send him drawings of their lives. He would also receive a copy of their report cards.

After Raymond purchased his Fiji Island, he brought six children from Naitamba to his California home. For the children old enough and able to pass entrance examinations, he paid for college educations. To earn their education, they did chores around his house. When they went back to Fiji, other children took their place. If families could not or did not want to be parted, Raymond brought the entire family over. The adults took care of his house, land, greenhouses, and gardens, and shared in some of the profits as well. One of Raymond's Fijian adopted sons went to medical school and returned to his homeland a doctor.

Once he took an entire busload of his Fijian children and adults on a holiday trip up the coast of California that included a visit to the television studio where Raymond was being interviewed on the "Merv Griffin Show."

In addition to providing for his adopted family, Raymond educated nieces and nephews. By September 1982, his private program had sponsored over 30 children from all over the world.

XVII

Canadian Films

From 1977 to 1979, Raymond was in Montreal to start filming his part in *Tomorrow Never Comes*, the first time in 41 years he had performed professionally in his native Canada. He wanted to study the production end of the Canadian movie business.

He signed with March Films, Ltd., for two theater films. Here he was able to observe, first hand, the temperamental antics of the stars. Raymond just sat back and watched during the making of the first film; his contract stipulated he would get overtime pay if his part went on longer than scheduled—$10,000 per day for a week's contract. Because of production difficulties and delays, he worked two weeks and then donated two more days of work on the film.

In *Tomorrow Never Comes*, Raymond portrayed a corrupt police commissioner. The character role was not very big, but he made the most of it and outshone the other stars. When reviews came out in newspapers and magazines, the notices were very bad.

Michael Springer, the producer, took the finished film to England. The film was so bad it was panned by reviewers and yanked out of theaters by the managers. However, five or six years later, this film showed up on cable television.

Raymond said, "There is a degree of excellence I wish was in the Canadian pictures I did. They were terrible and should never have been made. I did them only for tax purposes. Canada has some of the best film crews in the world and ... some of the best scenery."

One good thing came out of this experience: While on location in Vancouver, Canada, Raymond was able to visit his father often. He tried to persuade William to give up living in his beloved Canada and move to California with him.

Persistent persuasion by Raymond finally convinced William Burr to give up his apartment. On October 12, 1978, the elder Burr arrived in California to spend what he thought would be his final years with his son.

After Raymond's part was completed, he returned to the States to begin a new business venture in the manufacturing of soaps, colognes, and perfumes. He hoped in six years to have 12 different fragrances on the market. The products would be for both men and women, but there would be a long line of products for men only. In the meantime, he purchased property in Puerto Rico for more orchid growing.

Raymond filmed a cameo role for a television movie titled "79 Park Avenue." Portraying the godfather of a mob syndicate, he is talked about throughout the film but not seen until almost the very end. The public was shocked to find he had ballooned to over three hundred pounds.

Raymond had undergone dramatic surgery where he had to be put on a special diet to help him assimilate food. As a result, he had gained over 90 pounds in a year. The hospital stay had been kept secret and had not appeared in any newspapers or fan magazines. Appearing on Merv Griffin's show, Raymond shocked Merv when he walked out to greet him. Not only was he huge, but he had grown a beard and mustache for filming his part in "Centennial."

He was still wearing the beard when a role came along for a "Love Boat" episode. Gavin McLeod was a friend from early movie and television days, when he had appeared in several episodes of "Perry Mason." The "Love Boat" episode was called "Alas, Poor Dwyer." Filming was done on board ship during an 11 day cruise down the Mexican coast. He played the part of an English teacher with an alcohol problem who was attending a high school reunion planned by Julie McCoy, the ship's cruise director. Raymond was her favorite English teacher and gave an excellent, sensitive performance.

He also had a chance to sing Gilbert and Sullivan songs along with Gavin McLeod in several scenes. Raymond never got to sing in any of his films, so this was quite a delightful surprise to his audience and proved he still had a good voice.

When the cruise was over and his scenes completed, Raymond flew to Vancouver for a television interview on the "Alan Hamel Show" to talk about his television film, "The Jordon Chance," to be shown on Canadian television in a few days. He then flew to the West Coast to appear on Stephanie Edwards's "Everyday" show on October 13, 1978. Raymond mentioned how happy he was to have his 87-year-old father living with him. Just as the interview came to a conclusion, Edwards made an insulting remark about his weight. The audience and Raymond gasped as she quickly realized she had hurt him. She was still apologizing to him as the commercials came on and the show went off the air. The next interview was October 17, 1978, on Merv Griffin's show, to plug "The Jordon Chance." As the film clip was shown, true to form, Raymond would not look at the monitor and waited patiently until the end.

"The Jordon Chance" made its debut on television on December 2,

1978, and received good reviews. Raymond was disappointed because the film never became a series. Neither this film nor "Kingston Confidential" reached the potential he had hoped they would, yet from time to time both show up on television.

His next television movie was shown on May 20, 1979, a Civil War drama called "Love's Savage Fury." Raymond played the part of Jennifer O'Neil's father and was shot and killed by a cold-blooded soldier about ten minutes into the film. The pattern of being killed in his films still prevailed.

In the spring of 1979, Raymond went to Chicago to host and narrate a true story made into a dramatic television film titled "The Trial of Xavier Solorzana," based on a criminal trial that had taken place in and around Chicago. The film was shown in the Chicago area only. Raymond's summer plans took him to Frankfurt, Germany. After completing business there, he flew to Stockholm, Sweden, and spent a day and a half on business not related to show business.

Joe Don Baker was a young actor who had appeared in several "Ironside" episodes. He was given star status when he filmed his first pilot film, "Eischied," for a series. Raymond played the part of the police commissioner. The pilot was shown in two parts, on September 21 and 28, 1979. Raymond was seldom seen but was talked about in this five hour drama. When the actual series began, Raymond was talked about as the commissioner, the boss upstairs, but was never seen.

Raymond flew to New York to narrate "A Life on Paper," a PBS film based on the life and writings of William Faulkner. The film was shown on channel 13 in the New York area on December 17, 1979.

Before the close of the year, Raymond lost two friends. Kurt Kasznar, who had been the director of his first musical comedy in 1941, died of cancer. Collier Young, the creator and a producer of "Ironside," died of injuries received in an automobile accident. Young had lived long enough to know "Ironside" had been a success. In syndication, Raymond had received over $8 million for residuals and percentage points for sales around the United States, Canada, and the world.

Raymond went back to Vancouver to complete his second film for March Films. In *Out of the Blue*, he played a psychiatrist trying to help Linda Marz. His scenes were filmed in Canada while the rest of the film was done in various parts of the world. Script problems and personality conflicts dominated the production. "This was the worst film I ever worked on and the worst experience of my life," said Raymond. "It was a waste of time, money and talent. I'm sorry I ever agreed to make the film, as I realize now that filming in Canada was not done as strictly as it is done in the United States."

Raymond signed to play a role in "The Misadventures of Sheriff Lobo," in an episode scheduled to open the fall television season of 1980.

As the Godfather, Raymond was dressed in the same type of pinstriped suit and fedora hat he had worn in almost all his early gangster films. He pulled his hat down over his eyes and spoke in a menacing voice. His part was small, but he made the most of the scenes by stealing them from his friend Claude Akins. Years before, Akins had been a character actor in some "Perry Mason" and "Ironside" episodes.

Raymond traveled to Egypt for his role in "The Curse of King Tut's Tomb." Filming had started in December 1979 and continued into 1980. Some scenes were filmed in London, but most of the film was done on location in Egypt. Raymond was dressed in flowing robes and a turban as the Arab villain and collapsed one day from exhaustion as well as the extreme desert heat. As he fell from his chair his head struck an object, and he spent the next two days unconscious in the hospital.

Superstition about the curse of King Tut ran rampant as things began to happen to the cast and crew. The reporters watching the filming had a good deal of material to write about and created headlines in newspapers and magazines all over the world. A car accident caused a delay in production when Ian McShane broke his leg and had to be replaced by another actor. Eva Marie Saint was almost electrocuted. Raymond had his problems, and other near misses plagued the production. Filming was finally completed in March 1980, in London. Many years later, he told Larry King of CNN that he was still fanatical about not going into details about the film.

Arriving in Sydney, Raymond flew to Melbourne, where he attended a banquet for the winners of the Logie Award. Raymond presented the Logie Awards, the Australian version of the Emmy Awards, in Sydney, then flew home to California to face his next assignment. He hosted "Presto Chango, It's Magic," a 90 minute film for cable television, then made two more cable films, "Psychic Phenomena" and "The Alien's Return." Raymond portrayed Cybill Shepherd's father in the latter film, a science fiction movie made on location in Arizona and released in 1980.

Gradually, Raymond began accepting smaller parts on television and avoiding the headache of making another series. His role could be done in a few days, and he could move on to another film if he wanted to. This plan enabled Raymond to spread his film work over a year and attend to his business interests and his orchid farms.

Next role was as the president of a railroad in trouble in "Disaster on the Coast Train." The film was an ABC-TV two hour special.

Raymond then played the role of mayor of a town caught in a blackout. In his quiet, dignified way, he controlled a large city in crisis. The television film was titled "The Night the City Screamed."

As 1980 drew to a close, Raymond's business interests were beginning to take up most of his time, as were his travels around the world.

Raymond Burr and George Stanford Brown in "The Night the City Screamed," 1980.

On one of his trips to the main islands of Fiji, he discovered a wonderful Israeli artist, Triska Blumenfeld. Raymond arranged to exhibit her work in America. Her one woman shows were quite successful and won her a great deal of praise.

His next assignment brought him to Athens for the television film "The Acts of Peter and Paul." Raymond played King Herod Agrippa in this four hour special based on the book of Acts. During the month he spent there, he visited his adopted child, Maria, bringing her on a shopping spree and visiting her family. Shooting was completed on location in Rhode Island in 1981, but Raymond was already at work on another film. When "The Acts of Peter and Paul" was shown on television, Raymond's role had been cut to about four or five sentences and lasted about two minutes on the screen.

Raymond said at the time,

> I'm no longer interested in trying to have another series on TV. This stems from the financial setup of the studios. It leaves the actor poorer, the studios richer. Actors have to work extremely hard for long hours to make a series successful. The cost of putting one together keeps rising tremendously and it doesn't pay, these days, to gamble on its success or failure.

Burr as King Herod Agrippa in "The Acts of Peter and Paul."

Chances of succeeding become very slim if it is put on in an inappropriate time slot.

The public doesn't get a chance to voice their opinion about it before the show is canceled!

I would like to produce and direct films in Canada and the United States, for television and theaters, but the problems with the various unions spoil it for international actors like myself. Going back to the stage, touring on a limited basis, might be the answer. That way, *all* of my interests could be combined. I regret some roles I accepted, but never regretted turning down a particular role I felt was not right for me.

Raymond was in a position to pick and choose his roles — or not work at all. "No matter what happens with your life, you have to go on planning for your future. Never look back, never quit. Above all, never lose faith."

This philosophy gave him strength to cope with the loss of four women friends who had a great influence on his life. Luella Gear had been in *Crazy with the Heat*, the musical comedy Raymond had had small parts in back in 1941. She died after a long illness in 1980, at the age of 80. Gail Patrick Jackson died of leukemia at 69; she was the producer of the "Perry Mason" series and remained friends with Raymond long after the series ended. In 1981, Natalie Wood lost her life in a drowning accident. Then in 1982, Grace Kelly was killed in a tragic auto accident in Monaco. They had made *Rear Window* in 1953-54. Whenever Raymond traveled in France, he would always take time for a visit with Princess Grace and Prince Rainier.

The tragic deaths of Natalie Wood and Princess Grace forced Raymond to think about his own life. Hollywood and Los Angeles were changing into crowded, unpredictable towns. The television and film industries were turning out more and more violent films for the younger generation. He felt it was time to move on to a new area.

He put his home in the Hollywood Hills on the market for $2.5 million. Not long afterward, the house and grounds were sold for almost the asking price. "Since my father came to live with me we have gotten to know each other quite well. We have been making up for all the years apart. I feel it would not be wise to be away for long periods of time as he is in his nineties now," said Raymond.

The elder Burr had other ideas, however, and decided he had had enough of living in California. He insisted upon moving back to his beloved Canada when Raymond bought a 40 acre farm in Dry Creek Valley, a tiny town in the wine country of the Sonoma Valley in northern California, several hours outside San Francisco.

Nothing Raymond could do or say would change William's mind, so a very reluctant son flew to Vancouver with his father. Together they reopened the cottage on Boundary Bay, in British Columbia. "My father lives not far away from where we used to go swimming in the summertime," Raymond told a reporter. Raymond stayed long enough to make sure his father was settled and happy to be back home, close by his relatives and friends. He had his garden to attend to, and a housekeeper was hired to care for the cottage as well as William's needs. Raymond returned to his new farm, satisfied his father would be all right.

Sea God Nurseries grew and Raymond traveled around the country to flower shows and conventions. He was growing orchids on a grand scale, and investing in lumber production, cattle raising, coconut growing, and other enterprises in Portugal, the Azores, Fiji, and Puerto Rico.

He had transported his many greenhouses with all his orchid breeding plants and other plants he was experimenting with to the property in Dry Creek Valley.

> I have a vineyard growing 14 kinds of table grapes and I hope to make my own wine and champagne someday.
>
> I'm becoming the farmer I had always wanted to be. I have 60 sheep raised for 16 various colored wool. Natural colors of wool range from black to white, brown, taupe, grey, apricot, and tan.
>
> I hire men to shear the sheep each year and the wool is taken to a plant where it is washed, made into skeins and dyed other colors besides the color of the sheep. The skeins of wool are then sold to stores in town as well as in other stores across the country. This wool weaves better, knits better and wears better. This is also a money making project.
>
> The fruits and vegetables are collected by people I hired to do this work and what we don't use everyday is canned and stored for further use. My American grandmother and my mother taught me how to can food during the depression when food and money were scarce, so sometimes when I am on the farm, I'll do some of it. Otherwise my housekeeper and hired help will do it. I have my own label on all my products. These too are sold wherever there is a market for them.
>
> I also know how to milk cows since I once did it for a living!

Raymond, in the fall of 1982, became a professor of theater arts and university artist-in-residence at Sonoma State University in Rohnert Park, California. He enjoyed teaching a great deal and interested the faculty in extending the drama department to include all related theater subjects.

As a salesman, Raymond's life was beginning to come full circle. He had started out as a teenage door-to-door salesman and now, in the 1980s, was a super salesman via television, newspapers, and magazines. Through his real estate connections, Raymond became acquainted with Block Brothers Realty Company. The Vancouver based firm hired him to appear in their newspaper advertisements and television commercials throughout Canada. Bache, Halsey, Stuart Company, New York stockbrokers, hired him to do voiceovers for a series of television spot advertisements.

Raymond became the spokesman for the Independent Insurance Agents, appearing in their one minute series of commercials starting in 1981. When his contract was up in 1985, he signed on for another five years.

In one commercial for the television audience, Raymond appears in his trademark courtroom. As he walks toward the camera, he holds up a pair of locked handcuffs and pulls on them as he speaks to the audience: "Are you locked into one insurance agency?"

He attended organizations and national conventions, toured local agencies, and met with groups of insurance agents. He made radio and television commercials in cities all over the country. His soft-spoken, dignified, personable, and controlled sales pitch increased the Independent Insurance Agencies recognition factor over 20 percent. He used his own production company to film the tasteful insurance commercials. He believed in matching the man to the television commercial, not the other way around. To appear in commercials or do voiceovers for companies wishing to use his services, Raymond insisted on setting his own rules and a price high enough to attract the good products he believed in. He turned down over $20 million in offers for his endorsements of one product or another.

> I have a responsibility to the audiences who have supported me. When you get into products and the company is sold, they may change the quality and it turns out it isn't exactly as you told your audience. You might be talking about something you have no control over. When you can't have quality control, it is dangerous to get involved.

The Independent Insurance Agencies insisted he lose a lot of weight on a carefully planned diet and exercise program. He lost over a hundred pounds in a two year period.

"I have a great deal of confidence in what I do," he conceded. "I don't have a great ego. I don't even have a picture of myself in the house. I do have my memories of course, but tomorrow is important to me—not yesterday."

XVIII

Korea

Through the years, Raymond Burr gave his time to many causes he believed in, without publicity. He made 12 trips to Korea during the Korean War, visiting as many servicemen as he could on each mission. He brought news and messages from home, and the men gave him messages to take back to the States with him. Every chance he got, Raymond made it a point to visit the wounded in the hospitals.

The trips to Korea began in 1951 and continued until the conflict was over. In between he continued to make movies and radio and television shows.

Some of the servicemen wrote letters telling of their experience and impressions of him. They admired his guts for sharing foxholes with them under fire, crawling through the mud, and flying into their camp in bad weather to put on a show.

Raymond began by delivering messages and mail. After he came back stateside, he personally called the families to relay their messages. This continued until he got a telephone call: "My boy's dead."

Some of the trips were paid for and arranged by the Hollywood Coordinating Committee, or the USO, or the government. Most of the time Raymond paid his own way over and back. Four camp shows had the cooperation of government agencies.

Before the war, Bozy White operated Shoestring Records. When Raymond went to Greenland, he met White, who was stationed there. He recalled that Raymond was a great person and was glad he got the chance to meet this celebrity and shake his hand.

Edward F. Carnrite of Auburn, Washington, said, "I was in the 21st Artillery attached to 'C' Troop, 9th Cav. in Korea, 1963–64. Raymond Burr visited our unit and had supper with us. I have his autograph on a piece of notebook paper."

"I met Mr. Raymond Burr at Kemp Airbase, December 24, 1964, as he was returning home from Korea and I was going to Japan for R. and R.," recalled Theodore L. Strickland of Tampa, Florida.

I'm afraid our conversation was *not* pleasant, although I was pleased to talk to this great actor. Instead of me telling him how much I enjoyed his part in "Perry Mason" and other shows I had seen him star in, I talked of the pain, anger and hurt I felt inside. A few weeks earlier, I had lost my closest friend in the DMZ. The North Koreans had helped search for him and even permitted a general officer to enter the DMZ. The pain I felt inside that Friday was great. I was happy the North Koreans were helping and my feelings for them were friendship. But the following Sunday, at midnight, they ambushed and killed two Americans and wounded one. This compounded my hurt. At the time I met Mr. Burr my hurt was almost a sickness and he just stood and listened to me until I had gotten it all out of my system. I have often thought about that meeting and wished I had talked of something else.

"My introduction to Mr. Burr was made by another soldier," said Arthur Holliday of Hephzibah, Georgia.

I can't recall the soldier's name who introduced us.

It was December 31, 1963, at the Riviera Service Club, located at Camp Henry, Taegu, Korea. He rather jokingly introduced me to Mr. Burr as "Lieutenant Tragg." I was not overly impressed by his introduction of me to Mr. Burr, but I did enjoy a rather pleasant conversation with him. I explained to Mr. Burr that at the time I was both the Platoon Sergeant, Company A, 728th Military Police Battalion and the Operations Sergeant for the Taegu Subpost Provost Marshall's Office. This provided Military Police support to the Teagu Subpost. I was known by many friends and associates as "The Sheriff." Among my memorabilia I have a small poster which gives notice to Burr's arrival and a photograph with a short biographical sketch on the back. I also have a photograph on the wall of my den showing Mr. Burr cutting a cake at the service club with a hostess and an unidentified soldier in civilian dress and myself.

Mr. Burr was scheduled to visit the enlisted men's Mess Hall during the evening meal, which he did. He was invited to the NCO Club afterward. There were many parties going on at both places since it was New Year's Eve. I don't know if he visited any of them although he had been invited.

SFC Rodney D. Bryan of 503rd AG Company, APO, New York says,

I met Raymond Burr in December 1963 when he visited our compound during Christmas holidays.

He talked to soldiers in the Mess Hall on Christmas Day. I was a PFC assigned to B Battery, 7th Missile BN 2nd FA, 37th FA Group located on a (Hawk) missile Tac Site, four miles east of Inchon, Korea. I was the Battery Commander's driver and thus was privileged to drive Mr. Burr around the compound and Tac Site, during his visit. I took several pictures of him which I sent home to Portland, Oregon.

CWO Frankie L. Sharp of El Paso, Texas, says he was a staff sergeant when Burr visited them on Christmas Eve in 1953.

Mr. Burr visited our unit on top of Maybong Mountain, in Korea. We were known as the mountain men and the forgotten defenders. As a Hawk Missile Unit, part of the Air Defense in Korea, we were almost inaccessible. The weather year round was bad and travel to our unit was next to impossible! The rain, mud, rock slides, snow, ice, [and] washed out roads and bridges were only a few of the obstacles.

The creek would have to be crossed without bridges, and the small creek would become a raging river about halfway across and would rise over the vehicles in a matter of seconds. In the fall and winter, the fog would freeze and everything was a brilliant white (We called it a white-out), and you could not distinguish the size or shape of objects.

We couldn't even see the hood of our vehicles and the drivers would have the men walk in front of the vehicles holding hands to keep from getting lost while relaying back to the driver where the road was. We had to feel with our feet where the road was or—empty space approximately 4,000 feet below!

Raymond Burr braved the shifting winds, up and down drafts, wind shears, and sudden gusts of wind, and flew up to our missile site in a bubble helicopter. I don't know if he was aware of just how dangerous it was, but he was the *only* person who even tried to pay us a visit!

His visit to us, The Forgotten Mountain Men of Air Defense, on top of that godforsaken mountain, gave every one of us a tremendous lift in our morale. He even went out of his way to visit each and every one of us on that mountaintop. He took phone numbers and called our parents and wives when he returned to the USA—*and he paid for all those calls*! On behalf of all the men of B Battery, 5th BN 7th ADA on Maybong Mountain, we want to thank him even if it is over 40 years later. He did not forget us and we still remember him. On behalf of all the men who were in my unit, I say *thank you, as you are one in a million*!

"I had the pleasure of meeting Raymond Burr on two occasions while serving in the U.S. Army," recalls Lt. Col. Joseph E. Scanlin.

The first time, I was a Captain serving in Korea in 1953. I was the Assistant Plans and Operations Officer, G-5 Section Headquarters, 8th U.S. Army in Seoul. I was a sponsor of a group of Korean college students that met every Saturday morning in a USIA program, and Mr. Burr visited our group in the USIA building in downtown Seoul. We had a couple of hours and the students really got a thrill out of meeting "Perry Mason."

On the second occasion I was a Captain in Vietnam assigned to the 5th Special Forces Group in 1965. I was a patient in the hospital in Nha Trang and Mr. Burr was visiting the wards.

I remember him coming to my bed and looking at me and saying, "What are you doing here? Didn't I meet you in Korea?"

I said, "I was going to ask you the same thing." We talked for a few minutes and then he had to move on to another ward. We all enjoyed his visit, as he was very easy to talk with. I noted he traveled with a single escort officer.

After the Korean visit Mr. Burr contacted my parents to tell them he met me in Korea. In Vietnam I asked him not to, this time, as they didn't know I was in the hospital.

Everywhere Raymond went on his trips to Korea, the men had nothing but praise and admiration for him. He listened patiently to all he spoke with, even if it was gripes.

Lt. Col. Edwin S. Williams of Overland, Kansas, said,

> I was the Executive Officer of the 2nd BN, 76th Artillery, Camp St. Barbara, Korea. Mr. Burr came to our unit in late 1953, early 1954. I am a bit hazy on the dates, sorry about that. I met him briefly at the battalion headquarters but he wasn't interested in the officers—his main interest was the troops.
>
> We were a heavily indigenized organization (80 percent Katusa, with 12 Republic of Korea Officers). The ROK Executive, Major Kim, told me the Katusas did not believe this big person was Raymond Burr because he was only so big on the television screen! [Indicating several inches!]

James A. Dale of Decaturville, Tennessee, took pictures of Raymond Burr during one of his USO shows. The show took place in an empty cement warehouse. "We built a stage and dressing rooms and put heat in them, trying to heat the warehouse with portable heaters. Of course it cooled down fast during the program as it was about February or March and cold as H— — —."

Norman G. Laumeyer of Daleville, Alabama, met Raymond during his visit to Canto, Korea, late 1953 or early 1954. "Danny"—Harold E. Daniel from Aiea, Hawaii—has an autographed photo of Burr and a group of performers who went to the Navy Hospital in Oakland, California, to do a show for every ward filled with wounded men. They also went to Letterman General Hospital in Presideo, San Francisco, California. They did the show prior to going to Korea just before Christmas.

Danny said,

> One of the gags was to have Marla English advance on Raymond Burr trying to get his money and putting it in her fancy garter on her lovely leg!
>
> Another gag was to have a seaman throw a pie in Raymond's face. He really was a mess when the seaman got through with him.
>
> Raymond Burr was a very likable individual going out of his way to be helpful to everyone, whether he be a serviceman of the lowest rank or the top brass. He made sure he visited every man in the wards, talking, smiling and comforting them.

On May 14, 1967, James P. Gleason, a lieutenant colonel in the U.S. Marine Corps, was evacuated to the USS *Sanctuary* with a gunshot wound. Following surgery, he was assigned to a space in the sick officers quarters.

> About the third day, Raymond Burr came walking into our room—totally unannounced. There were six of us in the room and he spent time with each one of us. He asked about our wounds, where we were from,

usually relating a story about having performed in some stage production in that town, or nearby city, or having just visited that town in his early stage career. Two impressions of the visit remain with me today.

1. My first thought upon seeing him was what a great target he'd make! He was huge, not really fat, just massive. He seemed to fill the room!

2. The lack of fanfare that normally accompanied visiting Hollywood stars, such as Bob Hope, Martha Raye or Ann-Margret.

Mr. Burr just simply showed up. His one-on-one approach coupled with his earnest, sincere interest in our recovery. The talk of our hometown was probably the most important thing to all of us there. This served, if only for a short period of time, to pick up our spirits. Then, just as quickly as he arrived, he went on to the next ward.

Army Sgt. Gerald R. Shepard said,

Although I was not in combat during the Korean War, I was stationed in Japan for three years during that conflict. I was stationed at Osaka Army Hospital, and sometime in 1951, I don't remember the month, a couple of buddies and I went to a small tea room, located just outside the back gate of the Osaka Hospital. When we walked in the tea room, there was Raymond Burr sitting on the floor by a small table and we got to have a drink with him. He was really a friendly guy and we enjoyed it very much. He may not remember this event. After all it was over 35 years ago!

Leonard W. Pierson of Fair Oaks, California, came back from a mission in Korea in 1951-52 and went into the officer's mess to get a cup of coffee. He sat down opposite Raymond Burr. At first Pierson just told Raymond he looked familiar. Where had they met before?

"With a little indignity in his voice, Raymond told me his name and no one seemed to know that he was on the base! We only talked for a few minutes as I had to leave again."

Raymond was with a USO Tour in December 1951, when Allen T. Miller of Kailua, Hawaii, met him in Korea.

I was a pilot, a member of the 10th Liaison Squad (L-5's) and was assigned to fly Raymond to visit several army units who were stationed along the front lines. My memories are somewhat dim, but I was impressed with his desire to bring a bit of Christmas cheer to the troops. It confirms the impression I got from my brief encounter with him. He is a generous soul, ready and willing to do what he can to be a useful person in this world. I was a captain in the USAF assigned to a so-called Liaison Squadron, which had light, single-engine aircraft for short hops between the USAF and USA units. We were stationed at Seoul City Air Base (K-16), just southwest of Seoul on an island in the Han River. In mid–December a USO group appeared at our field, of which Raymond Burr was a member. I don't remember that he had a real part in the show that they put on. He seemed more interested in getting out with the fighting units.

At that point in the war, there was a general lull in the fighting, and each side was in a static position pretty much where the present demilitarized zone is.

The 3rd Division was on the line north of Seoul with headquarters at Chorwon, I believe, which was one of the anchors in the "Iron Triangle." Somehow Burr got permission to visit the troops of the Division, and I was assigned to fly him around.

We went in an L-5, a tandem two-seater, and his generous bulk made for a good load in the rear seat! The weather was exceptionally good for that time of year, and we made an uneventful flight, about 45 minutes, to the unit's forward airfield. We were driven in a jeep up to where the troops were actually dug in, something I had never seen before—sort of like trench scenes from World War I films!

Burr got out and introduced himself, engaged in friendly talk, and asked if he could take messages back to the home folk and so on. He wasn't well known at the time, and responses were a bit slow. I mentioned that he had recently acted with Elizabeth Taylor in a version of Dreiser's *American Tragedy*—that got the talk going. We did this at several places, using up all the available daylight.

By then we were getting pretty cold and got back to K-16 as fast as possible to get warmed up over a bottle of Johnnie Walker Red Label, which I had been saving for a special occasion, and I felt that this definitely was it. Can't remember much past that except he said he'd try to get back the next day for another visit forward. Evidently the USO troupe had to move on, and I never saw him again. Anyway, I had an enjoyable day with him.

On December 15, 1952, Raymond and other entertainers were honored at the National Guard Armory in Culver City, California. Immediately afterward, Raymond left to spend Christmas at the Greenland and Labrador bases.

This time he was accompanied by his brother, Edmond. Edmond played many percussion instruments, plus the piano. He was a composer, arranger, copyist, and conductor for the Los Angeles Police Band.

On one trip to Korea, Raymond, Jan Sterling and her husband, Paul Douglas, went to Tokyo Hospital to give blood. A boy's mother found out somehow that Raymond was about to go back to Korea on another trip. She took a chance and sent him her son's photograph. Attached was a letter explaining her son would be 21 years old on a date when Raymond would be in Korea. Raymond received the letter and inquired about the boy as soon as he arrived in the area. Afterward, the boy wrote home, "About two weeks ago I saw Raymond Burr at our airfield. He called me over and told me we had a dinner date in Saigon on May 28th. I told him that was my birthday when I would become 21 years old. He said he knew about it and proceeded to explain your letter to him. I was in a happy daze, believe me!"

Raymond took the boy and ten of his buddies to Saigon's Coco Club. They all had a fabulous dinner, including a huge birthday cake, all paid for by Raymond Burr.

James Maloney of South Plainfield, New Jersey, served in the Combat Engineers of the 36th Group of the 8th Army in Korea. He says,

We were assigned as armed escort security to the USO shows visiting the front, called "Iron Triangle" and "Old Smokey," in the Papason Sector. This was in the summer of 1952 and into 1953.

Mickey Rooney as well as Raymond Burr, Paul Douglas, Jan Sterling, and others performed for us. I designed the stage which we built from trees in the surrounding area. We built the stage strong enough to survive any heavy dancing or very heavy weights that would be using it.

Mick was a regular guy with the girls, but Raymond was somewhat of a loner. An immense man, we had to scour other supply outfits to get an XX large size or the biggest the U.S. Army made, fatigue outfit to fit him. Raymond had to wear the outfit during the finale of the show, which required that Burr receive pies made with shaving cream thrown in his face by servicemen. In those days Raymond was less known and most of us knew him not for television but as a villain in movies.

When Mr. Burr arrived, he immediately made off to the absolute front line, a short distance of about five miles away, in order to visit the frontline troops. He clearly presented a real danger to himself. The USO show he and other performers put on for us did more for our morale than anyone could reckon.

Life on the line was seven days a week with breaks for church or chapel, as it was available. It was dawn to dusk plus guard duty.

Two hours alone on an outpost midnight until two A.M., two to four, four to six, etc. Dark is a word one will never know until you have perceived it under conditions that were harsh in Korea anytime of the year. In dry periods road travel was like the 1930s dust bowl. Rain—one can't grasp R-A-I-N in ordinary terms. There were no trees, virtually due to the blitz of combat. Koreans also used up the wood to survive the cold and to use as fires to eat any dogs or cats they were able to catch, in order to stay alive.

Our Yalu River bridge washed out as the river rose to over 42 feet and twisted like a pretzel the steel trestles, which had been capable of supporting our tanks, trucks and heavy gun loads.

Snow! Cold! I personally recorded 27 degrees minus, Fahrenheit. We used small potbellied stoves to try to keep warm, but had to use outdoor latrines! If you were in a bunker and the bunker received a direct hit, you were buried alive with rats that were trying to keep warm also.

It is clear to me, today, many years after the Korean Conflict, that earth homes were practical and a sandbag reinforced tent was the alternative, or—a foxhole.

The USO was a Godsend beyond words, when they showed up with music, laughter and girls!

I found out later that Raymond Burr talked to the men at the dangerous outposts taking letters, messages, and phone numbers, promising to deliver the letters and if possible, personally phoning the loved ones of the men. The men later heard that he kept his promise.

A few trips later, Raymond wangled a ride up to the front lines and promptly got shot at. He flew on a fighter bomber mission over enemy territory in a tiny, slow, unarmed L-5 liaison plane. He was on his way to visit the men who drove the tanks and some Air Force personnel. At the same time, he got a good look at Heartbreak Ridge and The Little Bulge fighting area.

Matt Weinstock of the *Los Angeles Daily News* was on this trip with Raymond. He later published an article which said:

> There is no way to describe the stink and destruction, or the kind of fighting our men had to do. Put together all the unprintable words and you have Korea. It is that kind of hell hole. The city of Seoul isn't there anymore. A new kind of fever attacks the men, because there is no water, except what they carry in their canteens. The young age fast in the front lines. Raymond Burr gave blood in a Yokohama hospital and visited the patients there.
>
> The biggest shock came when Raymond got up at three in the morning to visit a Korean hospital and helped to unload the wounded men from the ambulances. One of the men he unloaded and helped carry was one of his best friends from Northern California. The man was so badly wounded he required nine transfusions.

Robert F. Shaw recalls:

> I was headquarters Commandant of the 179th Infantry Regiment in Korea. It was the time of Raymond Burr's USO tour in the area, the winter of 1952–53. He and his escort officer arrived at our headquarters one morning for 6:30 A.M. breakfast, after they had traveled from division headquarters, ten miles or so over hairpin turns of a few mountains. His escort officer was doing more talking than Mr. Burr was.
>
> Mr. Burr's purpose was to go up to the front line positions along "Heartbreak Ridge" and spend the day talking with the men there. It was dark when he finished breakfast and left. He didn't return until after dark that evening. GIs were asking, "Who is this guy Burr?" He was really friendly and said he'd write to our folks in the States. In the ensuing weeks, the same GIs were reporting that their folks had indeed had letters from Raymond Burr, assuring them of their son's or husband's welfare.
>
> Burr was quietly doing all he could to boost the morale on a personal, genuine basis. He did more with those interviews and letters than he accomplished in all of his shows, excellent as they were. Suffice it that those of us who met him there have wished him all success ever since and have been darned happy to see how much success he has had.
>
> He showed himself to be not only a gracious gentleman, but a credit to the USO and the world of entertainers—many of whom stayed close to their comforts and preferred the company of the brass to that of the men in the lines.

Lt. Col. Robert L. Chase of San Marcos, California, met Raymond

Burr while on duty with KMAG in Wonju, Korea, in 1953-54. Chase says he was quartered with the Wonju Area Command.

I went to see a USO show one evening and Burr was one of the entertainers. I had never met him before, and I never even heard of him until that USO show played Wonju. His style and mannerisms were uncannily a duplicate of another thespian friend of mine named Patrick T. Miller. There was absolutely no physical similarities between these two men. Burr was a big man with dark hair. Pat was small, blond, and handsome. After the show was over, Burr came over to the Officer's Club (Quonset Hut) to chat.

I was so intrigued by the stark similarities of Burr and Miller on stage that I just *had* to question him. I introduced myself to him and told Raymond of the similarity between him and my friend Pat and asked by any chance if he knew him. Burr replied that he sure did know Pat and the two of them had attended the Pasadena Playhouse at the same time! It seemed to me that the Pasadena Playhouse must have had one way of training actors in order for those two to have almost identical techniques and stage mannerisms.

Raymond asked me to say hello to Pat when I saw him again and to ask Pat to tell me of an amusing incident when the two of them were in a play together with Raymond portraying George Washington.

I lost track of Pat so have been unable to relay the message. I was impressed with Mr. Burr's friendliness and stage presence and have not seen him in person since.

That tour of duty with the Army in Korea was one of the few memories that I cared to bring home. However, the USO shows were great, even though I never heard of Raymond Burr until I saw this USO show. Needless to say, I have admired his acting ever since then.

"My association with Raymond Burr was early in 1953, in Korea," said Col. Paul Fojtik, USAF (retired), of Truckee, California.

I was the Commander of the 6147th Tac Control GP, an Air Force unit flying World War II T-6s.

We were located at K-47 Chun Chon, Korea, and our mission was to locate enemy targets and mark them with smoke rockets for the Air Force jets to bomb. We were dubbed Mosquitos by the North Koreans because no matter how much they tried to hide, we could find them and apply the "sting."

Raymond Burr headed up a USO show that visited our base. Inasmuch as we were the most remote Air Force base, USO shows generally spent the weekend with us. Our mission was considered the most unusual in Korea. Raymond decided to extend his stay in Korea after his show returned to the States.

Our mission included providing a Tac Control Party of three men with each ground unit on the front lines. They coordinated by radio the location of targets with our Mosquito pilots and jet fighters. We were located with United Nations units as well and had a total of about 60 individual control parties on the line.

Burr insisted on a personal visit to each of the 60 Tac Control parties over several weeks, living with them under quite primitive conditions.

Fojtik added, "As you would realize, he was an outstanding hit—much appreciated. No other personality of the many that did visit extended themselves to be one of the boys. Burr was great!"

Lt. Col. John A. Estock of North Providence, Rhode Island, recalls an amusing incident when he met Burr.

> I spent an evening with Raymond Burr at the Officer's Club, 10th Corps Headquarters in Korea in late 1953 or early 1954. A pilot friend of mine flew him in from Seoul, introduced him to me at the club, and asked me to keep him company for the evening, since the pilot had to fly back to Seoul immediately. This was about 5:00 P.M.
>
> During the introduction, I understood the man to be Raymond *Brown*. About 10:30 P.M., after making an arrangement to meet Raymond the next day, I decided to leave. Halfway out of the club I was asked by another officer how I knew Raymond Burr the movie actor. I said he was introduced to me as Raymond Brown! I then decided to go back to the bar and asked Raymond if his last name was Burr and was he a movie actor. Burr said yes and mentioned a picture with Elizabeth Taylor in which he played the part of a lawyer. I stayed another hour and we talked about his career. My friend the pilot was scheduled to leave the service and go to work for Raymond Burr. I don't know if he ever did work for him.

"Mr. Burr, you owe me an undershirt!" So says Jeremy K. Schloss.

> I was the commanding officer of the 5th Communications Group in Seoul, Korea, from November 1952 until November 1953. During that time Raymond Burr visited my organization with a group, in approximately June of that year, performing several skits, and during one of those skits Raymond took a pie in the face. Needless to say, he was quite a mess after the session and found himself short of an undershirt. I loaned him one of mine since we were about the same size. I believe that he had dinner with the enlisted personnel in the main dining room of Seoul University, my headquarters at the time. His performance was wonderful and the men constantly referred to his visit as one of the entertainment highlights of Korea. There weren't too many of those! Incidentally, he still owes me an undershirt, but since I no longer wear such clothing I'll settle for a drink when he visits the Bay area.

However, Colonel Orvil T. Unger had a different view of Raymond's performance for the GIs. Col. Unger served from January to September 1953 as Wing Chaplain at Chinhae, Korea. During this tour, a USO show performed in the base theater, and Raymond Burr was the master of ceremonies.

Colonel Unger says,

I had never seen him before and later I learned to admire his performances and regretted that he was in the position to receive my censorship.

Before hundreds of sex-starved men (of which I was one, so my
response was not objective) Raymond and an attractive female rubbed
and fondled each other, punishing the viewers as if tasting a steak dinner
before the starving. After the show, I censored him for indulging in a public display. A public display of oral orgasms, imaginary intercourse, and
mental masturbation (I've been a sucker for alliteration). Mr. Burr was
apologetic and I feel genuinely contrite, stating that he was required to
transmit my protest to the USO. I believe the troupe performed at Mason
the next morning. I never received any response or reaction from any
source. However, I suspect Mr. Burr will recall one irate chaplain, who
I'd like him to know, is now one of his fans.

Arvin O. Meredith of Phoenix, Arizona, had a casual acquaintance
with Raymond in Korea in 1953 and found him to be one whom he held
in high regard.

You must recognize that after more than thirty or thirty-five years,
memory blurs somewhat as to the details of most any given subject.

However, I do remember more or less clearly my encounter with Raymond Burr in Chun Chon, Korea, which represents only one facet of his
activities with the USO troupes throughout where American troops were
on duty.

I was Executive Officer of a large battalion in 8th Army area immediately
to the rear of American Xth Corps. Also the Korean I ROK Corps, and
where we had erected a rather large prefabricated building for use as a
theater for USO shows and attended by such troops as could be spared
from duty, who were trucked from forward areas. There were wooden
benches for seating and we built a makeshift stage for the performers.

At our location, shows were given on a Saturday afternoon, after which
the members of the troupes had Saturday night and Sunday off before
resuming their tours on Monday morning, a rest after their always ar-
duous weeks.

They stayed in our compound the weekends and for whose use we
had erected large squad tents, separate quarters of course, for males and
females. We even had a female latrine which was somewhat of a novelty
in an all-male soldier atmosphere. We had an enlisted men's club and a
small officer's club where beer and liquor were available along with canned
music.

On Saturday night the performers would split up and spend some time
in the clubs, talking and having a drink or two with the men. They seemed
to enjoy themselves as much as the men did. They ate the same rations
as did the troops and stood in line before the mess hall like any other
soldier. Indeed, they looked like soldiers, being dressed in the same fatigue
clothes and boots as the men, except that on visiting the clubs, the females
managed to rake up female clothing and looked like women, a sight for
which the men were of course hungry. With few exceptions they were truly
good troopers and performed a valuable service in enhancing morale.

Raymond Burr was an exception to the Saturday night parties at the clubs. He didn't attend them. Instead, after the Saturday afternoon shows, we would provide him with a helicopter and he would be flown to forward division areas, where he could go from place to place visiting the men in forward outposts and who were not to be spared to go to the rear areas. He didn't put on a performance, but would talk and visit with the men. This was invariably his weekends. While most USO performers had contracted for a period of six to ten weeks in Korea, Raymond Burr, to my knowledge, spent in excess of six months in Korea.

He never seemed to tire and was always gracious and kind in his association with the men. For that he was extremely well regarded.

In the early 1950's, Burr was not a star nor was his name well known, but dating from the latter 1940's he had appeared in numerous motion pictures, always playing a role of a dirty-bastard, killer-type gangster, making his face fairly well known among movie goers.

Therefore, it was a surprising innovation to see him performing as a country bumpkin, slapstick comedian, a foil for a straight man or straight woman, who always ended up covered with a litter of numerous pies thrown in his face, which he would climax with putting his own pie in the face of both the straight man and of the prettiest, or most handy, woman on stage!

This was received with even greater approval because of the total change from "Bad Guy" to comedian, a role in which not everyone had seen him, nor pictured him, because of his already having been typed as a bad guy.

Off stage he was quiet, serious, and a good conversationalist. Uppermost in his mind was his desire to entertain troops wherever he could reach them and for as long as the day and time allowed.

In short, he seemed dedicated to the task. In all the years since that experience with him I have admired him and was pleased to see his subsequent successes in "Perry Mason" and "Ironside," etc. This is the gist of my knowledge of Raymond Burr.

"I recall having the pleasure of meeting actor Raymond Burr in Sokdro, Korea, in the winter of 1953–54, even though it was a brief but very pleasant encounter," says G. J. Hamilton of Grand Island, Nebraska.

I encountered Mr. Burr at the Officer's Club of the Port Operations Detachment at Sokcho-ri, Korea, which is a little north of 38 degrees and was in North Korea *before* the Demarcation Zone was established in July 1953. In fact, when the villagers erected a statue in memory of refugees, they put the figures facing north. It's on the East Coast.

I had been up some 36 hours and was really needing a drink, dinner, and bed. Mr. Burr and I shared several beverages and a strong ration of conversation before he went off to entertain the troops and I got my dinner. It was a congenial exchange, and I think Mr. Burr gave me more than my share of attention because I was able to cite a couple of his cinematic performances that I particularly enjoyed, rather than just saying something meaningless like, "I'm your biggest fan."

Meanwhile, I've enjoyed the few "Perry Mason" shows I've seen and we must have watched every "Ironside" segment. Of course I see Mr. Burr in ads for the insurance folks, and I wish him a broken leg with his play. I also wish I had more to pass along, but the meeting was unplanned and unexpected and no photos were taken, nor was there a tape made. It was just a brief encounter between a celebrity and one overtired Marine.

"Roland Sorenson, lieutenant junior grade, USNR, and I had had to make an emergency landing at King 18," said Walter Barbu of Brookfield, Wisconsin.

This was in Kangnung, South Korea, after an air strike into North Korea March 16 or April 12, 1953. As I recall, King 18 was a South Korean Air Force Facility that was protected by the U.S. Army. The U.S. Navy and Air Force also had splinter units stationed there to afford emergency assistance and repair for aircraft that couldn't make it home. Our home at the time was the CVA-34 USS *Oriskany*-UF124.

We landed around 1630 hours and by the time we checked over Rollie's problems with the Navy maintenance and repair crew it was about 1730 hours—just in time to make the "Happy Hour," which was not afforded us on the *Oriskany*!

I found $5.00 in script in my emergency kit, which I placed on the bar, advising the custodian of spirits to cut us off when it was spent. We were on our second glass when the base CO, an Army colonel whose name I can't recall, and Raymond Burr joined Rollie and me. They were very interested in our health and activities and were very friendly as well as gracious. I don't know how long we talked, but from the way my head and stomach felt the next morning, I knew it had to be quite some time.

Ray was on tour with an Armed Forces Entertainment Group, who were putting on a show for the base personnel that evening. His role was that of a comedian, and I was told by the Navy crew who attended the show that Ray was exceptionally funny and was well received.

Rollie and I couldn't attend since our attire under the Poopy Bags we wore was not fit for mixed company. Also we had to make an early morning takeoff to return to the USS *Oriskany*, as the much patched up repairs were completed and our presence was requested. I talked with some of the Army and Navy personnel at early breakfast before we took off. This is where I learned Ray was such an excellent comedian. I always thought of him to be a heavy, as this is what I had seen him play.

Ray and the base CO had a very late night after we had partied with them. I believe the show was a three hour affair—2000–2300 hours, after which Ray and the CO hopped into an armed jeep and went north looking for game, North Korean vintage. At the time King 18 was about 40 miles south of the Line and there were reports of North Koreans infiltrating south of that Line.

I was favorably impressed, as was Rollie, by Ray—he was warm, friendly, down to earth, with a great sense of humor. I also recall that I found that $5.00 script in one of my pockets on my return to the USS *Oriskany*. It was the nicest night I spent in the eight months we were policing North Korea.

Edwin L. Draper, from Wichita Falls, Texas, says he flew Burr wherever the American forces were stationed in Thailand.

I was a young Captain at the time, stationed in Korat, Thailand. I spent three days with Ray; talking and observing. Burr visited the troops to thank them for what they were doing for their country. There wasn't any television crews, no great publicity, and no money to be made on this trip. I found him to be a *great* American.

He was well received wherever he went. His sincerity was evident to all of us. His "thanks" was appreciated. I treasure the memory of my time spent with this great man. I have dreamed of meeting him again and possibly visiting his island, which he had just purchased at the time. I hope this gives some additional insight to a great human being.

"I know for sure Raymond Burr had many interesting experiences and a few close calls," said John J. Clark from Prescott, Arizona. "I was an Army pilot flying Artillery Missions with the 9th Corps Artillery. Mr. Burr would spend the night with the front line troops and I would pick him up at the front in a L-19 and bring him back to the rear."

"Mr. Burr brought a small group to North Korea in 1952, before the DMZ was formed," recalls Richard J. Best of Jacksonville, Florida. "Burr and his troupe spent the night with my battalion, staging two performances for us the following day. We built a small amphitheater specifically for the occasion, using natural materials, ROKA and KATUSA labor for dressing rooms and the stage. It was quite a success. I learned later that Mr. Burr wrote to our project officer expressing his pleasure with the facility." Best managed to get some slides of one performance.

Maj. Gen. S. L. McClellan of Carmel, California, states,

> In the Spring of 1953, as a Captain of Infantry, I was serving as a Rifle Company Commander of Company L, 7th Infantry Regiment, 3rd Infantry Division, in combat in Korea. My unit occupied a defensive position on the Central front, near Kumwha. Action in our area was heavy, and contact with the North Korean/Chinese enemy was on a daily basis. The unit occupied and manned a 1,700 yard defensive line, with dug-in machine gun bunkers and mortar positions connected by a meandering frontline trench. During daylight hours it was a suicidal act to walk upright outside the trench line. At night, we were subjected to intense artillery and mortar attacks, usually accompanied by an enemy probe of our positions.
>
> To our front, the hillside we occupied was strewn with antipersonnel mines and several bands of barbed-wire barriers. Our sleeping positions were in dug-in earthen bunkers, just off the hilltop, connected with our fighting positions by zigzag communication trenches.
>
> Late one afternoon during this period, I was surprised to see our Battalion Commander, Major Decatur P. Butler III, trudge up the hill accompanied by a large civilian dressed in yellow slacks, loafers, and a red-checked shirt. I was introduced to Raymond Burr, who would like to spend a few days with us to get a closer feel of combat in Korea! While shaking his hand, I dimly recalled seeing this character in a 1951 or 1952 movie with Elizabeth Taylor and Montgomery Clift. I recalled that I had

not liked his arrogant portrayal of a prosecuting attorney. At any rate, somewhat confused by the bizarre circumstances, I welcomed Mr. Burr and took him to my command post for a cup of coffee. The Battalion CO left soon, informing me to "look after Ray Burr, as we wouldn't want him to become a casualty in our area."

Over coffee, I learned that Ray was in Korea heading up a USO Troupe which was playing our rear area, some 15 miles away. The previous night, he had had a few drinks with Major Butler in the 3rd Division Officer's Club.

Ray had requested a visit to a frontline unit. They had traveled up by jeep that afternoon; the USO troupe was left in someone's hands and Ray told me he would like to stay with us for, as he put it, "a couple of days."

The whole situation was irregular in the extreme. On one hand, civilians were *not* authorized to be in an active combat area. On the other hand, he had been brought up by my superior officer, apparently with Major Butler's blessing, to stay with us. There was another factor: we were damn busy trying to kill the enemy and stay alive in the process. Frankly, I didn't appreciate a visit from an actor out on a lark. I concealed this feeling, however, and made him welcome.

As darkness fell, and after a supper meal of hot C-Rations, I set out to check departing night patrols. My Executive Officer, 1st Lt. Desmond O'Keefe, had been clued in to keep our visitor company. Also he was to see to it that he stayed out of danger.

As I strapped on my pistol and got into my steel helmet and flak-jacket (bullet-proof vest), Ray asked if he could go along with me.

I said to myself, "What the hell!" and told him he could. I outfitted him in O'Keefe's flak-jacket and steel helmet and led the way over the hilltop to the frontline trenches.

Except to make sure he stayed on my heels, I paid him little attention as I checked out six or seven patrols moving out on ambush missions into no-man's-land, which divided friendly and enemy positions.

Several times we had to hit the dirt in reaction to incoming artillery and flares. By the time we returned to the Command Post, both Ray and I were tired out and covered with mud. While I settled in to monitor progress of the patrols by radio, I had a cot set up for him in the corner of the bunker and advised him to get some rest. He was asleep and snoring loudly in five minutes. I wasn't able to follow suit until 5:00 A.M. due to several enemy contacts during the night.

About 6:00 A.M., less than an hour after I turned in, I was awakened by Ray as he clattered around the bunker, fiddled with the stove trying to heat water to shave—whistling all the time. In less than courteous tones I told him to "Quiet-the-hell-down and go back to bed!" He followed my orders. I slept undisturbed for two more hours, until awakened by O'Keefe bringing in a steaming pot of coffee. After a breakfast of heated C-Rations, another day was underway.

Ray stayed with us for five more days and voluntarily experienced everything he had hoped for—and more too!

He accompanied me day and night, visiting every single soldier in the outfit, crawling through the mud to check engineer work to our front, diving to the ground to make smaller target for enemy fire, and through it all he was cheerful and uncomplaining.

Believe me, when anyone of the 240 soldiers of Company L first saw this apparition from another world, eyes were wide and jaws were slack! He soon won over all of them and became a most popular "visitor."

Morale in the unit was top-notch before Ray came, but was setting a record by the time he left.

Long before the day came for him to leave, we had become warm friends—a friendship renewed over the intervening years. When he departed Company L, with Lt. O'Keefe to guide him back to Division Headquarters, he asked if he could do anything for us. We needed toilet paper and had been unable to jar any loose through Army supply channels. I asked him to see if he could get some up to us. A truckload of toilet paper arrived the next day.

Prior to his departure, I presented Ray with a Combat Infantryman's Badge in recognition of his week in combat and thanked him sincerely for cheering us all by his visit.

O'Keefe returned after dark, with Ray safely in the hands of his USO Tour Group. Des smiled sheepishly as he ducked into the bunker entrance, covered with lipstick from kisses received from the female members of Ray Burr's troupe.

Both then and now, we considered his perseverance in learning the actualities of Korean combat both unusual and commendable.

Somehow, although we afterward met several times in Washington, D.C., Hollywood, and his home in Santa Monica, we are out of contact— although I believe he, too, is in California.

Naturally I followed his successful career, but I choose to remember him covered with mud, grinning with pride and elan, on a hillside in South Korea, over 35–40 years ago!

As a final aside, Ray later repaid my gift of the CIB award by presenting my wife Phyllis with a miniature of his golden Emmy Award for the "Perry Mason" series in 1959 or 1960, as I recall.

Lt. Colonel Stewart G. Real, from Charleston, South Carolina, says,

I met Raymond Burr in Korea and shared with him an exciting experience that required bypassing regulations to satisfy Burr's determination to visit the forward area where there was combat, despite the so-called truce. During this period of the conflict, the combat troops were dug in along the Main Line of Resistance on the United Nations side of the demilitarized zone. The headquarters, administrative, supply and reserve units were in the rear area out of range of incoming artillery fire.

Between the two was a series of checkpoints manned by MPs called the Helmet Line. When you reached one of these checkpoints, you had to wear a flak-jacket and helmet because you were then within range of enemy fire.

Raymond visited the 45th (Thunderbird) Infantry Division, assigned to X Corps, defending the most northeast sector of the MLR that included historic battle sites: Pork Chop Hill, Heartbreak Ridge, and Sandbag Castle.

I was the Public Information Officer of the 45th and was assigned to escort the Burr group during the visit.

Mr. Burr graciously and tactfully accepted VIP treatment heaped upon him at Division Headquarters. He was (as I would later summarize in a report on his visit) at his best when he was one-on-one or one-on-a-few with the enlisted men. He was delighted (and the delight was contagious among the soldiers) as we toured the rear area.

Raymond would ask to stop to talk with lonely guards at an ammunition dump. He would stop a truck driver to chat and tell him how important his job was—tell a mail clerk how important his job was to morale.

I have to digress to remind everyone that at this time the name of Raymond Burr wasn't synonymous with "Perry Mason" or "Ironside." In fact, more than once I heard such remarks as, "This guy's great, but—who the hell is he?"

All the while he was making the rear area troops happy, I could sense that Mr. Burr wasn't totally happy. He wanted to be where there was action, no matter how sparse or sporadic. I would have been happy to oblige him, but for one *small* detail. There was a regulation, decreed by higher headquarters, that *no* personnel in Raymond's category would be permitted to go beyond the Helmet Line.

Perhaps it was that the man's sincere determination was contagious; perhaps it was that I learned the hard way that the old Army adage "Regulations were made to be broken" had to be considered if I was to be effective in the precarious assignment I had. Whatever, I decided to get the man where he wanted to be! The regulation prohibiting the mobility of the Raymond Burr type didn't pertain to accredited news correspondents. I had taken quite a few newsmen through a checkpoint on the Helmet Line that led to an outpost on the MLR, that was less than a couple of footfields in distance from the North Koreans. From this observation post you could traverse a maze of trenches and dugouts where there were soldiers as close to the enemy as any point in Korea.

It was a great showpiece for someone like me, engaged in the care and feeding of correspondents; to portray the Army at its finest.

Fortunately, I had a close working arrangement with the troop commander in this forward area. A phone call established that I was bringing a "special" newsman into his sector and there would be no questions about credentials.

The checkpoint was a breeze. Raymond, the jeep driver, and I arrived in flak-jackets, helmets, and goggles to combat the dust. I identified myself, was recognized and waved on through with an "he's got another one" attitude.

Believe me, when we got to where Burr wanted to be, he was a hit! Again I must remind everyone that he was meeting and talking to those individual fighting men *before* his TV acclaim to follow. His personalized one-on-one was outstanding. You can't expect one to quote verbatim after more than three decades, but I recall such as, "So you're from Chicago. Ever been to that place near Central Station that has great barbecued ribs...?" "No, I haven't been to Topeka, Kansas, but we were doing a western...."

I do recall there were references to a "purple" something or other, and maybe it's not verbatim—but close to it—a soldier saying, "Now I know you! You're that big mother that kills all those other mothers!"

A Texan from Austin, John J. Cleary writes,

> I was an Air Force Officer serving in Korea in 1963-64. I was stationed
> at a remote radar site on an island named Paengnyongdo (P.Y. Do) about
> 125 miles from the city of Inchon and only four miles off the coast of North
> Korea, in the Yellow Sea near the 38th Parallel.
>
> Raymond Burr went far out of his way and at no small risk to himself
> just to visit a few American servicemen, Army and Air Force, on a cold
> winter day. The airplane that brought him to the island landed on the
> beach at low tide. I shall always remember him fondly for coming to our
> remote outpost.

Cleary has a photo of Raymond Burr taken on Paengnyongdo. The
man in the center of the photo is Father Jim Bishop, a Maryknoll priest
assigned to a Catholic mission on the island, and Cleary is at left in the
photo.

Cleary notes,

> I was part of a small detachment of five United States Air Force officers
> and about 50 enlisted men assigned in an advisory capacity to help the
> ROK Air Force at the radar site.
>
> The USA had a radio facility on the island with about six enlisted men
> assigned. Also, I recall that three American technical representatives, em-
> ployees of Philco, were there.
>
> I regret that I don't remember the exact date of Raymond's visit to the
> island. I do remember that it was the winter of 1963 and the weather had
> been miserable for several weeks—low cloud cover, cold and windy with
> drizzle. As you can see in the photo there wasn't any snow, which came
> shortly after Mr. Burr's visit.
>
> The day Burr visited our unit, the weather was threatening to ground
> all aircraft except emergency flights. We were expecting Mr. Burr and
> were somewhat dismayed to learn that U.S.A.F. officials at Osan Air Base
> were advising him to cancel his trip to the island due to safety reasons.
> However, we were cheered upon learning by radio communications that
> Burr had insisted on not disappointing us and that he was already airborne
> en route to our little island.
>
> I was one of the small group meeting the C-47 "Gooney Bird" at the
> beach when it landed at low tide. We used to say our "airport" had the
> only runway in the world which was resurfaced twice daily by the tide.
> When Mr. Burr got off the plane, he let it be known immediately he came
> primarily to talk with the enlisted men.
>
> He shook hands with the officers present, exchanging a few pleasantries.
> He asked where I was from and I told him Tucson, Arizona. He told me
> he owned an art store or museum there. When we drove from the beach
> to our living quarters, he went straight to the enlisted men's dining hall,
> where the men were all gathered. He remained for nearly two hours chat-
> ting with them. I don't recall if he shared a meal with them, but he may
> have.
>
> Before he left, Raymond offered to phone the wife or parents of anyone
> who cared to have him do so when he returned to the States.

John J. Cleary, Father Jim Bishop, and Raymond Burr.

I personally spent only moments talking with Mr. Burr, but I did appreciate his visit very much. I was in sympathy with his desire to spend his limited time with the GIs rather than the officers. I do know the American servicemen on that remote, windswept island were moved by the selfless generosity of this famous man who gave of himself for a handful of guys consigned to the backwaters of Korea. As a matter of fact, we sometimes felt unappreciated and overlooked. It felt so good when Raymond Burr felt we were important enough to go out of his way to visit our remote island.

I heard later during that trip to Korea, Burr purchased uniforms for one of the municipal Korean police departments.

Asa McCranie of Cape Coral, Florida, says, "I was a Second Lt. pilot in the 5th Light Aviation Section HQ X Corps, at Inji Airfield K-47 from February 1954 until we moved south to Wonju, Korea, about August 1954. I remember flying Raymond Burr in an Army L-20 during that period. I flew him north somewhere to a smaller unit, then flew him back to X Corps. I also remember him as a very nice but large man, since he could barely fit in a center seat in the L-20."

"Raymond was with the U.S. Army Special Services in Germany in 1954 and it was one of the low periods in his career when he couldn't get acting roles and went to work for the Army to earn beans and bread!" was the mistaken impression of Lt. Col. Hal D. Steward. In fact, Raymond decided to turn down many roles in order to work for the Army and to tour Korea on the first of many handshaking tours as well as to work for the USO entertaining troops all over the world. In all, his manager said Raymond Burr lost over $85,000 by turning down film offers. He lost the role in *From Here to Eternity,* which Ernest Borgnine won an Academy Award for, portraying a cruel serviceman.

Instead, Raymond provided up to 18 hours of entertainment per day, averaging four shows daily, sometimes playing to three people as close to the front lines as any show could get. At other various locations he would play to about 12,000 servicemen. Always he made it a point to visit local service hospitals.

Raymond even rewrote *Charley's Aunt* to fit a GI background, with the help of three GIs dressed as sergeants and three dressed as WACs. The real aunt was a delegate to the United Nations. They used whatever props were available or made their own. Because sometimes there was a language barrier, they learned to do a lot of visual shows to get across their comic message.

Mike Sheehan kept calling Raymond "Bob" in December 1963, when he served in Korea. He was General Houze's mess officer and also ran the VIP billets in which Raymond Burr stayed for five days and four nights.

Raymond had told Sheehan at the time to contact him, but Sheehan was not able to get Burr's address. Mike spent quite a bit of time with "Bob" while he was there and says Burr participated in many events and was a great person. "He has done many helpful things for the people he has known."

Dean D. Fish recalls that he met Raymond Burr briefly at Camp Red Cloud, Uijongbu, Korea, at the Service Club in 1964 or 1965.

"He was being interviewed by young GIs who queried him on the 'Perry Mason' TV series." Why did Hamilton Burger, District Attorney, always lose the cases?

"Burr explained that was the way the script was written. Most of the GIs mentioned his size—'Bigger Than Life!' I'm sure he showed up in Vietnam in 1966-67, but I was so busy I didn't get the opportunity to see any of the USO or other shows in Saigon."

Back in the States, Raymond complained to the appropriate congressional committees when he found paralyzed veterans in hospitals suffering from bedsores and crusaded for more recreational facilities for American combat troops still serving in Asia.

He showed this same compassion to civilians here at home. Irving Pringle, a makeup man on the "Perry Mason" show, was rushed to the hospital with a bleeding ulcer. Raymond went in the ambulance with him and stayed there all night, making sure Pringle got careful attention.

He got angry when reporters found out about his visit to a Massachusetts girl who had been burned in a fire and was not expected to live. Raymond found out she was a fan of "Perry Mason" when her mother wrote a letter to him requesting an autographed picture for her daughter. Instead of mailing the photo, he flew up to the hospital in Massachusetts and visited the child, Elizabeth (LiLi) Sargis, spending as much time as he was allowed, talking to the little girl and her mother. Elizabeth won her battle for life after many skin grafts.

There was a terrible fire in Malibu, where he lived at the time. Residents lost everything. Raymond's house was spared, so he opened his doors to the families, cooking meals for them, helping them find shelter, and letting a few stay in his house until they could arrange to find housing elsewhere.

XIX

Vietnam

Raymond had a short vacation in New York, then went on his first trip to Vietnam in 1963 to entertain the troops as he had done in Korea. The *Observer*, the official newspaper published for the U.S. forces in Vietnam, ran an editorial thanking Perry Mason for coming on this trip.

While in Vietnam, Raymond often played to a mere handful of men and dodged bullets many times, spending many grueling and physically dangerous weeks hedgehopping by Army helicopter, going from one Vietnamese outpost to another. He shook hands with more than 13,000 service personnel.

Raymond Burr arrived in South Vietnam on May 10, 1965. This was his seventh visit to U.S. troops, and he remained three weeks to meet with the servicemen and diplomatic personnel. This trip took Raymond 8,500 miles within the borders of South Vietnam. He traveled by helicopter and airplane, visiting 147 different outposts. Many were remote outposts, and he personally made contact with 200 separate units, from village outposts of three or four men to huge bases with many thousands of troops.

"I didn't go over there as an entertainer because it wasn't that kind of war. I entertained by just talking and listening to the soldiers while they were at their posts," said Raymond.

Estimations were that he visited a total of 27,000 men during that period. On his six other trips to Vietnam, plus Thailand, Japan, and Korea, Raymond logged more than 25,000 miles and 1,200 hours of helicopter flying—the equivalent of two years of duty for the U.S. Army helicopter pilots that were over there.

During his visit, Raymond was fired on at least six times during the flights from Song Be and Dak Pek. The Song Be post was attacked May 11 by the Vietcong. Kan Nack was attacked March 8, and he arrived May 12. He celebrated his birthday, May 21, in between attacks. Hill 159 had been attacked on February 8, but Raymond did not arrive until May 16. May 13 he visited Dak Pek, which was attacked with Vietcong mortars the next day.

Other outposts Raymond visited came under fire. On one trip he was traveling with dignitaries. When Raymond's visit was finished, he and all the dignitaries boarded a helicopter. As it gained speed over the barbed wire surrounding the camp, the helicopter passed about ten feet over a so-called friendly minefield. As it did so, the wash of dust stirred up by the helicopter blades detonated one of the mines just below Burr's craft. For just a moment, the helicopter faltered but then quickly gained altitude and got the hell out of the area. After that incident, Raymond came to Bangkok, Thailand, and asked for permission to go upcountry into the mountains to visit the troops stationed there.

One of the correspondents who traveled with Raymond Burr dubbed him Mr. South Vietnam. During the three weeks he spent there, he went into exposed battlefield conditions and ate his meals with the enlisted men in their mess hall. On this particular tour he suffered from a pinched nerve in his leg, but he just kept going from one outpost to another.

Raymond said,

> There were more than 70,000 Americans in South Vietnam then. I had pledged to do what I could for these people.
>
> I supported the *men* in Vietnam, *not* the war. I got into a lot of controversy about my trips to Vietnam. I didn't have any definite answers to the complex problem. The point wasn't whether we were there in the best way, or the best time, or whether we should have remained there as long as we did. The point is, *WE WERE THERE*. I went because there were Americans there and they wanted to see someone from home. We all had a job to do.

Norman E. Hardy met Raymond in 1969 when he visited Firebase Oasis near Pleiku and was caught in an attack of mortar, rockets, and ground fire. This was a particularly vicious attack, lasting several hours and forcing Raymond to stay overnight with the men, remaining in the Tactical Operations Center throughout the action. Hardy recalls Raymond as being very "cool" about all of the action. They played chess late into the night.

CSM Glenn E. Owens of Panama City Beach, Florida, said, "I was a Sergeant Major of the 13th Combat Aviation Battalion stationed in Cantho, Vietnam, in 1964-65. I was invited to visit and lunch with Raymond Burr. What amazed me was the size of him compared with seeing him on TV! There were about eight of us present, all noncommissioned officers, which he had requested. The luncheon took place at the MACV Compound at Cantho and was a very delightful experience, for I had always admired him."

"Late in 1963, early 1964, Raymond talked and joked with both officers and enlisted men, sometimes in small groups and sometimes just one man at a time when he came to the Team Camp in the Long Than

District of Bien Hao Province of Vietnam," says Col. Clark L. Kershner of Sanford, North Carolina, who was able to get quite a few photos of Raymond.

"I had the pleasure of meeting and being photographed with Mr. Burr in 1963 in Rach Gia, Vietnam," recalls Col. Martin L. Ganderson from Carlisle, Pennsylvania. "I recall being very appreciative that a 'star' took the time and interest in us at such an unknown place."

SGM Paul J. L. Soublet says he has vivid memories of Raymond Burr's visit to Vung Tau, Vietnam. Raymond came in at Christmastime in 1964, and all Paul had was a coin collector's record book, which he asked Raymond to autograph on the inside front cover.

> It was all I had on me at the time we met. So little of his visits with the troops have ever been publicized since he was not the large audience, publicity seeking type. Raymond preferred to visit the remote, out-of-the-way areas where troops were isolated from the built-up command headquarters. He arrived at my station without fanfare and I think without an escort. I had recently arrived in the country and was with the 73rd SWAD awaiting reassignment to the 5th Special Forces Group, headquartered at Nha Trang, RSVN. Mr. Burr arrived about midday and I was in my sleeping quarters having "Poc-Time."
> He came up to me in a very casual manner, shook my hand and said, "Hello, I'm Raymond Burr."
> I recognized him straightway from seeing him on his television detective series. He was dressed in a bush jacket and matching pants but no headgear. We spoke for a few minutes, and I asked him to autograph the coin book, mainly because he was the first, and turned out to be the last, celebrity I was ever in personal contact with throughout my 25 year military career. Shortly after he autographed my book he wished me luck and departed alone, seeking out other troops around the airfield. He acted as if he had been there all the time. I was surprised at his manners—quiet, casual, and friendly—because most of the celebrities I had seen at a distance were always surrounded by a large escort or in the company of high brass.

Derhyl L. Bray met Raymond Burr on his second visit to Vietnam in 1964. He was stationed at Da Nang Airbase. He found Raymond to be a very personable, likeable individual. He believes all the men who met him felt the same way. "I suppose we were overwhelmed that he would travel a great distance just to visit us GIs, who were sweating out a year in Nam."

A one hour special, "Raymond Burr Visits Vietnam," was shown on NBC October 6, 1967. He let the men and the country speak for themselves and added little commentary aside from the voiceover narration. He is shown as he travels with the Navy's Assault Flotilla One up the Mekong River on a search and destroy operation. The cameras follow Raymond as he narrates what he sees and talks to the people he meets. His last words about Vietnam in the documentary were, "Vietnam is not a happy place to visit. Perhaps one day it will be." As a Navy veteran of World War II, Raymond arranged some of his treks to Vietnam via old Department of Defense contacts and was able to get into areas where others were not allowed. He was remarkably quiet on the subjects of his trips to Vietnam and Korea. He never demanded press conferences at the end of his trips in order to explain his personal views.

Roger D. Winslow served 30 months in Vietnam and had the pleasure of flying Raymond Burr throughout the delta area. Daily, Winslow and a copilot picked up Burr for visits to the numerous outstations, Special Forces Camps, and other major American bases within the entire area. Winslow vividly recalls playing tennis with him and other advisers. After he got back from this trip, Raymond had his office telephone Winslow's parents to tell them he was okay, that he had talked to Winslow while he flew him to wherever Raymond wanted to go.

Lt. Col. Violet D. Nemky was a nurse and first met Raymond Burr in Okinawa, at Camp Kue Army Hospital, in 1963. At the time Okinawa was the jumping off area for Vietnam. She was the head nurse on the enlisted medical ward.

> We knew Mr. Burr was coming to the hospital and was told he would be on our ward at 1100 hours. The corpsmen and patients who were ambulatory worked like beavers to have the ward in tip-top condition. The bed patients were scrubbed, bed linens were wrinkle free, floors were shining — no mess, no dust anyplace. This was a very busy day patient wise — new patients in, well patients out.
>
> Our ward doctor, Captain Speed, was swamped with work, as were we all. The 1100 hour came and *no* Mr. Burr! We were disappointed but not discouraged. We thought he had gotten delayed and would come soon. So we waited and worked until 1500 hours, when we were told Mr. Burr was at the Red Cross and he wouldn't be coming to our ward. In our disappointment we sent as many patients as we could and gave permission to the corpsmen to go on a rotating schedule of ten minutes each.
>
> One of the corpsmen knew I liked Mr. Burr very much and was eager to meet him. When this young corpsman came back from the Red Cross, he told Dr. Speed and me that he had spoken to Mr. Burr and had expressed our disappointment in not seeing him in our ward. Naturally Dr. Speed and I thought he was telling us a tall tale. Finally, Dr. Speed said, "Major Nemky, I will hold the fort here. Why don't you go see Mr. Burr?"
>
> I knew Mr. Burr didn't have much time, so I rushed to the Red Cross. As I approached the Red Cross, Mr. Burr was coming out the hallway. I stepped against the wall with other personnel. When he came to me he stopped and shook my hand saying, "Major Nemky, I'm sorry I didn't come to your ward."
>
> I was flabbergasted. The young corpsman *had* told him of our disappointment and Mr. Burr *had* remembered.
>
> This should be the end of my story, but there is one final note. This will

emphasize how thoughtful he is. When I returned to the ward the next morning at 0630 hours, the patients told me Mr. Burr came to the ward and talked with all the patients, spending about two hours with them.

The next time I met Mr. Burr in Vietnam at the 8th Field Hospital at Nha Trang.

I was the chief nurse there. I can't remember if he was there in late 1968 or early 1969. On this visit, again he saw all the patients where permitted and then spent several hours in the mess hall talking with patients and personnel.

From San Antonio, Texas, Malcolm R. Dixon recalls the time he met Raymond Burr, who was visiting his advisory team in Quang Ngai in June 1964.

I had gone out early in the morning and returned to the compound at 1500 hours. Another Captain was with me and we went to the Mess Hall for a cup of coffee. Raymond Burr was sitting at one of the tables talking to several others of our team. We were surprised and very happy to see him sitting there and we sat down at the table and chatted with him. He was very friendly and so personable; he just wanted to talk with us and see how we were doing. He had brought some Special Service flyers with his picture on them. I had him autograph one for me, which I might add, I have on the wall of my den. As he was leaving I took two pictures of him outside the Mess Hall. We all appreciated his taking the time to visit us and was a big boost to our morale.

Roger E. Willcut from Yankton, South Dakota, shares a true story that he frequently tells on himself regarding Burr's visit.

I was overseas from late 1960 until 1965 and had watched very little television—but I was of course familiar with who he was and had seen him on television. My first comment to him when he walked into our mess hall was, "You are heavier than you appear on television."

I don't recall his response to my crass observation. I was embarrassed at the time for my crude comment, especially nowadays when I think of it, given the amount of weight I have put on since I was a sergeant!

"The year was 1964," recalls Ken A. Davis of Stage Coach Farms in Walla Walla, Washington.

I was the Province Adviser in Phuc Long Province in the city called Song Be. Raymond Burr visited my Advisory Team and spent the night with them.

Mr. Burr has never been given the credit he deserves for the fine work he did during those days. He visited us under extremely dangerous conditions with no fanfare or publicity. I had the pleasure of dealing with other VIPs who received great publicity, but did nothing *but* obtain publicity.

Raymond was able to help us in Phuc Long Province where it really counted. This was the mountain villages long before the American liberal even knew where Vietnam was located.

Although my contact with Mr. Burr was very short in time, he left a very lasting impression on my career and he accomplished a great deal while in Vietnam. No one will ever know how much.

Ray Mullen wrote from Amphue Maetaeng, Chiangmai, Thailand, to say he met Raymond Burr in Vietnam.

> It was the summer or early fall of 1965 when one evening we got a message that Raymond Burr would be arriving by chopper at our location, about nine o'clock the next morning. We were positioned just north of Bien Hoa Air Base at the time. I was the S2 of the 173rd Airborne Brigade. We were advised Raymond didn't want briefings. He didn't want to talk to any officers, only the enlisted men, the lower the rank the better.
>
> We advised our units and when Burr arrived I met him and shook hands with him. He asked me if I was his escort and I said no. I proceeded to tell him there was a jeep with a driver waiting who knew where to go. As a precaution I sent a sergeant along with them. I recall Mr. Burr stayed a couple of hours; then I heard his bird take off. Later I asked my sergeant how it went. His only comment was to the effect that the man really moves!

On his last trip to Vietnam there were over a half million Americans there. When Raymond got back to Los Angeles, he made a long speech to the World Affairs Council about Vietnam.

Raymond Burr did not support the war in Vietnam. He did support the servicemen and women who had to be there. He was severely criticized for his own efforts in trying to keep up their hopes and morale.

In 1986, five servicemen and their wives had a reunion dinner with Raymond Burr at a hotel in Colorado Springs, Colorado. One of them paid Raymond the highest compliment he could think of: he called him the "Old Soldier."

XX

Underground *and*
"The Return of Perry Mason"

Raymond went to England in February 1983 to appear on stage in a dramatic play called *Underground*. Raymond toured Scotland and the provinces with the play, then took the play to Toronto for six weeks. While in Toronto, he tripped and fell over a wire lying on the backstage floor, which injured and pulled the cartilage in his knee. Though in pain, Raymond performed leaning on a cane. After the Toronto run of the play, Raymond returned to tour the provinces outside of London.

The tour was completed in August 1983 at the Prince of Wales Theatre in the heart of London's theater district. Throughout the tour Raymond and the British cast broke box office records, despite the bad reviews. Raymond felt there was always a challenge for him to come back to England, with its tradition of fine acting. "It was one of the reasons they got a long list of big British names for this play," he said with a dry chuckle. "Actually, I'm thrilled that people in Britain remember me."

Raymond told British reporters who interviewed him, "The quality of theater in Britain is different from the United States. We don't have the opportunities anymore in the States or Canada for the great early training that people have in Britain, both in theater and drama schools. Young actors and actresses have a superb base for their craft, which we in the United States have to build up as we go along. Customs, styles, and attitudes of actors are so different in Britain, and I am still learning."

Underground takes place on a stalled subway car left stranded in a tunnel. An American lawyer (Burr) on a holiday in London is caught in the car with a group of people. Little by little, each character divulges his or her thoughts to the audience. When the lights come on again, someone has been murdered. The rest of the play is taken up solving the murder.

It was reported that Raymond would have received $35,000 for perhaps a day or two of filming a cameo role in the television comedy "Night Court" but that he turned it down because he had other commitments. He was asked to play a small role in a new version of *Godzilla,* a film he had originally appeared in, in 1956. This one was titled *Godzilla '85,* and his character in the film was Steve Martin, a retired reporter who witnesses the second destruction of Tokyo by the monster.

However, since 1956, another Steve Martin had become a famous comedian. To get around this situation Raymond is addressed as Mr. Martin whenever he appears in a scene. All of his scenes were filmed in a Hollywood studio, and the rest of the film was made in Japan. As in the 1956 film, there is a Japanese as well as an American version.

The 1985 version comes across as a science-fiction disaster movie with the use of miniature cars, bridges, buildings, tanks, and the like. The special effects were spectacular. The American version lost a great deal of money, however. At least Raymond received a great deal more than the ten thousand dollars he had gotten for the 1956 version.

"Nine years ago I had the idea of resurrecting 'Perry Mason' in a two hour format for a limited run," he told a reporter. "No one in the television industry seemed interested at the time. Then in 1985, when I resurrected my role of Steve Martin in *Godzilla '85,* suddenly the network executives got the message."

Raymond signed a contract with Viacom, through Fred Silverman, to make an updated television film titled "The Return of Perry Mason." Raymond Burr Productions (RBP) worked in tandem with Viacom. The new version was made entirely in color, and the title was changed to "Perry Mason Returns." Shooting was scheduled to start in June 1985, but Barbara Hale fell in her home while celebrating the birthday of her husband, Bill Williams. Barbara broke her hip and production had to be delayed until late July, when she was well enough to resume her role as Della Street. When she was able to travel, the cast and crew flew to Toronto, Canada, to a courtroom with old English mahogany wood panels that looked like the courtroom in the original series. Some of the courtroom sequences were filmed in the city council's chambers.

Barbara, who would not fly, arrived by train, and almost all her scenes were shot with her sitting down. When she had standing scenes, she was supported by or leaned against Raymond or her son, William Katt. Her walking scenes were done by a double.

At first William Katt balked at playing the part of Paul Drake, Jr. He was starring in the play *The Music Man* in Kansas and had his own television series in syndication, "The Great American Hero."

Raymond said, "I've had him on my knee when he was a little boy and he called me 'Uncle Ray.' He has a certain amount of respect for me, since I put him in a couple of 'Ironside' episodes when he was a teenager. I *did* interfere with his life this time when I called him in Kansas and persuaded him to join us in the cast."

"Perry Mason Returns"

The wardrobe department decided not to plan a wardrobe to make Raymond look slimmer. They could not make him look like he was at the peak of the 1957 "Perry Mason" days—rusty or not, Perry was thirty years older and wiser and an appellate court judge.

When the first scene was being filmed, Raymond sat at the defense table and Barbara sat next to him. They looked at each other while they were waiting for the scene to be set up. It was like yesterday—1957 all over again. William Hopper, Ray Collins, and Bill Talman were not in the courtroom scene, however. They had all passed away in the years since the series had ended.

"I would give anything in the world if Erle Stanley Gardner could see the two hour version," Raymond said.

> Although they aren't the stories he wrote, at least he could have seen the fullness of the character as it was done thirty years later.
>
> Erle wrote a Perry Mason story once, with clues about the running board of an automobile. That was the year cars were being designed *without* running boards! That book was never published and Gardner, after that, never tied himself down to a piece of physical evidence that didn't last through the years. That's why Erle never described what Perry looked like nor what the other characters were like. Erle wanted to leave these characters up to the reading audience's imagination and why the Perry Mason character has worked after thirty years. The audience *can* visualize an older man still doing his job and even becoming a judge! What people were after in "Perry Mason" was the dream becoming a reality; to the allure of nostalgia.

Barbara Hale says of Raymond Burr:

> As both Barbara and Della, I think of Raymond as an actor who is not only handsome but in perfect control, authoritative in manner, and thorough. He knows his lines and how to react to everyone else's lines so as to give them more added value. He takes the trouble to continue studying and his knowledge of law and TV production is amazing.
>
> He finds out what's going on with the people around him. When someone is in trouble, he immediately gives them a helping hand. An example of his kindness: A crew member had his garden washed away in a flood due to heavy rains. Raymond heard about this and had a number of plants delivered to his door so he could replant immediately.
>
> Another crew member heard Raymond was going to Chicago soon and jokingly suggested he call his family and say hello. Raymond visited the man's relatives for two hours!
>
> What impresses me are Raymond's blue hypnotic eyes with their steady, piercing gaze. His voice and manner of a gentleman, which is in contrast to his sloppy way of dressing when he is wearing his leisure-time outfit of blue jeans, sweat shirt and tennis shoes.

Christian I. Nyby, II, director of quite a few of the "Return of Perry Mason" series, learned from his father, who directed some of the 1957–66 series, to watch out when Raymond was angry and his temper flared. Everyone stayed out of his way until he calmed down.

Most of the time Raymond was a warm, friendly, humble, caring human being who dominated any room he walked into. Reporters who interviewed him were sometimes in awe of his size and his steel blue eyes. He could charm them into other questions when he refused to answer something personal he did not want to reveal.

The "Return of Perry Mason" swept away all the ratings on December 1, 1985, and was number one across the nation. Perry beat his closest competition, "The Bill Cosby Show."

The second episode of the updated Perry Mason was titled "The Case of the Notorious Nun." It was filmed in Vancouver in February and March 1986. Some scenes were filmed in the downtown YMCA, others at the University of British Columbia. At one point, Raymond had the filming stopped because someone forgot to put Perry's briefcase on a table in the imaginary office outside the courtroom. Perry would never have left it in the courtroom, since Della would have automatically picked it up as she followed her boss out of the room.

The third episode, called "The Case of the Shooting Star," was filmed late in July 1986 for a November 9, 1986, release date. Filming for "The Case of the Lost Love" began in Denver, Colorado, for a January 1987 release.

Raymond was riding in a golf cart when the driver made a sharp sudden turn to avoid a small animal darting into the path of the cart and threw Raymond out onto the ground. He had just completed some scenes as a judge for a television movie titled "Grass Roots." His character had just completed a round of golf and was talking to another player in the scene right before the accident. He hit his right leg and knee on a rock in the road. He tore ligaments, had the leg treated and thought it was healing until he tripped over a cable on the set. His knee was injured again and had to be operated on to repair the damage. All the rest of the episodes show him walking with a cane and limping. The operation was written into the script of "The Case of the Murdered Madam," shown on December 4, 1987, to explain the use of the crutches and then the use of the cane again.

Raymond complained of poor scripts and slipping ratings. The last episode had the weakest script, and scenes were being refilmed a month before it was shown on television. However, "The Case of the Lady in the Lake" received the highest ratings, much to the surprise of everyone, including NBC.

Raymond had gained a great deal of weight since he had stopped smoking. Supermarket tabloids blazed headlines for June 7, 1988, that the 320 pound Burr had been warned by doctors to diet or die.

Meanwhile, NBC asked for three more episodes of "Perry Mason." Raymond said he would end with "Perry's Last Case" and refused to do anymore. However, he changed his mind when ratings continued to be excellent and the audiences demanded more episodes.

More and more Raymond turned toward teaching acting between his other activities. While teaching at Sonoma State University he met President Hugh La Bounty and an invitation was extended to him to teach at California Polytechnic State University. Raymond became interested in their television production, hotel management, restaurant, and travel departments. He sent hybrid orchid seedlings from some of his rare orchids to Cal Poly in Pomona. They went on sale in February 1986 with ten other orchid varieties, collectors items, and novelty breeds Raymond had cultivated for two to five years. A total of 4,500 seedlings were put in pots ranging from four to eight inches for Cal Poly's nursery to sell. They hoped to sell 25,000 to 28,000 orchid plants in the spring of 1986, and over 105 different seedling crossbreeds were offered for sale. Since then, each spring the proceeds of these sales go to Cal Poly.

Beginning in September 1986 Raymond taught drama for one semester at his alma mater, the University of Southern California, and planned to keep on teaching whenever and wherever he found time to do so. "I haven't accomplished all I plan to do, but I have learned it is perfectly marvelous just to be alive. Why breathe if you don't enjoy life? I don't have any spare time because I get more out of life than most people. I enjoy everything I'm doing! Let's say I'm satisfied with what I can do in a 24 hour period. That is a good deal for a man to say."

While most people his age thought about retiring and living off the fruits of their labors, Raymond worked harder than ever as a farmer-rancher, a teacher, real estate investor, business investor, and importer and exporter of rare flowers from his orchid farms around the world.

"I guess I haven't grown up yet," said Raymond with a smile. "Perhaps I'd do everything the same in my career, if I had a second chance. That is — everything except 'Perry Mason' for so long. Five years is enough for any series. If I still had the chance I'd like to be a newspaperman. I would try to interview the Dali Lama of Tibet. That would be interesting.

"Another thing I won't do is whistle in any dressing room because it destroys all the other actors."

Raymond still wanted to make a feature film about Pope John XXIII about the life and death of the beloved Pope—not just one incident, as he had portrayed on television in 1973. He also wanted to make one on Henry the Navigator, and hoped to film in Portugal, where there is a great deal of history about the father of navigation.

Raymond's first visit to Denver was in 1944, when he performed at the Elitch Gardens Theater. When Raymond filmed episodes of "Perry Mason" in Denver, he became interested in getting school boards in the area to reopen the theater in order to use it as a magnet school for the performing arts. He tried to raise $2–3 million in order to interest school-children in the theater. He had been successful in opening a similar magnet school in Cincinnati, Ohio.

(Clockwise from upper left): **Charles Rocket, David Rasche, Mariel Hemingway, John Candy, Emma Samms, Raymond Burr, and Dylan Baker star in MGM's comedy** *Delirious.*

Raymond finished filming "The Case of the Glass Coffin" in Denver in February 1991. He was about to start filming another episode when he decided to fly up to New Westminster, British Columbia, on February 13, 1991, to make a serious decision and to put his affairs in order.

He returned to Denver and told everyone on the set that he had decided to take a vacation, starting February 19. Raymond flew back to his farm for a few days, and then flew to Los Angeles in order to enter Cedars Sinai Hospital under the name of Raymond Burrows. Eight hours of tests revealed a tumor in his colon that had to be operated on immediately. The 330 pound Burr was in danger of hemorrhaging. The operation took over four hours. Raymond was in the intensive care unit for two days, fed by tubes and swallowing ice chips, then was moved to a private room. He was discharged in six days with a clean bill of health.

Robert Benevides drove Raymond up to Sacramento, then drove to the farm, where he recuperated for the next two weeks. He came back to the hospital for a followup checkup before he resumed filming the next "Perry Mason" in Denver on March 25. During the checkup he received more bad news: A cancerous tumor had been removed from the base of his spine during the colon operation, and he required more radiation treatments. In May, and all during the filming of the Perry Mason episode, he received radiation treatments which sometimes left him tired and sick.

As usual, the tabloids carried huge headlines stating that Raymond was dying of cancer and had only months to live. He finally appeared on "Entertainment Tonight" where he stated "I am not dying of cancer. I am in reasonably good health. I leave for Denver, Colorado, on March 18th to continue to film three more 'Perry Masons.' Then I still want to film an 'Ironside' episode. I have plans to the year 2001, which may or may not come true."

Raymond continued to be examined once a month to make sure the colon cancer had not spread to his other organs. Unfortunately, in January 1993, cancer was found in his left kidney and doctors suggested he have surgery right away.

He postponed the operation for almost six months because he wanted to complete the last two "Perry Masons" and the "Ironside Reunion." The money he would receive was earmarked for special charities he had committed himself to.

Tentative plans called for a "Perry Mason" to be filmed in Japan, but rumors persisted that the series would end before 25 episodes were completed. Because of his operations and the weight problem, his contract with the Independent Insurance Agents of America, Inc., was canceled.

Raymond came down to Los Angeles on January 29, 1993, to have lunch with the president of the National Association for the Advancement of Perry Mason, a club started in December 1985 by Jim Davidson. Also at the luncheon was a ghostwriter Raymond had hired to write about the television years 1957 through 1975. The two men listened as Raymond complained about everything he felt he had to get out of his system.

Hours later Raymond entered Cedars Sinai Hospital, and on February 1, his cancerous left kidney was removed. The cancer was thought to be present only in the kidney. It was hoped that the cancer had not spread to his other organs. He was up walking around his room in two days.

Raymond was discharged a week later and stayed at a nearby hotel so that he could continue radiation treatments. Raymond had to be examined at the hospital before being allowed to return to his farm. He spent the rest of February recuperating and during the second week of March turned up in Paris.

The twenty-fifth "Perry Mason" episode was postponed while he was on this business trip for Viacom. George Faber, the public relations man for Viacom, was with him to keep reporters away. Raymond had lost some weight and looked healthy once more.

The radiation treatments continued while he filmed "The Return of Ironside," and another "Perry Mason" titled, "The Case of the Tell-Tale Talk Show Host."

"The Return of Ironside" reunited all the former cast members. Barbara Anderson and Elizabeth Bauer had retired from acting to raise families. Don Mitchell was in politics, and Don Galloway had been in several "Perry Masons" and was still active in television. They all responded to Raymond's call to come to Denver to make the film. In publicity interviews they all said it seemed like only yesterday that they were on the set doing "Ironside" episodes. The ratings were excellent when it was shown May 4, 1993, which inspired Raymond to think of doing more "Ironsides."

Meanwhile, Raymond had started filming the "Perry Mason" episode on February 28, 1993, with talk show host Regis Philbin as the murder victim. Several other talk show hosts had parts in the film as suspects. The "Perry Mason" "Case of the Tell-Tale Talk Show Host" aired on May 21 to very good ratings, although it got mixed reviews in the papers. On the strength of this NBC ordered six more episodes. Filming was scheduled to begin in Denver on four of them and continue until the end of 1993, with the last two done sometime in 1994.

On May 12, 1993, he was honored with a resolution for his support of human rights and his education efforts to eliminate discrimination. The ceremony took place at the Denver City Council and was witnessed by Barbara Hale and William Moses.

Instrumental in creating the School of the Arts for the Denver Public Schools, Raymond was given the degree of Doctor of Humane Letters on Saturday, May 15, 1993, at the University of Colorado, in Denver, and recognized for his artistic contribution to television and the movie industry.

Raymond Burr reflected on the art of acting in an interview:

> I guess you could call it the art of giving yourself away.
> You have to identify the beauty of a sunset, the feel of mud, the rain; the sound of laughter; the cry of pain, and the taste of tears. Also the charm and beauty of a wonderful woman.
> Early in my career when I played all those villains and brutal gangster parts, I think my Canadian relatives were all embarrassed and ashamed of me. As the years and the parts changed, I hope they enjoyed my work.
> I think I would rather have been a doctor instead of an actor and since

I did the "Perry Mason" series, I have the highest respect for the legal profession. Sometimes I wish I had taken time to study law more thoroughly! Thinking back to those early years at the Pasadena Playhouse, I realize that theatrical lives, like performances, sometimes grow a thick covering of moss of memory. Events can take on nostalgic greatness that might not have really been there to begin with. Even so, in careers of any length, like mine of over fifty years, a continuity emerges that comes from a base. That base I believe comes from training.

What we are here on earth for is to be of service. What difference where we serve?

The good Lord and I have an understanding. One day I will be here on earth and the next day I won't. It is as simple as that! Until that day arrives I live life to the fullest and have enjoyed those fifty years in show business, traveling all over the world many times, meeting famous people from all walks of life and enjoying every minute of my life that God grants me.

A few months later when he was examined again, the doctors gave him the bad news that the cancer had spread to his other organs and was inoperable.

He decided to give his friends a number of farewell dinners but not tell them the reason they were gathering. Most of them had guessed since he looked gravely ill.

Raymond insisted on filming the "Ironside Reunion" in Denver with all the cast of the famous series. The cast never realized he was receiving radiation treatments between filming and never acted as if they knew he was ill and in pain.

In July 1993, Raymond filmed the last "Perry Mason," "The Case of the Killer Kiss." He arrived on the set in Denver at four o'clock in the morning in a wheelchair. Everyone on the set knew he was very ill and in extreme pain. Scenes were rewritten so he could work sitting down.

Raymond was bedridden on his farm in August as the cancer had spread to his liver, lungs and brain. On September 12, 1993, Raymond Burr died.

Appendix A: Radio Shows

Raymond worked steadily in radio throughout the 1940s and 1950s, until his film career demanded more and more of his time and energy. There are a great many undocumented radio shows, since he made over a thousand of them. Some of the shows that he took part in and that are documented on tape are listed below.

"Family Theater," Mutual Network.

"Stranger in Town," with Virginia Gregg

4/21/47 "CBS Workshop/Son of Man." Bible verses narrated by Burr. Robert Young, Vincent Price, and Herbert Marshall read verses from Matthew, Mark, Luke and John.

1948–49 "Pat Novak for Hire," with Jack Webb

1949–50 "Dragnet," with Jack Webb

1949–50 "Lights Out"

1950 "Dr. Kildare" series. Played Dr. Conlan, a quack doctor, starred Lew Ayres as Dr. Kildare, Lionel Barrymore as Dr. Gillespie, Agnes Moorehead as Nurse Parker; "The Fire and the Jenkins Boy," played the arsonist using an accent and disguised voice; "Operation on Ship," played the captain of the ship in trouble. Jack Webb was helicopter pilot.

3/24/50 "Chicago Deadline," a Screen Directors Playhouse show. Alan Ladd starred, with Burr in several episodes.

12/20/50 "The Line-up," as Matt Klein catching bank robbers. Also disguised voice as an Englishman who was in the lineup. Played various parts as policemen or people in the lineup.

1949–50 "Screen Directors Playhouse." Original role as MacDonald in 1948 movie *Pitfall*, 10/17/49.

1950 "The Whistler." "Break Away," as Walter Stone; "A Matter of Time."

1950 "Mike Shayne," Jeff Chandler starred. "Case of the Eager Victim"; Raymond played two parts in one episode—Mr. Sik with a disguised voice and the man with an artificial leg. Ted De Corsica also in cast.

1951 "The Line-up"; "The Candy Store," played Albert, a killer; Jeanette Nolan in cast.

4/19/51, "The Pendleton Story." Ran for 39 episodes, with Raymond Burr in
debut some of them. A series about history with Lamont Johnson starring as Patriot Robert Pendleton.

179

4/19/51	"The Declaration"
6/15/51	"The Warning"; "The Mischianza"
7/18/51	"Escape"; "Macao"
8/4/51	"The Line-up"; "Irene Oldin & John"
1952	Promo for "What You Can Do for Your Country"
4/7/52	"The Homecoming"
4/16/52	"The Child"
11/23/52	"Errand of Mercy" #216, "Jimmy Is for Luck"
1/11/53	"Favorite Story," Adolphe Menjou host, "How Much Land Does a Man Need?"
8/1/53	"The Railroad Hour," Gordon McRae; "Trilby," Burr as Svengali
1953	"Bud's Bandwagon," AFRS #172, interview with Raymond Burr
1956	"Fort Laramie," as Captain Lee Quince of the U.S. Cavalry. 40 episodes.
3/9/56	"CBS Radio Workshop," report on ESP
3/10/57	"Suspense/The Peralta Map"
4/21/57	"CBS Radio Workshop/The Son of Man," repeat broadcast of 4/21/47
7/14/57	"CBS Workshop/The Silent Witness." Perhaps his best part on radio. For a half hour he dramatically questions a woman who cannot speak in a courtroom. Sound effects signify she is writing her answers on paper.
7/57	"CBS Radio Workshop/Gettysburg"
7/28/57	"Suspense/Murder on Mike"
10/27/57	"Suspense/Country of the Blind"
9/07/58	"Suspense/The Treasure Chest of Don Jose"
12/21/58	"Suspense/Out for Christmas"
1958	"Frontier Gentlemen," several episodes. John Dehner starred.
4/2/59	"Suspense/Copper Tea Strainer," Betty Grable in dramatic role
6/7/59	"Suspense/The Pit and the Pendulum"
8/24/69	"Special Delivery: Vietnam"
6/2/76	"Jack Benny Show," from television version; Jack calls on Perry Mason to defend him
6/22/76	"Crop Dusters"; Jack Benny turns a drama into a comedy
12/22/77	"Arlene Francis Show," interview

Raymond Burr recorded over three thousand Armed Forces radio shows, which included voiceovers for training films. Many radio shows never mentioned the cast members, so Burr's radio shows are hard to find. In some shows Raymond had only one line to speak. Actors were paid by the words they spoke, and rehearsals were rare.

"Pat Novak for Hire"

No. Episode   *Date Shown*

1.	Debut	2/12/49
2.	Jack of Clubs	2/19/49
3.	Jockey Checked Out	3/5/49

No.	Episode	Date Shown
4.	Jockey's Horse Disappears	3/13/49
5.	Jockey's Horse Disappears (Repeated)	3/16/49
6.	Rory Malone Prizefighter (Frank Lovejoy)	3/20/49
7.	Doreen Wilde and Gambler (Ted DeCorsia)	3/27/49
8.	Father Leahy and Alcatraz Escape (Also known as Find Joe Feldman)	4/02/49
9.	Sam Tolliver and China Star (Also known as Sgt. Grimes, who was played by Raymond Burr, who also was Lt. Hellman)	4/09/49
10.	Go Away Dixie (Also known as Lee Underwood)	4/16/49
11.	Gunsel: Key to Novak's Boat	4/23/49
12.	Pat Watches a Lady Drunk	4/30/49
13.	The Wrong Shirts	5/07/49
14.	Patsy Gets $50 for a Delivery	5/14/49
15.	John St. John	5/21/49
16.	Follow Agnes Bolton (Burr not in this)	5/28/49
17.	Pat and the Emeralds	6/11/49
18.	Pat's Boat Riddled with Bullets; Fat Lady with Green Package	6/14/49
19.	Joe Dineen	6/18/49
20.		6/25/49
21.		7/02/49
22.		7/09/49
23.		7/16/49
24.		7/23/49
25.	Wendy Morris and Lost Husband	7/30/49
26.	Jack of Clubs (repeated broadcast of 2/19/49)	8/3/49

Blank spaces are for missing cassette tapes not located by radio show collectors.

"Dragnet"

Raymond Burr did not appear in all episodes, since his movie career was going strong. Episodes he was in are marked with an asterisk. Many 1949 and 1950 episodes are difficult to locate and are left blank, except for the date.

Date	Episode
7/7/49	
7/14/49	
7/21/49	
7/28/49	Missing Girl* (with Lurene Tuttle)
8/4/49	
8/13/49	The Wolf* (with Jeff Chandler; listed as 15th show. This show is also listed for 9/10/49)

Date   *Episode*

8/18/49	Jewel Thief* (with Harry Morgan; listed as 11th show)
8/24/49	Stolen Car*
9/14/50	Shooting in Bakery Shop
9/21/50	House Stripper
9/28/50	Mr. Trudeau, Paid Killer
10/5/50	
10/15/50	Doc Burglar*
10/19/50	Sick Naval Officers
10/26/50	Trapping a Narcotics Gang
11/2/50	
11/9/50	Stolen Stricker Baby
11/16/50	Guthries and Parrot Burned
11/23/50	Obituary Bunko
11/30/50	
12/7/50	Linda Drake, Juvenile Prono
12/14/50	George Hoffman, Armed Robbery*
12/21/50	Gun for Christmas

"Dragnet" became a television show December 16, 1951, with "The Human Bomb." Raymond Burr was in this debut film.

"Fort Laramie"

Ken Greenwald of Pacific Pioneer Broadcasters compiled this list, with additional information supplied by the author.

The first episode titled, **"Playing Indian,"** was written by John Meston. Transcribed January 19, 1956, the series began on January 22, 1956. Besides the main cast of Raymond Burr as Captain Lee Quince, Vic Perrin as Sergeant Goerss, Harry Bartell as Lieutenant Siebert, and Jack Moyles as Major Daggett, this episode featured Dan Riss, Clayton Post, Larry Dobkin, Joyce McClusky, Paul Dubov, and James Nusser.

Episode 2: "Boatswright's Story" Writer, John Meston. Transcribed January 26 and aired January 29, 1956. Cast: Bob Sweeney, Jan Arvan, Lou Krugman, Sam Edwards, and Joseph Cranston.

Episode 3: "Square Man," also titled **"Will Granby, Scout"** Writer, John Dunkel. Transcribed February 2 and aired February 5, 1956. Cast: Eleanor Tanin, Frank Cady, Ralph Moody, and Edgar Barrier as Grey Feather, Rappahoe Indian Chief.

Episode 4: "The Woman at Horse Creek" Writer, Les Crutchfield, *not* Kathleen Hite. Transcribed February 9, aired February 12, 1956. Cast: Virginia Gregg as Mrs. Dennis, Widow; Barney Phillips as the barkeeper; and John Dehner as Flint.

Episode 5: "Boredom," also titled **"Unknown Disease at Fort"** Writer, Les Crutchfield, *not* John Meston. Transcribed February 16 and aired February 19, 1956. Cast: Joseph Cranston, Parley Baer, Sam Edwards, Jack Kruschen, Vivi Janiss, and Howard Culver.

Episode 6: "The Captain's Widow" Writer, John Dunkel. Transcribed February 23 and aired February 26, 1956. Cast: Jack Kruschen, James Nusser, Helen Kleeb, Virginia Gregg, and Joseph Cranston. This was a love story about Captain Lee Quince and the widow.

Episode 7: "Shavetail," also titled **"Spotted Tail's Daughter"** Writer, Les Crutchfield. Transcribed March 1, aired March 4, 1956. Cast: John Dehner, as Chief Spotted Tail, and Joseph Cranston.

Episode 8: "Hattie Pelfry" Writer, Kathleen Hite. Transcribed March 3, aired March 11, 1956. Cast: Virginia Gregg, as Hattie, and Sam Edwards.

Episode 9: "The Beasley Girls" Writer, Kathleen Hite. Transcribed March 8 and aired March 18, 1956. Cast: Sam Edwards, Lou Krugman, James Nusser, Larry Dobkin and Lillian Buyeff.

Episode 10: "The Coward," also titled **"Lt. Robbie Wendt"** Writer, Les Crutchfield, *not* John Dunkel. Transcribed March 10, aired March 25, 1956. Cast: John Dehner as Lt. Robbie Wendt; Lynn Allen as Mrs. St. Cloud; Paul Dubov; Clayton Post; and Joseph Cranston.

Episode 11: "Lost Child," also titled **"Major Barlow's Survey"** Writer, Les Crutchfield, *not* Gil Doud. Transcribed March 1, aired March 15, 1956. This episode was to be aired April 8, but was preempted by the Master's Golf Tournament. Cast: Larry Dobkin, Harry Bartell, Clayton Post, Joseph Cranston, Richard Beals, and Ralph Moody as Chief Weissiren.

Episode 12: "Stage Coach Stop," also titled **"Major Jesse Hale Buried"** Writer, Kathleen Hite. Transcribed March 22, aired April 15, 1956. Cast: Howard McNear, Jack Kruschen, Sam Edwards, Frank Cady, Shirley Mitchell, and Eleanor Tanin.

Episode 13: "The New Recruit," also titled **"Will Banyon"** Writer, Les Crutchfield, *not* E. Jack Neuman. Transcribed March 29, aired April 22, 1956. Cast: Paul Dubov, Larry Dobkin, James Nusser, Sam Edwards, John Dehner, and Joseph Cranston.

Episode 14: "Quince's Capture," also titled **"White Dog's Tribe"** Writer, Kathleen Hite. Transcribed April 5, aired April 29, 1956. Cast: Lou Krugman, Ralph Moody, Frank Cady, Lee Miller, and Jeff Silver.

Episode 15: "Never the Twain" Writer, William M. Robson. Transcribed April 12, aired May 6, 1956. Cast: Ralph Moody, Don Diamond, John Stephenson, John Dehner, and Lillian Buyeff.

Episode 16: "War Correspondent" Writer, Kathleen Hite. Transcribed April 19, aired May 13, 1956. Cast: Sam Edwards, Parley Baer, Larry Dobkin, and Lou Krugman.

Episode 17: "Black Hills Gold" Writer, Kathleen Hite. Transcribed April 26, aired May 20, 1956. Cast: Frank Gerste, Virginia Gregg, Ralph Moody, Howard McNear, and Clayton Post.

Episode 18: "Sergeant Goerss's Baby," also titled **"Stella Merchant's Ordeal"** Transcribed May 10, aired May 27, 1956. Cast: Richard Crenna as Billie Merchant, Ann Morrison, Virginia Gregg, and Helen Kleeb.

Episode 19: "Don't Kick My Horse," also titled **"Mrs. Wentner, Widow"** Writer, Les Crutchfield. Transcribed May 3, aired June 3, 1956. Cast: Virginia Gregg as the widow, Mrs. Wentner; Barney Phillips, Larry Dobkin, Tim Graham, and Jack Kruschen.

Episode 20: "Young Trooper" Writer, Kathleen Hite. Transcribed May 17, aired June 10, 1956. Cast: Eve McVeagh, Frank Cady, and Jeff Silver.

Episode 21: "Winter Soldier," also titled **"Conflict"** and **"Two Deserters"**

Writer, Les Crutchfield, *not* John Dunkel. Transcribed May 24, aired June 17, 1956. Cast: Joseph Cranston, Paul Dubov, James Nusser, and Howard Culver.

Episode 22: "The Loving Cup" Writer, Kathleen Hite. Transcribed May 31, aired June 24, 1956. Cast: Helen Kleeb.

Episode 23: "Trooper's Widow" Writer, Kathleen Hite. Transcribed June 7, aired July 1, 1956. Cast: Lynn Allen, Larry Dobkin, and Jeanne Bates.

Episode 24: "Talented Recruits," also titled **"Two Actors"** Writer, Kathleen Hite. Transcribed June 14, aired July 8, 1956. Cast: Parley Baer as Posie Finney, the first actor; John Dehner as Granville Merriweather; Arnie Botkins, ham actor.

Episode 25: "Old Enemy," also titled **"The Search for Sitting Bull"** Writer, Les Crutchfield, *not* Kathleen Hite. Transcribed June 21, aired July 15, 1956. Cast: John Dehner as Sitting Bull, Sam Edwards, Paul Dubov, James Nusser, Joseph Cranston, and Herb Vigran.

Episode 26: "Spotted Tail Returns," also titled **"Spotted Tail Leaves the Reservation"** and **"Fleet Bear's Unknown Plans"** Writer, Les Crutchfield, *not* Kathleen Hite. Transcribed June 28, aired July 22, 1956. Cast: John Dehner as Spotted Tail, Tim Graham, Lou Krugman, Ralph Moody, and Joseph Cranston.

Episode 27: "Nature Boy," also titled **"The Quiring Family"** Writer, Les Crutchfield, *not* Kathleen Hite. Transcribed July 7, aired July 29, 1956. Cast: Howard McNear as Horace Quiring, Virginia Gregg as Winifred Quiring, Parley Baer, Shirley Mitchell as Gussie, and John Dehner.

Episode 28: "The Massacre," also titled **"Snowfoot, Renegade"** Writer, Les Crutchfield, *not* Kathleen Hite. Transcribed July 12, aired August 5, 1956. Cast: John Dehner as Snowfoot, Larry Dobkin, Sam Edwards, Lou Krugman, Tim Graham, and Joseph Cranston.

Episode 29: "Assembly Line," also titled **"Red Deer, Pow Wow"** Writer, Les Crutchfield, *not* Kathleen Hite. Transcribed July 19, aired August 12, 1956. Cast: John Dehner as Chief Red Deer, Joseph Kearns as Mr. Lack, Vivi Janiss as Mrs. Lack, and Joseph Cranston.

Episode 30: "Goodbye, Willie," also titled **"Captain Quince's Romance"** Writer, Les Crutchfield, *not* Kathleen Hite. Transcribed July 21, aired August 19, 1956. Cast: Virginia Gregg as Miss Willa, Dolores Pinard Brown, Parley Baer, and John Dehner.

Episode 31: "The Chaplain" Writer, Kathleen Hite. Transcribed July 26, aired August 26, 1956. Cast: Parley Baer, Paul Dubov, and Larry Dobkin.

Episode 32: "The Return of Hattie Pelfry" Writer, Kathleen Hite. Transcribed July 28, aired September 2, 1956. Cast: Virginia Gregg as Hattie Pelfry, Paul Dubov, and Sam Edwards.

Episode 33: "The Buffalo Hunters" Writer, Les Crutchfield, not Kathleen Hite. Transcribed August 2, aired September 9, 1956. Cast: James Nusser and Barney Phillips.

Episode 34: "The Payroll," also titled **"Waiting for the Paymaster"** Writer, Kathleen Hite. Transcribed August 4, aired September 16, 1956. Cast: Clayton Post, Sam Edwards, and Howard McNear.

This was the last of the series, as announced on the recording.

Episode 35: "The Woman at Horse Creek" Writer, Les Crutchfield. Transcribed originally on February 9 and aired February 12, 1956. This episode was repeated on September 23, 1956, under the title of **"Mrs. Dennis, Widow"** Cast: Virginia Gregg as the Widow Dennis, John Dehner as Flint, Barney Phillips as the barkeeper, and Joseph Cranston.

Episode 36: "A Small Beginning," also titled **"Breaking in Lt. Siebert"** Writer, Les Crutchfield, *not* Kathleen Hite. Transcribed September 20, aired September 30, 1956. Cast: Sam Edwards, Jess Kirkpatrick, Jack Kruschen, Joseph Cranston, Howard Culver, Larry Dobkin, and John Dehner as Square Dog.

Episode 37: "Galvanized Yankee," also titled **"Two Ex-Cons"** Writer, Kathleen Hite. Transcribed September 22, aired October 7, 1956. Cast: Frank Cady as the Depot Man; Paul Dubov as Medford; the second ex-con, Sam Edwards; Larry Dobkin; and Parley Baer as Spencer, the first ex-con.

Episode 38: "Still Waters" Writer, Kathleen Hite. Transcribed September 27, aired October 14, 1956. Cast: Jeanette Nolan, Howard McNear, and Sam Edwards. Ended 13 week cycle. Raymond Burr sang a few bars of "Around Her Neck She Wore a Yellow Ribbon."

Episode 39: "Indian Scout" Writer, Kathleen Hite. Transcribed October 6, aired October 21, 1956. Cast: Larry Dobkin.

Episode 40: "Army Wife," also titled **"Lt. Stocker's Wife"** and **"Hester's Gun"** Cast: Richard Crenna as Lt. Blade Stocker, Helen Kleeb as Hester Stocker, Virginia Gregg as Mrs. Mead, Parley Baer, Ann Morrison, and Sammie Hill. This was a repeat of episode 18.

"Fort Laramie" was canceled after the second show in the cycle. Raymond Burr had been chosen to play Perry Mason and was committed to filming 18 episodes for a September 21, 1957, debut.

Appendix B: Films

Abbreviation Key

RKO	Radio-Keith-Orpheum	REP	Republic
COL	Columbia Studios	REAL	Realart
UA	United Artists	LIP	Lippert
PAR	Paramount	AA	Allied Artists
UNIV	Universal	EJ, JAP	Japanese
MGM	Metro Goldwyn Mayer	CAN	Canadian
EL	Eagle-Lion	TCF	20th Century–Fox
WB	Warner Brothers	DCA	Distributors Corp. of America

No. Title	Studio	Year
1. Earl of Puddlestone	REP	1940
2. Without Reservations	RKO	1946
3. San Quentin	RKO	1946
4. Code of the West	RKO	1947
5. Desperate	RKO	1947
6. Fighting Father Dunne	RKO	1948
7. Pitfall	UA	1948
8. Raw Deal	EL	1948
9. Ruthless	EL	1948
10. Sleep, My Love	UA	1948
11. Adventures of Don Juan	WB	1948
12. Walk a Crooked Mile	COL	1948
13. Stations West	RKO	1948
14. I Love Trouble	COL	1948
15. Criss Cross (his part cut out of released film)	UNIV	1949
16. Bride of Vengeance	PAR	1949
17. Black Magic	UA	1949
18. Abandoned	UNIV	1949
19. Red Light	UA	1949
20. Love Happy	UA	1949
21. Unmasked	REP	1950
22. Borderline	UNIV	1950

No.	Title	Studio	Year
23.	Key to the City	MGM	1950
24.	A Place in the Sun	PAR	1951
25.	The Magic Carpet	COL	1951
26.	His Kind of Woman	RKO	1951
27.	Bride of the Gorilla	REAL	1951
28.	New Mexico	UA	1951
29.	M	COL	1951
30.	FBI Girl	LIP	1951
31.	The Whip Hand	RKO	1951
32.	Meet Danny Wilson	UNIV	1952
33.	Mara Maru	WB	1952
34.	Horizons West	UNIV	1952
35.	The Blue Gardenia	WB	1953
36.	Fort Algiers	UA	1953
37.	Bandits of Corsica	UA	1953
38.	Tarzan and the She-Devil	RKO	1953
39.	Serpent of the Nile	COL	1953
40.	Casanova's Big Night	PAR	1954
41.	Gorilla at Large	TCF	1954
42.	Khyber Patrol	UA	1954
43.	Rear Window	PAR	1954
44.	Passion	RKO	1954
45.	Thunder Pass	LIP	1954
46.	They Were So Young	LIP	1955
47.	You're Never Too Young	PAR	1955
48.	Count Three and Pray	COL	1955
49.	A Man Alone	REP	1955
50.	Double Danger (released in London only)	AA	1955
51.	The Brass Legend	UA	1956
52.	Please Murder Me	DCA	1956
53.	Godzilla	EJ	1956
54.	Great Day in the Morning	RKO	1956
55.	Secret of Treasure Mountain	COL	1956
56.	A Cry in the Night	WB	1956
57.	Ride the High Iron	COL	1956
58.	Crime of Passion	UA	1957
59.	Affair in Havana	AA	1957
60.	Desire in the Dust	TCF	1960
61.	P.J.	UNIV	1968
62.	Tomorrow Never Comes	CAN	1978
63.	Cebe (title changed to Out of the Blue and rereleased as Never Look Back)	CAN	1979
64.	Airplane II	PAR	1982
65.	Godzilla '85	JAP	1985
66.	Delirious	MGM/UA	1991

In the Movies Raymond Burr Was

Shot 17 times
Beaten 3 times
Stabbed 2 times
Drowned 1 time
Killed in a duel 2 times
Trampled to death 1 time
Arrested 6 times

Fell to his death 3 times
Blown up 1 time
Killed by blow to head 1 time
Dead by alcohol poisoning 1 time
Killed in fights 2 times
Suicide victim 1 time

In the Movies Raymond Played a

Detective 4 times
Police chief 4 times
Crook 13 times
Spy 2 times

Lawyer 3 times
Gangster 10 times
Bank robber 2 times
Tycoon 3 times

Played a politician, soldier, rancher, psycho, desperado, ivory poacher one time each; played a Hindu, Arab, Egyptian, Muslim, Italian, German and a revolutionary American.

Appendix C: Television Shows

Date	Show/Episode	Network
1947	"Mr. & Mrs. North," with Barbara Britton, and Richard Denning, Jeanne Cagney, Mike Connors	
4/29/51	"Bigelow Theater/The Big Hello," with Cesar Romero, Jeanne Cagney	NBC
12/16/51	"Dragnet/The Human Bomb," debut, with Jack Webb	NBC
1952	"Favorite Story/How Much Land Does a Man Need?"	SYN
4/24/52	"Gruen Guild Playhouse/The Tiger"	SYN
6/25/52	"ZIV-TV/Merry Go Round"	
8/20/52	"ZIV-TV/The Magnificent Lie"	
9/9/52	"Gruen Guild Playhouse/The Leather Coat"	MCA
9/23/52	"Gruen Guild Playhouse/Face Value"	
10/10/52	"Mr. Lucky at Seven/Pearls from Paris"	ABC
10/16/52	"ZIV-TV/The Unexpected"	
1953	Commentator for Academy Awards	
—	"Hollywood Showcase/Paris Calling," with Mary Astor as Host, Raymond Burr in the George Sanders role	
2/10/53	"Four Star Playhouse/The Room," with Dick Powell	CBS
6/1/53	"Twilight Theater/Mask of Medusa," with Steven Geray	ABC
1/7/54	"Ford Theater/The Fugitives"	NBC
2/12/54	"Lux Video Theater/Shall Not Perish," with Fay Bainter	CBS
1955	"Robert Montgomery Presents"; debut of Elizabeth Montgomery in "Top Secret"	—
—	"Crime and Punishment," with Jean Pierre Aumont	—
7/1/55	"Schlitz Playhouse/Ordeal of Dr. Sutton," with Marilyn Erskine	CBS
7/1/55	"Undercurrent/The Web," several episodes	CBS
9/17/55	"Counterpoint/The Wreck"	SYN
11/2/55	"20th Century Fox Hour/The Oxbow Incident," with Robert Wagner, E. G. Marshall, Cameron Mitchell	CBS
12/1/55	"Lux Video Theater/The Web"	NBC
3/1/56	"Climax/The Sound of Silence," with Jean Pierre Aumont and Lloyd Bridges	CBS
5/1/56	"Ford Theater/Man Without Fear," with Joseph Cotten, John Bernadino, Angela Green	NBC
5/24/56	"Climax/The Shadow of Evil," with Jan Sterling and Richard Boone	CBS

Date	Show/Episode	Network
10/18/56	"Lux Video Theater/The Flamingo Road"	NBC
11/5/56	"Arizona/Ames"	CBS
12/6/56	"Climax/Savage Portrait," with Joanne Woodward and John Cassavetes	CBS
1957	"Undercurrent/No Escape"	CBS
1/31/57	"Playhouse 90/The Greer Case," with Melvyn Douglas, Anita Louise, Zsa Zsa Gabor	CBS
9/21/57–5/22/66	"Perry Mason"	CBS
10/16/57	"Strange Stories/Face Value" (repeated)	
10/18/57	"Strange Stories/Leather Coat" (repeated)	
12/26/57	"Playhouse 90/The Lone Woman," with Kathryn Grayson, Virginia Grey, Jack Lord, Scott Brady, Vincent Price	CBS
1956–57	"Chevron Hall of Fame," several episodes	
12/25/58	"Special/A Star Shall Rise"	CBS
12/25/59	"Special/A Star Shall Rise" (repeated)	SYN
—	"You and the Law," opening and closing	
1959	"11th Emmy Awards," wins first award. With Jack Benny, Shirley Temple, James Arness, Fred Astaire, Ed Sullivan, Richard Nixon	—
7/30/59	"Peter Potter's Juke Box Jury," as a juror	CBS
11/7/59	"Jack Benny Show," as comedian	CBS
5/16/60	"Jack Benny Show," repeated	CBS
1960	"The Triumphant Hour/Father Patrick Payten"	SYN
1960	"Person to Person," with Edward R. Murrow	CBS
6/9/61	"Meet the Stars, *TV Guide*," first guest	
6/14/61	"Meet the Press," Melbourne, Australia	HSV7
6/18/61	"Questions and Answers," Melbourne	HSV7
6/18/61	"Variety Show," Melbourne	HSV7
6/18/61	Host of "Perry Mason" episode	HSV7
11/5/61	"Jack Benny Show," "Perry Mason" spoof	CBS
7/16/62–9/13/68	"Actuality" specials; narrator of news documentaries	
1964	Art Linkletter's "House Party"	CBS
5/1/65	"Phillip Morris Show/Kentucky Derby Festival"	
2/25/65	"Jack Benny Show," repeated	CBS
2/25/65	"What's My Line?" mystery guest, with Arlene Francis, Dorothy Kilgallen, Bennett Cerf, John Daly	CBS
7/28/65	Art Linkletter's "House Party"	ABC
8/25/65	"This Is Canada," special narrated and produced by Raymond Burr	CBS
11/15/65	"Johnny Grant's Stand by Stage 5"	KTLA
4/10/66	"Big Picture/Why Vietnam?"	CBS
9/12/66	"Jean Arthur Show"	CBS
10/20/66	"Red Skelton Show," comedy sketches	CBS
3/28/67–1/16/75	"Ironside"	NBC
10/6/67	"Special Report," Burr's visit to Vietnam, filmed by his Harbour Productions	NBC

Date	*Show/Episode*	*Network*
1/1/68	Orange Bowl Parade, Miami, Florida, with Anita Bryant	CBS
1/1/68–	Rose Parade, Pasadena, California, Betty White cohost	NBC
1/1/72		
1968	"It Takes a Thief," with Robert Wagner and Fred Astaire	ABC
—	"Password," with Allen Ludden	NBC
1/12/68	"Hollywood Squares," one week and one night	NBC
9/3/68	"Tonight Show"	NBC
9/22/68	"Beautiful Phyllis Diller Show"	NBC
10/26/69	"Leslie Uggams Show"	—
—	"Kaye Ballard Show"	CBS
5/16/70	"Jimmy Durante Show"	ABC
9/21/70	"Red Skelton Show"	CBS
10/15/70	"Flip Wilson Show"	NBC
11/18/70	"Don Adams Show," ad-libbed comedy with David Janssen	NBC
12/15/70	"Don Knotts Show"	NBC
—	Tribute to Alfred Lunt and Lynn Fontaine, with Carroll O'Connor	—
1/21/71	"Dean Martin Show"	NBC
2/5/71	"Andy Williams Show"	NBC
2/20/71	"Glen Campbell Show," whistles "The Colonel Bogey March"	CBS
2/23/71	"Kopykats," in London; Rich Little imitates Raymond Burr	ABC
9/30/71	"Flip Wilson Show"	NBC
11/15/71	"Ford Theater Special," for President's Festival at Ford's, with Bob Hope and Carol Channing	NBC
9/14/72	"The Bold Ones/Five Days in the Death of Sgt. Brown,"	NBC
9/19/72	parts 1 and 2	
1/27/72	"Dean Martin Show"	NBC
11/30/72	"Flip Wilson Show"	NBC
3/27/73	"Keep America Beautiful," guest with Lena Horne, Ruth Buzzi, Don Knotts	NBC
4/19/73	"Flip Wilson Show"	NBC
4/22/73	"Portrait: A Man Whose Name Was John," two hour special on Pope John XXIII, with Don Galloway	NBC
8/9/74	"John Denver Show." This was never shown, due to President Richard Nixon's resignation	NBC
2/3/76	"Tonight Show"	NBC
2/6/76	"Merv Griffin Show"	MM
2/8/76	"Sonny and Cher Show"	CBS
2/8/76	"Mallory," produced by RBI Co.	NBC
2/25/76	"Dinah Shore Show"	CBS
3/5/76	"Donny and Marie Show"	ABC
4/11/76	"Phil Donahue Show"	NBC
4/27/76	"Dinah Shore Show"	NBC
6/29/76	"Psychic Phenomena"	PBS
7/3/76	"Inventing of America," with James Burke	NBC
7/13/76	"A.M. Chicago"	ABC

Date	Show/Episode	Network
8/22/76	"Dinah Shore Show"	CBS
9/2/76	"Phil Donahue Show"	NBC
9/15/76– 8/10/77	"Kingston Confidential," produced by RBI Productions	NBC
11/22/76	"Captain and Tennille Show"	ABC
11/76	"Dick Van Dyke Show"	NBC
3/22/77	"Tonight Show"	NBC
4/5/77	"Merv Griffin Show"	MM
10/16/77	"79 Park Avenue," cameo role as the Godfather, with Leslie Ann Warren	NBC
12/21/77	"Good Morning, America"	ABC
1977	"Victory Gardener," talked with Jim Crockett about orchid growing	—
12/23/77	"Good Day, Boston"	NBC
12/24/77	"Christmas Around the World," first use of satellites, live and then on tape 12/25/77	PBS
1/9/78– 2/17/78	"Hollywood Squares"	NBC
2/19/78	"The Flower Spot," with Betty Thompson	CAN
10/1/78	"Centennial"	NBC
10/13/78	"Stephanie Edwards Show"	CBS
10/17/78	"Merv Griffin Show"	MM
11/3/78– 11/9/78	"Match Game," with Gene Rayburn, Elaine Joyce, Joyce Bulifant	CBS
12/2/78	"The Jordon Chance," 2 hour special produced by RBI	NBC
1/17/79	"Psychic Phenomena," host and narrator	NBC
2/3/79	"Loveboat/Alas, Poor Dwyer"	ABC
2/16/79	"Dinah Shore Show," interviewed "Loveboat" crew, with guest Raymond Burr	CBS
5/20/79	"Love's Savage Fury," small part, with Jennifer O'Neill	NBC
1979	"Trial of Zavier Solorzana," host and narrator, shown in Chicago only	WTTW
9/21/79	"Eischied/Only the Pretty Girls Die," part 1, as Police Commissioner	NBC
9/28/79	"Eischied," conclusion, with Joe Don Baker	NBC
10/23/79	"The Misadventures of Sheriff Lobo," with Claude Akin	NBC
10/28/79	"Disaster on the Coastliner," small part with William Shatner	NBC
12/17/79	"William Faulkner, His Life on Paper," narrator, NYC area only	PBS
1980	Logie Awards, Melbourne, Australia	
1980	"The Alien's Return," with Jennifer O'Neil	Cable
4/20/80	"Presto, Chango—It's Magic," host	HBO
5/8/80 & 5/9/80	"Curse of King Tut's Tomb," parts 1 and 2	NBC
12/14/80	"The Night the City Screamed," with Robert Culp	NBC
4/12/81	"The Acts of Peter and Paul," with Anthony Hopkins	NBC
2/12/82	Telethon for Variety Clubs Int'l in New Westminster, Canada	CAN

Date	Show/Episode	Network
1984	"Good Morning, America"	ABC
11/25/85	Emmy Awards	NBC
12/1/85	"Return of Perry Mason"	NBC
9/29/87	"Larry King Live"	CNN
10/1/87	"Charlie Rose Nightwatch"	CBS
10/1/87	"Morning Program"	CBS
10/2/87	"Live at Five"	NBC
10/2/87	"Showbiz Today," with William Katt	—
10/2/87	"Entertainment Tonight"	CBS
—	"Legend of Perry Mason"	Showtime
10/4/87	CNN, one-on-one interview	CNN
2/25/88	"Hour Magazine," with Gary Collins	Fox
2/25/88	"Sonya Live in LA"	—
2/26/88	"Today Show"	NBC
1981–88	Commercials for the Independent Insurance Agents. Commercials for Block Brothers Real Estate in and around Vancouver, Canada.	
8/28/89	"Larry King Live"	CNN
8/30/89	"This Morning"	CBS
4/8/90	"Bloopers and Bleepers," with Dick Clark and Ed McMahon	NBC
9/1/90	"Good Day, America"	Fox
9/11/89 –1990	"Trial by Jury." Raymond Burr played Judge, explaining legal terms used, and a jury member, talking directly to the viewer. Joseph Campanella, Charles Siebert, Madelyn Rhue, and others played attorneys or judges. Show dramatized a case and viewers decided guilt or innocence of person on trial. Ran 5 days per week.	
10/21/90	"Bloopers and Bleepers," repeat	
1990	"Regis and Kathie Lee, Live in New York"	ABC
9/30/90	"Joan Rivers Show"	NBC
1/18/91	"Disaster on the Coastliner," repeat	NBC
5/14/91	"Entertainment Tonight," about new episode of "Perry Mason," with John Tesh	NBC
5/14/91	11 o'clock news tells of cancer operation	NBC
—	Narration of "My Nuclear Neighbors," about nuclear energy.	—
2/24/92 2/25/92	"Grass Roots," parts 1 and 2, as Judge Henry Bogg	NBC
3/1/92	"Case of the Fatal Framing"	NBC
5/5/92	"Case of the Libeled Lady"	NBC
6/1/92	Documentary, "Handicapped in Wheelchairs," on Irish television stations	—
7/4/92	"Portraits of Freedom," host and narrator. Not documented are live performances on the West Coast only during 1950 "Stars over Hollywood"; two plays in 1951, "The 13th Day" and "The Story of Esther"; and "The Frank Sinatra Show"	NBC

Appendix D:
"Perry Mason" Episode Guide

These episodes were compiled by David Javorsky in 1974-75, while he was attending the University of Rhode Island. His interest was in the character of Perry Mason, not in the man who portrayed him.

REGULAR CAST

Perry Mason	Raymond Burr
Della Street	Barbara Hale
Hamilton Burger	William Talman
Lieutenant Tragg	Ray Collins
Paul Drake	William Hopper
Gertie Lade	Connie Cezon

The Case of the Restless Redhead,
9/21/57 (series debut)

Perry Mason receives a call for help from redheaded Evelyn Bagby, who has found a strange gun in her apartment. He learns she was recently tried for diamond theft but was acquitted for lack of evidence. Later she is chased by a hooded man and, after shooting at him, is picked up by the police for the man's murder. Perry defends her.

Evelyn	Whitney Blake
Mr. Boles	Vaughn Taylor
Mrs. Boles	Jane Buchanan
Mervyn Aldritch	Ralph Clanton
Sgt. Holcomb	Dick Rich
Helene Chaney	Gloria Henry
Judge Kippen	Grandon Rhodes

Sleepwalker's Niece, 9/28/57

A divorce case almost costs Perry his life, as it involves blackmail, perjury, and murder.

Edna Hammer	Nancy Hadley
Peter Cole	John McNamara
Steve Harris	Darryl Hickman
Lucille Mays	Helen Mowery
Ralph Duncan	Thomas B. Henry
Frank Maddox	John Archer
Doris Cole	Hillary Brooke
Judge	Kenneth MacDonald

Nervous Accomplice, 10/5/57

Sybil Granger's husband is involved with the beautiful Roxy Howard, and Sybil wants him back. The lovely woman hires Perry to help her keep her husband and some land supposedly rich in oil, but then she is charged with murder.

Sybil	Margaret "Maggie" Hayes
Roxy	Greta Thyssen
Bruce Granger	William Roerick
Gertie	Connie Cezon
Hurley	Robert Bice
George Lutts	Richard Hale
Herbert Dean	Robert Cornthwaite
Judge Hoyt	Morris Ankrum

Drowning Duck, 10/12/57

In Logan City to investigate a blackmail racket and free a client, Perry faces hostile people who block his efforts, and his involvement eventually leads to murder.

Helen Waters	Carolyn Craig
Don Briggs	Harry Landers
George Norris	Don Beddoe
Martha Norris	Paula Winslow
Lois Reed	Carol Kelly
Mrs. Adams	Olive Blakeney
Clyde Waters	Vic Sutherland
Mr. Marv Adams	Gary Vinson
Dr. Wall	Joseph Crehan
Cortland	Phil Tonge
Judge Meehan	Nolan Leary

Sulky Girl, 10/19/57

Young heiress Frances Celand wants to manage the trust fund now controlled by her uncle. A blackmailer contacts her, her uncle is killed, and Frances is jailed for the murder.

Frances Celane	Olive Sturgess
Clara Mayfield	Lillian Bronson
Ed Norton	Raymond Greenleaf
Don Graves	William Schallert

Silent Partner, 10/26/57

Mildred Kimber learns her husband lost some stock in a crooked poker game. Perry finds an ex-con won the stock.

Mildred Kimber	Anne Barton
Bob Kimber	Mark Roberts
Lola Florey	Peggy Maley
Harry Marlow	Dan Seymour
Sam Lynk	Michael Emmet
Welsh	Dan Sheridan

Angry Mourner, 11/2/57

Perry learns that all lipstick is not kissproof when defending a woman's honor and, later, against a charge of murder. His defense leads to verbal dynamite.

Hale	Paul Fix
Marion Keats	Joan Weldon
Harvey Delano	Peter Nelson
Carla Adrian	Barbara Eden
Belle Adrian	Sylvia Field
Sheriff Elmore	James Westerfield
Betsy Burris	Dorothy Adams
Sam Burris	Malcolm Atterbury

Crimson Kiss, 11/9/57

A lipstick print found on a dead man's forehead may explain why Fay Allison and her roommate took overdoses of sleeping pills. Louise Marlow calls Perry when she finds her niece Fay and her roommate near death from the overdoses; later, the dead man is found in the same building. Evidence in his apartment points to Fay.

Carver Clement	John Holland
Dane Grover	Douglas Dick
Fay Allison	Sue England
Anita Bonsal	Jean Willes
Louise Marlow	Frances Bavier
Dr. Hawley	Howard Culver
Shirley Tanner	Gloria McGhee
Gertie	Connie Cezon
Don Ralston	Doug Evans

Police Sergeant and Sideman	Larry Hudson
Lab Man	John Harmon
Judge Randolph	Frank Wilcox
Clerk	Jack Gargan
Vera Payson	Joi Lansing

Vagabond Vixen, 11/16/57

(Based on Gardner's novel *The Vagabond Virgin*) A movie mogul desiring secrecy asks Perry to secure the release of a beautiful hitchhiker jailed for vagrancy. After Perry does so, he learns a blackmail plot is the reason for secrecy. He baits a trap for the blackmailer, which nearly fails as the client is arrested for murder.

Myrtle Northrup	Peggy Converse
Veronica Dale	Carol Leigh
Peter Handsel	Jim Anderson
Sergeant Brent	Robert Carson
John Addison	Robert Ellenstein
Lorraine Ferrell	Catherine McLeod
Mrs. Dale	Barbara Pepper
Deputy Neffs	Russell Trent
Ed. Ferrell	Paul Cavanagh
Judge Keetly	Pierre Watkin

Runaway Corpse, 11/23/57

A dead man leaves a letter naming his wife as the killer. The wife, Myrna Davenport, asks Perry's help but he runs into trouble with the law. Trying to defend her for two murders, Mason is accused of violating the law by Hamilton Burger, as a one-year-old body keeps vanishing.

Myrna Davenport	June Dayton
Jason Beckmeyer	Adam Williams
Louise Ansel	Sarah Selby
Rita Norge	Rebecca Welles
Ed Davenport	John Stephenson
Gertie	Connie Cezon

Crooked Candle, 11/30/57

Perry's client is charged with killing her husband, but then another woman arrives and claims also to be his widow. Which one is lying?

Martha Bradford	Nancy Gates
Rita Bradford	Doris Singleton
Joe Bradford	Bruce Cowling
Larry Sands	Whit Bissell
Nikolides	Henry Corden
Captain Noble	Francis McDonald

Negligent Nymph, 12/7/57

An attractive blond, Sally Fenner, claiming she had to swim for her life, is pulled from the water by Perry Mason, who is on a fishing trip. The woman says she fled when she was caught burglarizing her former boss's home.

Ysidero Martinez	Robert Tafur
Nina Santos	Nadja Posey
Sally Fenner	Peggy Castle
George Alder	David Lewis
Karen Alder	Joan Banks
Arthur Dorian	James Griffith
Alex Hess	John Cliff
Dr. Murray	Forrest Lewis
Judge Summerville	James Nusser

Moth-Eaten Mink, 12/14/57

A scared but beautiful waitress runs for her life from the café where she works, leaving a moth-eaten mink coat and her check behind. Later she is struck by a speeding car, and a murder charge results.

Sergeant Jaffrey	Douglas Kennedy
Morey Allen	Bob Osterloh
Dixie Dayton	Kay Faylen
Frank Hoxie	Than Wyenn
Mae	Roxanne Arlen
George Fayette	Marc Krah
Judge Lennox	Grandon Rhodes
Gertie	Connie Cezon
Parking Attendant	Brian Hutton
Bailiff	Jack Gargan
Drake's Operator	Lynn Guild
Cop	Jack Shea
Burger's Assistant	Jim Waters
Stunt Man	Richard Geary

Baited Hook, 12/21/57

Perry gets half of a $10,000 bill from a heavily veiled woman and a man. They say he will get the other half when his services are needed, which is soon as a murder takes place.

Robert Dawson	Willard Sage
Enid Shaw	Mary Castle
Albert Tydings	George Neise
Gertie	Connie Cezon
Rich Ellis	Alfred Hopson
Carol Stanley	Judith Braun
Abigail Leeds	Geraldine Wall

Receptionist	Peg Whitman
Officer	Lyle Latell
Janitor	Frank Marlowe
Drake's Operator	Lorraine Martin
Operative	Maurice McEndree

Fan Dancer's Horse, 12/28/57

John Callender comes to Perry Mason about his stolen riding horse. His ex-wife, shapely exotic dancer Lois Fenton, is charged with his murder, as fragments of her ostrich plume fan are found in the fatal wound. Later another fan dancer is also charged with the murder, causing problems.

Cherie Chi-Chi	Judy Tyler
Lois Fenton	Susan Cummings
Arthur Sheldon	Scott Elliott
Frank Faulkner	Robert Bice
Jasper Fenton	John Brinkley
John Callender	Hugh Sanders

Demure Defendant, 1/4/58

Hamilton Burger charges Perry Mason with tampering with evidence in a murder case. Perry's client, a young girl charged with killing her uncle, confessed to the murder while under the influence of a truth serum.

Gertie	Connie Cezon
Nadine Marshall	Christine White
Martin Wellman	Alexander Campbell
Captain Hugo	Clem Bevans
John Locke	Sherwood Price
Judge	Morris Ankrum
Marian Newburn	Fay Baker
Dr. Denair	Barry Atwater
Korbell	Steven Geray
Lester Newburn	Walter Coy

Sunbather's Diary, 1/11/58

Clad only in a beach towel, Arlene Dowling reports the theft of all her belongings, including a diary she desperately wants back.

Arlene Dowling	Susan Morrow
George Ballard	Ralph Moody
Thomas Sackett	Paul Brinegar
Helen Rucker	Gertrude Michael
Dr. Ralph Chandler	Carl Betz
Gertie	Connie Cezon
Judge	Kenneth MacDonald

Mr. Hartsel	Nesdon Booth
Bill Emory	Peter Leeds

Cautious Coquette, 1/18/58

While working on a financial statement for a hit-and-run victim, Perry becomes involved in blackmail, a frameup, and murder.

Harry Pitkin	Harry Jackson
Elaine Barton	Kipp Hamilton
Ross Hollister	James Seay
Sheila Cromwell	Virginia Gregg
Frederick Arms	Sid Clute
Robert Finchley	Brett Halsey
Stephen Argyle	Donald Randolph

Haunted Husband, 1/25/58

Mason arranges bail for a woman charged with auto theft, but when a man's body is found in her hotel room, the woman, Claire Olger, is charged with his murder.

Claire Olger	Patricia Hardy
Doris Stephanak	Karen Steele
Mike Greeley	John Hubbard
Harold Hanley	Harlan Warde
Jerry Heywood	Grant Richards

Lonely Heiress, 2/1/58

A young, vengeful heiress is charged with the murder of the man whom she believed responsible for her sister's death. She tries to set a trap for the man, but he is killed and she is arrested.

Marylin Clark	Kathleen Crowley
Charles Barnaby	L. Q. Jones
George Moore	Richard Crane
Agnes Sims	Betty Lou Gerson
Ed Lacey	Robert H. Harris
Dolores Coterro	Anna Navarro
Lieutenant Kramer	Robert Williams
Judge	Frank Wilcox
Dr. L. J. Palmer	Robert McQueeney
Margo	Gail Kobe

Green-Eyed Sister, 2/8/58

Perry helps attractive Harriet Bain fight her father's blackmailer, who has a tape that could convict him of embezzlement. Perry tries to help, but his client is charged with murder.

Harriet Bain	Virginia Vincent
Sylvia Bain	Tina Carver
Addison Doyle	Robin Hughes
Ned Bain	Carl Benton Reid
Arthur West	Dan Riss
J. J. Stanley	James Bell
Judge	Morris Ankrum
Gertie	Connie Cezon
Dr. Hanover	Dennis King, Jr.

Fugitive Nurse, 2/15/58

Young Janet Morris asks Perry's help on a tax matter, but she is then charged with murdering a man who happens to be her husband.

Janet Morris	Bethel Leslie
Dr. Charles Morris	Shepperd Strudwick
Gladys Strome	Maxine Cooper
David Kirby	Dabbs Greer
Detective Ron Jacks	Lee Roberts
Detective Ralston	Sydney Mason

One-Eyed Witness, 2/22/58

Perry receives a telephone call from a woman about paying off a blackmailer, but after he agrees to handle the matter, his client is arrested for murder.

Mrs. Marian Fargo	Angie Dickinson
Sam Carlin	Luis Van Rooten
Arthur Fargo	Peter Adams
Pierre	Jan Arvan
Diana Maynard	Dorothy Green
Detective	Ray Kellogg
Charles Gallagher	Paul Picerni

Deadly Double, 3/1/58

Helen Reed dreams of killing a man. Her brother fears it will come true and hires Perry Mason.

Helen Reed	Constance Ford
Cora Dunbar	Carole Mathews
Robert Crane	Denver Pyle
John Hale	Murray Hamilton

Empty Tin, 3/8/58

Young Doris Hocksley hires Perry to prove she, not several others, is the rightful heiress to a disputed fortune. She is framed for murder when she is found in a locked room with a corpse and a gun in her hand.

Alan Neil	Warren Stevens
Doris Hocksley	Toni Gerry
Rebecca Gentrie	Olive Deering
Miriam Hocksley	Mary Shipp
Gow Loong	Benson Fong
Judge	Frank Wilcox
John Lowell	Otto Waldis

Half-Wakened Wife, 3/15/58

An old wartime buddy of Perry's sends him a telegram, denies having sent it, and then is arrested for the murder of his employer.

Scott Shelby	Tom Palmer
Marion Shelby	Phyllis Avery
Frank Lawton	Stewart Bradley
Arthur Williams	Jonathan Hole
Ellen Waring	Barbara Lawrence
Howard Black, DA	Peter Hansen
Richy	Paul E. Burns
Phil Dix	Claude Akins
Mitchell Ellsworth	Jason Johnson

Desperate Daughter, 3/22/58

Teenager Doris Bannister has amnesia and consults Perry. As she tries, with his help, to establish her identity, the district attorney arrests her for murder.

Doris Bannister	Gigi Perreau
Gary Marshall	Don Durant
Stefan Riker	Werner Klemperer
Lisa Bannister	Osa Massen
Ed Bannister	Robert F. Simon
Helene	Gere Craft
Detective Davis	Paul Genge
Detective Marlowe	Ivan Bonar

Daring Decoy, 3/29/58

A fight for control of the voting stock in a firm leads to murder. Perry's client is charged with the killing after his prints are found on the murder gun.

Mavis	Natalie Norwick
Daniel Conway	H. M. Wynant

Rose Calvert	Pamela Duncan
Linda Griffith	Marie Windsor
Amelia Corning Armitage	Jacqueline Scott
Fred Calvert	Jack Weston
Warner Griffith	John Mack Brown
Miss Eastman	Louise Lorimer
Judge	Grandon Rhodes
H. B. Varnell	Donald Foster
Court Clerk	Jack Gargan

Hesitant Hostess, 4/5/58

Albert Sanders is on trial for murder after being on trial before for robbery. The victim is cab driver Lane.

Albert Sanders	Fred Sherman
Fred Archer	Les Tremayne
Kim Lane	Betty Utey
Inez Kaylor	Karen Sharpe
Martha Rayburn	June Vincent
Ralph Faulkner	Gil Frye
Joe Gibbs	Ned Wever
Sergeant Brice	Lee Miller
Detective	Robert Karnes

Lee Miller is Raymond Burr's stand-in.

Screaming Woman, 4/26/58

Perry's client, charged with murder, has already confessed to Hamilton Burger, who calls Della Street to the stand to prove Perry Mason withheld evidence and to discredit him.

Leona Walsh	Josephine Hutchinson
Mary K. Davis	Marian Seldes
Dr. George Barnes	Arthur Shields
Eugene Jarech	Berry Kroeger
Connie Cooper	Ruta Lee
Ralph Davis	Philip Ober

Fiery Fingers, 5/3/58

Charming, elderly Nora Mae Quincey knows her boss will be killed but is then charged with her murder after an amused Perry becomes involved with the eccentric lady.

Gertie	Connie Cezon
Charlotte Lynch	Fay Spain
Nora Mae Quincey	Lenore Shanewise
Louise Gordon	Susan Dorn

Vicky Braxton	Mary La Roche
Court Clerk	Jack Gargan
Judge	Sydney Smith
George Gordon	Edward Norris
Dr. Williams	Charles Lane
Detective	Gilbert Frye
Dr. Fremont	Robert Burton
Matron	Jean Andrew
Dr. Meecham	Charles Davis

Substitute Face, 5/10/58

Perry and Della's ocean cruise is ruined by a shipboard murder.

Carl Houser	Theodore Newton
Laura Houser	Maureen Cassidy
Anna Houser	Lurene Tuttle
Roland Carter	Ralph Dumke
Daniel James	Don Lawton
Evelyn Whiting	Joan Tabor
Captain Walters	Gavin Gordon

Long-Legged Models, 5/17/58

Lovely Stephanie Faulkner's father dies mysteriously and a prospective buyer of her property is slain. She is charged with his murder. A friend of her father's hires Perry to defend her.

Stephanie Faulkner	Peggy McCay
Glenn Faulkner	Russell Thorson
George Castle	Joe De Santis
Mike Garvin, Sr.	Lyle Talbot
Mike Garvin, Jr.	William Swan
Eva Elliott	Alix Talton

Gilded Lily, 5/24/58

Stewart Brent agrees to pay Arthur Binney several thousand dollars to suppress damaging information about his wife. Later Brent is found standing over the blackmailer's corpse with his prints on the gun, and Perry must defend him for the murder.

Anne Brent	Mari Aldon
Stewart Brent	Grant Withers
Arthur Binney	Richard Erdman
Enid Griffin	Barbara Baxley
Sheila Bowers	Peggy Knudsen
Harry Lake	Wally Brown
Dr. Cortley	Alan Dexter

Court Clerk .... Jack Gargan
Judge .... Fay Roope
Dr. Parsons .... Carleton Young
Janitor .... Max Wagner
Garage Man .... Cy Malis

Lazy Lover, 5/31/58

Lucille Allred sends Perry a $2,500 check with no explanation. When he tries to reach the woman who signed the check, her husband says she has run away with another man, Bob Fleetwood.

Lucille Allred .... Ann Lee
Patricia Faxon .... Yvonne Craig
Bertrand Allred .... Neil Hamilton
Bob Fleetwood .... Harry Townes
Bernice Archer .... Frances Helm
P. E. Overbrook .... James Bell
Judge Colton .... Kenneth MacDonald
Gertie .... Connie Cezon

Prodigal Parent, 6/7/58

Perry is retained by Ethel Harrison to defend her ex-husband, charged with killing his stepson. To complicate matters, the death weapon has the man's fingerprints on it.

Claire Durell .... Ann Doran
Ethel Harrison .... Fay Wray
George Durell .... Herbert Rudley
Joseph Harrison .... John Hoyt
Philip Harrison .... Terry Becker
Lorraine Stevens .... Andra Martin
Irene Collaro .... Virginia Field
Sarah Winslow .... Nancy Kulp
Judge .... Morris Ankrum
Mr. Alcorn .... Chet Stratton
Court Reporter .... Richard Bull
Policeman .... Leo Needham
Detective Sanchez .... Dean Casey
Dr. Anders .... Michael Fox

Black-Eyed Blonde, 6/14/58

Wearing a coat, bathrobe, and a black eye, Diana Reynolds claims she is being framed for a jewel theft, and an intrigued Perry Mason decides to investigate.

Diana Reynolds .... Whitney Blake
Tony Davis .... Jan Merlin

Norma Carter	Phyllis Coates
Mathew Bartlett	R. G. Armstrong
Helen Bartlett	Irene Hervey
Marian Shaw	Judith Ames
Judge	Grandon Rhodes
Otto Kessler	Ludwig Stossel

Terrified Typist, 6/21/58

A South African diamond company is robbed of a fortune in gems. A messenger, Baxter, is murdered during the robbery. Another company employee is arrested, and the firm asks Perry to defend him.

Gertie	Connie Cezon
James Kincaid	Alan Marshal
Patricia Taylor	Joanna Moore
Mrs. Lumis	Joan Elan
Duane Jefferson	Steve Carruthers
Walter Lumis	Ben Wright
George Baxter	Jack Raine
Jack Gilly	Hank Patterson
Henrich	Harold Dyrenforth

Rolling Bones, 6/28/58

Perry was making progress keeping rich Daniel Reed out of a mental hospital, but he now becomes a murder suspect. His relatives previously had wanted him committed to an institution as mentally incompetent.

Daniel Reed	Edgar Stehli
Donna Knox	Joan Camden
Arlene Scott	Mary Anderson
Willard Scott	Arthur Space
Maury Lewis	King Calder
Millie Foster	Kitty Kelly
George Metcalf	Simon Scott
Judge Treadwell	Richard Gaines
Victor Kowalski	Sid Tomack

Corresponding Corpse, 9/20/58

Perry is called by George Beaumount, whose funeral he attended three years before and for whose death $90,000 in insurance was paid.

George Beaumount	Ross Elliott
Ruth Whittaker	Joan Camden
Harry Folsom	Vaughn Taylor
Laura Beaumount	Jeanne Cooper

Lucky Loser, 9/27/58

In an auto crash, young Ted Balfour is charged a lesser charge of manslaughter. While waiting for the second trial, his lawyer suddenly waives rights to a new trial and has Ted plead guilty to involuntary manslaughter. His grandfather, aghast, asks Perry to take the case; then it is learned that the victim died of a bullet wound.

Ted Balfour	Tyler MacDuff
Addison Balfour	Richard Hale
Steven Boles	Douglas Kennedy
Harriet Balfour	Patricia Medina
Lawrence Balfour	Bruce Bennett
Fred Haley	Woodrow Chambliss
Florence Ingle	Heather Angel
Roger Faris	Guy Rennie
Autopsy Surgeon	Herb Lytton
Policeman	Len Hendry
Detective	Paul Genge
Schmidt	John Bleifer
Judge Cadwell	Morris Ankrum
Thurston	John Eldredge
Ballistics Expert	Jack Holland

Pint-Sized Client, 10/4/58

A teenage boy appears in Perry's office seeking legal advice on whether "finders keepers" is ethical. His grandfather is charged with murder, and the case becomes more serious.

George Koch	Joseph Mell
Nicky Renzi	Bobby Clark
Frank Anderson	James Anderson
Arthur Crowley	Elisha Cook
Lois Gilbert	Eleanor Audley
Iris Anderson	Nita Talbot
Gramp Renzi	Eduardo Cianelli
Judge	Raymond Greenleaf
Cagle	Ed Marr
Harry Bender	Paul Bryar
Ed Merlin	Than Wyenn
Charles Hays	Robert Lieb
Kolichek	Otto Waldis

Sardonic Sergeant, 10/11/58

Army Sergeant Joseph Dexter asks Perry to defend him at a general court-martial on the charge he murdered another Army officer, who earlier had wanted to see Perry about a matter of importance.

Joseph Dexter	Paul Picerni
Sergeant McKnight	Lee Torrance
Captain Kennedy	Grant Richards
Lt. Walker	Rand Harper
Blake	Hal Torey
M. Sgt. Wm. Smith	Larry Jackson
Helen Lessing	Lori March

Curious Bride, 10/18/58

Young Rhoda Reynolds seeks advice for a friend about the legality of a marriage, but Perry suspects it is for herself.

Dr. Harris	James Seay
Rhoda Reynolds	Christine White
Frank Lane	Tommy Cook
Carl Reynolds	Casey Adams
Arthur Kane	Michael Emmet
Philip Reynolds	John Hoyt
Edna Freeman	Peggy Maley

Buried Clock, 11/1/58

The son-in-law of Dr. Blane is blackmailing the physician, but he is killed, and the doctor is suspected of the crime.

Judge Norwood	Jamie Forster
Dr. Blane	Don Beddoe
District Attorney Hale	Paul Fix
Jack Hardisty	Fredd Wayne
Rodney Beaton	Robin Hughes
Court Clerk	Harry Tyler

Married Moonlighter, 11/8/58

Young teacher Danny Harrison has taken two jobs to support his family. One night in the café where he works, friend Frank Curran is too drunk to drive, so Danny takes him home. Later the friend is killed, and lots of money is missing from the body. Danny is charged with the murder but he will not seek help. His wife sees old friend Perry Mason for help.

Danny Harrison	Arthur Franz
Frank Curran	Stacy Harris
Eileen Harrison	Anne Sargent
Phil McCabe	Douglas Evans
Linda Kennedy	Frances Helm
George Palmer	Tom Palmer
Judge Carwell	Richard Gaines
Luke Hickey	Jesse White
Sergeant Brice	Lee Miller

Jilted Jockey, 11/15/58

Jockey Tic Barton's wife threatens to leave him if he won't throw a race, as she is in cahoots with a gangster. Barton asks Perry's help in the divorce case, but the gambler Starr is killed and the jockey is arrested for the crime.

Tic Barton	Billy Pearson
Gloria Barton	Barbara Lawrence
Johnny Starr	Don Durant
Eddie Davis	Joe di Reda
Dion Bannion	Hugh Sanders
Victoria Bannion	June Vincent

Purple Woman, 11/22/58

Art dealer Milo Girard is threatened with a lawsuit for fraud for selling an alleged forgery. His wife talks to Perry about the matter, but her husband is killed and she is arrested.

Milo Girard	George Macready
Evelyn Girard	Bethel Leslie
Rufus Varner	Rhys Williams
Wayne Gordon	Don Murphy
Doris Andrews	Doris Singleton

Fancy Figures, 12/13/58

Charles Brewster was guilty of the crime of embezzlement, for which Martin Ellis was in prison. Perry gets him out of prison on this charge, but now Brewster is murdered, with evidence pointing to Ellis.

Martin Ellis	William Phipps
Charles Brewster	Ralph Clanton
Valerie Brewster	Joan Banks
Jonathan Hyett	Frank Silvera
Victor Squires	Harvey Stephens
Richard Hyett	Ray Kellogg
Carol Ellis	Anne Barton
Sergeant Brice	Chuck Webster
Judge	S. John Launer

Perjured Parrot, 12/20/58

Casanova, a murdered man's parrot, is called at an inquest as a witness. Ellen Monteith, Perry's client, is accused of killing Fremont Sabin.

Ellen Monteith	Jody Lawrance
Fred Bascomb	Robert Griffin
Sprague	Jason Johnson
Sheriff Barnes	Frank Ferguson

Mr. Bangley	Joe Kearns
Stephanie Sabin	Fay Baker
Richard Wald	Dan Barton
Voice of parrot	Mel Blanc

Shattered Dream, 1/3/59

Mason learns that Sarah Werner's missing husband, a gem expert, is posing as a diamond cutter under another name. He left her and her child after taking her inherited fortune. He also has the Pundit Dream, a valuable stone owned by the wealthy Virginia Trent, whom he romances.

Sarah Werner	Osa Massen
Virginia Trent	Virginia Vincent
Irene Bedford	Marion Marshall
Hans Breel/Hugo Werner	Kurt Kreuger
Jerry Morrow	Chris Alcaide
Adolph Van Beers	Ludwig Stossel
Lawrence David	Robert Carson
Judge	Lillian Bronson
William Walker	Theo Marcuse

Borrowed Brunette, 1/10/59

A young woman seeks Perry's advice on a strange business transaction. She has accepted a rent-free apartment and one hundred dollars a day expense money from private detective Slater. The girl and her aunt move in but feel they are being watched and become suspicious of the legality of the arrangement. Later, Slater is killed and the aunt is held for his murder.

Sam Dixon	Howard Van Proyen
Eve Martel	Maggie Mahoney
Melvin Slater	Joe De Santis
Agnes Nulty	Sheila Bromley
Barbara Slater	Adrienne Marden
Helen Reynolds	Paula Raymond
Grant Reynolds	John Stephenson
Judge Bates	Morris Ankrum
Tom Folsom	Herman Rudin
Secretary	Gisele Verlaine

Glittering Goldfish, 1/17/59

Tom Wyatt and Frederick Rollins, working on a cure for a disease fatal to fish, need more money to finish their research. To do so, Rollins sells his business to Jack Hoxley, who later claims the sale terms make him sole owner of the formula. Perry is called in, but Hoxley is killed.

Tom Wyatt	John Hudson
Frederick Rollins	Gage Clarke

Jack Hoxley	Murvyn Vye
Nora Hoxley	Catherine McLeod
Donna Sherwood	May Wynn
Judge	S. John Launer
Darrell Metcalf	Cecil Kellaway
Sally Wilson	Jacqueline Scott
Clerk	Olan Soule

Foot-loose Doll, 1/24/59

Mildred Crest's fiancé, Bob Wallace, leaves with embezzled money from the office and manages to frame her for the theft. She is charged with murder after being involved in an auto accident in which another woman is killed. She becomes Perry's client.

Mildred Crest	Ruta Lee
Senator Baylor	Barton MacLane
Bob Wallace	John Bryant
Laura Richards	Eve McVeagh
Fern Driscoll	Helene Stanley
Fred Ernshaw	Sam Buffington

Fraudulent Foto, 2/7/59

District Attorney Brander Harris, preparing evidence of graft for a grand jury, is threatened with blackmail. He hires Perry to get the blackmailer, but Harris is charged with murder soon afterward.

Brander Harris	Hugh Marlowe
Jim Castleton	Mark Roberts
Marshall Scott	Bartlett Robinson
Leora Mathews	Carole Mathews
Helen Preston	Carol Nugent
Eva Scott	June Clayworth
Mr. Duclerc	Peter Brocco
Cleveland Blake	Wilton Graff
Judge	Kenneth MacDonald
George Fairbanks	Francis DeSales

Romantic Rogue, 2/14/59

Stacey Chandler romances a rich young woman to marry her for her money but later realizes he really loves her. He is approached by Irene Wallace, who knows his original motives toward his fiancée and who threatens to reveal those reasons and his shady past unless he takes part in an extortion plot against his fiancée.

Stacey Chandler	John Bryant
Helen Harvey	Marion Ross
Irene Wallace	Jean Willes

Florence Harvey	Sara Haden
Margo Lawrence	Peggy Maley
Pete Daniels	Jack Daly

Jaded Joker, 2/21/59

Small-time agent Charlie Goff jokingly double-crosses well-known comic Danny Ross. Goff is killed, and Ross is arrested. It seems Ross's career was in decline and the unhappy man turned to Goff to resurrect his success of the past. Perry's investigation on Goff's behalf leads to a beatnik coffeehouse.

Danny Ross	Frankie Laine
Buzzie	Bobby Troup
Charlie Goff	Harry Jackson
Sheila Hayes	Martha Vickers
Cleve Niles	Tom Drake
Judge	S. John Launer
Freddie Green	Walter Burke
Lisa Miller	Mary LaRoche

Caretaker's Cat, 3/7/59

Carpenter James Hing is charged with arson and murder after his boss is found dead in the ruins of his mansion, but Hing says Peter Baxter told him to burn the house.

James Hing	Benson Fong
Kenneth Baxter	John Agar
Stuart Baxter	Robert Knapp
Peter Baxter	Anthony Jochim
Edith Devoe	Maxine Cooper
Winifred Oakley	Judy Lewis
Medical Examiner	Michael Fox

Stuttering Bishop, 3/14/59

Perry's visitor says he is an Australian bishop and needs his help in awarding a multimillion dollar inheritance to the rightful claimant, a young woman.

Wallace Lang	Ken Lynch
Bishop Mallory	Vaughn Taylor
Carol Delaney	Rebecca Welles
Janice Burroughs	Joan Vohs
Charles Burroughs	Carl Benton Reid
Phil Burroughs	Jonathan Kidd

Lost Last Act, 3/21/59

Theatrical angel Frank Brooks is accused of killing a playwright. The murderer stole the last act of the victim's play. Perry's client, Brooks, had recently withdrawn his financial backing from the play and had asked his actress girlfriend to drop out of it.

Frank Brooks	Stacy Harris
John Gifford	David Lewis
Ernest Royce	Jerome Cowan
Jim West	Richard Erdman
Michael Dwight	Robert McQueeney
Helen Dwight	Katharine Bard
Faith Foster	Joanne Gilbert
Gertie	Connie Cezon
Judge	Richard Gaines

Bedeviled Doctor, 4/4/59

Blackmailer Mark Douglas steals a tape of a session between Hollywood producer Peter Heywood and his psychiatrist. He uses the tape to blackmail the doctor, who is later arrested for Mark's murder.

Dr. David Craig	Dick Foran
Peter Heywood	Phil Terry
Mark Douglas	Barry McGuire
Edith Douglas	Marianne Stewart
Ron Fowler	Allen Case
Barbara Heywood	Andrea King
Dana Lewis	Norma Moore
Dr. Hoxie	Michael Fox

Howling Dog, 4/11/59

Clinton Forbes remarries and his former wife is angry, as his new wife formerly was married to his former wife's brother. Forbes is slain, and her rancor toward him leads to her arrest for the killing. Perry's investigation turns up a secretary who wears glasses she does not need as well as an impersonator.

Evelyn Forbes	Ann Rutherford
Clinton Forbes	John Holland
Thelma Brent	Fintan Meyler
Polly Forbes	Elaine Edwards
Arthur Cartwright	Robert Ellenstein
Bill Johnson	Gregory Walcott
Rod Andrews	Tom Greenway
Judge	S. John Launer

Calendar Girl, 4/18/59

To finish a job, building contractor George Andrews is forced to negotiate with a gangster and political racketeer. The gangster is soon killed, and Perry has to defend Andrews in the matter, which involves three fierce dogs and a has-been football player.

Wilfred Borden	George Neise
George Andrews	John Anderson
Beatrice Cornell	Evelyn Scott
Frank Fettridge	Dean Harens
Store Owner	Ralph Moody
Foreman	Charles Tannen
Judge	Richard Gaines
Autopsy Surgeon	Jon Lormer
Models	Kasey Rogers
	Dolores Donlon
	Diana Crawford

Petulant Partner, 4/25/59

Harry Bright is accused of killing his business partner's wife. Perry defends him, despite circumstantial evidence and the fact that he considered the woman a self-seeking gold digger.

Harry Bright	R. G. Armstrong
Chuck Clark	William Wright
Salty Sims	Francis McDonald
Nell Gridley	Geraldine Wall
Howard Roper	Myron Healey
Margaret Clark	Nan Leslie
Bill Shayne	Bill Swan

Dangerous Dowager, 5/9/59

An unpaid gambling debt and IOUs could hurt Sylvia Oxman's chances in a child custody hearing. Before Perry can get the notes, the man who holds them is killed and the gun belonging to his client is found beside the body.

Frank Oxman	Gene Blakely
Arthur Manning	Michael Dante
Sylvia Oxman	Patricia Cutts
Danny Barker	Robert Strauss
Matilda Benson	Kathryn Givney
Robert Benson	Barry Atwater

Deadly Toy, 5/16/59

Claire Allison receives frightening newspaper clippings and tells boyfriend Dick Benedict about them. He in turn consults Perry Mason about the matter: harassment from a jealous suitor.

Dick Benedict	Robert Rockwell
Claire Allison	Mala Powers
Martin Selkirk	Dennis Patrick
Darrel Reed	Norm Alden
Ralph Jennings	Max Adrian

Spanish Cross, 5/30/59

Runyan, owner of a jeweled Spanish Cross, talks to an antique dealer interested in buying it. As they talk, it is stolen and Runyan accuses young Jimmy Morrow, a former juvenile delinquent who is on probation, of the theft in his store. The frightened boy runs away, since he had been convicted of stealing Runyan's car. His rehabilitation is set back when Mrs. Runyan's jewelry piece vanishes. Later, the boy is charged with murder.

Jimmy Morrow	Peter Miles
Curtis Runyan	Donald Randolph
Mrs. Grace Runyan	Linda Watkins
Felix Karr	Jacques Aubuchon
Everett Wormser	Jonathan Hole
Judge	Richard Gaines
Miriam Baker	Josephine Hutchinson
James Morrow, Sr.	Arthur Space

Dubious Bridegroom, 6/13/59

One night Perry spies a gorgeous blond intruder climbing into his office window. The woman claims she is not a burglar but a detective working on a case.

Virginia Colfax	Joan Tabor
Ethel Garvin	K. T. Stevens
Lorrie Garvin	Betsy Jones-Moreland
Ed Garvin	Harry Ellerbe
Frank Livesey	Neil Hamilton
District Attorney Covington	Patrick McVey
Sergeant Holt	Keith Richards
Filomena	Rosa Turich

Lame Canary, 6/27/59

Walter Prescott is found dead, with his wife holding the murder weapon. Perry defends her of the crime and must persuade a canary who saw the crime to tell who is guilty.

Walter Prescott	William Kendis
Ruth Prescott	Stacy Graham
Harry Jonson	James Philbrook
Jim McLain	Biff Elliot
Margaret Swaine	Susan Cummings
Ernest Wray	Berry Kroeger
Hotel Clerk	Chet Stratton
Cal Carpenter	Ray Phillips
Dr. Fowler	Emerson Treacy
Dr. Hoxie	Michael Fox
Judge	S. John Launer
Court Clerk	George E. Stone
Sergeant Brice	Lee Miller

Spurious Sister, 10/3/59

Bruce Chapman is charged with killing his wife, but the dead woman turns up alive and sues him for divorce.

Bruce Chapman	Karl Weber
Marie Chapman	Peggy Knudsen
Ginny Hobart	Marion Marshall
Grace Norwood	Mary La Roche
Helen Sprague	Marianne Stewart

Watery Witness, 10/10/59

George Clark asks Perry to look into the possibility that his wife is the daughter of actress Lorna Thomas. The child was abandoned when a baby by the actress. He asks Perry to legally establish the relationship. The actress is furious when he mentions the matter to her.

George Clark	John Bryant
Lorna Thomas	Fay Wray
Betty Clark	Dusty Anders
Fred Bushmiller	Douglas Dick
Dennis Briggs	Malcolm Atterbury
Harriet Snow	Kathryn Card

Garrulous Gambler, 10/17/59

Steve Benton wants Perry to protect his brother, who has forged checks to pay off his gambling debts. The brother, Larry Benton, will not admit what he has done, so Perry is called in.

Steve Benton	Dick Foran
Larry Benton	Wynn Pearce
Johnny Clay	Tony Travis
Ben Wallace	Steve Brodie
Earnshaw	Robert Nash
Doris Shackley	Paula Raymond
Mickey Fong	Victor Sen Yung
Nora Bradley	Anne Barton
Judge	Morris Ankrum
Dr. Victor	Law Green
Mike Granger	Gordon Wynn

Blushing Pearls, 10/24/59

Hudson Nichols hires a detective to follow Mitsou Kamuri, who he believes has taken his wife's pearls. Perry is surprised when the man offers him a large fee to clear the girl of suspicion.

Mitsou Kamuri	Nobu McCarthy
Grove Nichols	Steve Terrell

Hudson Nichols	Ralph Dumke
Toma Sakai	George Takei
Edgar Beals	Joe Di Reda
Thelma Nichols	Angela Greene

Startled Stallion, 10/31/59

Old John Brant takes Jo Ann Blanchard's horse, Spindrift, in lieu of a mortgage payment. When she cannot make the payment, he refuses to extend the matter and decides to foreclose on the deed he holds on her property. The man, a mean old buzzard, wants to keep her prize horse too.

Clara Hammon	Melora Conway
Jo Ann Blanchard	Patricia Hardy
Peter White	Richard Rust
John Brant	Trevor Bardette
Terry Blanchard	Elliott Reid
Earl Mauldin	Paul Richards

Paul Drake's Dilemma, 11/14/59

Perry has a strange client charged with murder: his old friend Paul Drake. Trying to clear Paul, Perry runs into a powerful patriarch who bribes witnesses to protect his family.

Henry Dameron	Basil Ruysdael
Donna Kress	Vanessa Brown
Tad Dameron	Dean Harens
Frank Thatcher	Bruce Gordon
Charles Dameron	Simon Scott
Mrs. Colin	Sheila Bromley
Anders	Robert Cornthwaite
Jacob Wiltzy	Ralph Moody

Golden Fraud, 11/21/59

Executive Richard Vanaman, a competitor for an important company position, is being blackmailed. Jealousy and intense business rivalry—plus a murder—are involved in the blackmail.

Richard Vanaman	Arthur Franz
Frances Vanaman	June Dayton
Sylvia Welles	Joyce Meadows
Rip Conners	David Sheiner
Fred Petrie	Alan Hewitt
Hale	Alex Gerry
Bunny Lee	Asa Maynor
Doris Petrie	Patricia Huston
Henry Noble	Neil Hamilton

Bartered Bikini, 12/5/59

Wally Dunbar, a swimsuit manufacturer, suspects his girlfriend, a model working for him, is stealing samples of a new line of swimsuits. Mason is hired to find the girl after she vanishes. A murder takes place, for which she is wanted.

Macready	Herbert Patterson
Rick Stassi	Stephen Bekassy
Wally Dunbar	John Lupton
Kitty Wynne	Terry Lee Huntingdon
Madge Wainwright	June Vincent
Lisa Ferrand	Rita Lynn
Simon Atley	Paul Langton
Yvonne	Maura McGiveney
Bud Ferrand	John Anderson

Artful Dodger, 12/12/59

Allen Sheridan is obligated to provide for his Aunt Sarette. He is shiftless and decides to stop giving her money. She becomes indignant, and matters get worse when she is charged with his murder.

Ralph Curtis	Douglas Henderson
Sarette Winslow	Lurene Tuttle
Victor Latimore	Jerome Cowan
Lou Caporale	Peter Leeds
Allen Sheridan	William Campbell
Joyce Fulton	Patricia Donahue
Doris	Terry Loomis
Sergeant Brice	Lee Miller
Dr. Hoxie	Michael Fox

Lucky Legs, 12/19/59

Two men offer Perry the same job, finding missing beauty contest winner Marjorie Cluny. She vanished when she was offered a worthless movie contract. There is a murder warrant out for her and she has disappeared.

Marjorie Cluny	Lisabeth Hush
J. R. Bradbury	John Archer
Bob Doray	Michael Miller
Frank Patton	Douglas Evans

Violent Village, 1/2/60

Perry Mason's fishing trip in a small town goes sour when young Phil Beecher is accused of murder. The local people are in an ugly mood, since the man was sent to prison for killing the victim's sister in a car accident, and are in a lynching mood. The possibility of a fair trial is threatened.

Phil Beecher	Ray Hemphill
Sheriff Eugene Norris	Barton MacLane
Kathi Beecher	Jacqueline Scott
Judith Thurston	Ann Rutherford
Norman Thurston	Bart Burns

Frantic Flyer, 1/9/60

Carol Taylor hires Perry Mason to prove her late husband did not steal money from his rich father. In the meantime, she is charged with the murder of her father-in-law's trusted business manager.

Carol Taylor	Rebecca Welles
Wade Taylor	Wilton Graff
Howard Walters	Simon Oakland
Janice Atkins	Patricia Barry
Ruth Walters	Virginia Vincent
Roger Porter	Ed Kemmer
Zack Davis	James Bell

Wayward Wife, 1/23/60

Author Ben Sutton's troubles are more than fiscal, as a second man, Arthur Poe, claims to be the author of his successful book about his Korean war experiences. Even though Sutton is receiving plenty of royalties, he borrows money from his wife's brother.

Arthur Poe	Marshall Thompson
Ben Sutton	Richard Shannon
Harry Scott Wilson	Frank Maxwell
Marian Ames	Madlyn Rhue
Gilbert Ames	Alex Davion
Sylvia Sutton	Bethel Leslie

Prudent Prosecutor, 1/30/60

Hamilton Burger asks Perry Mason to defend a good friend charged with murder. It seems the man once saved Burger's life.

Jefferson Pike	J. Pat O'Malley
Denver Leonard	Walter Coy
Asa Culver	Phil Bourneuf
Fred Pike	Ron Foster
Vita Culver	Ruta Lee
Joan Leonard	Barbara Fuller

Gallant Grafter, 2/6/60

A corporate executive, Ed Nelson, may lose his company when a blackmailer finds a lot of money missing with Nelson's name on the checks. To complicate matters, Frank Avery and his wife threaten him with loss of reputation as well.

Judith	Joan Staley
Ed Nelson	Herbert Rudley
Sylvia Nelson	Virginia Arness
Frank Avery	John Stephenson
Robert Doniger	Phillip Terry
Arthur Siddons	Charles Aidman
Norma Williams	Charlotte Austin
Patricia Martin	Fintan Meyler

Wary Wildcatter, 2/20/60

Wildlife photographer Roger Byrd films an unusual event—Charles Houston killing his wife by pushing her over a cliff—and then blackmails the man and his sweetheart.

Roger Byrd	Harry Jackson
Charles Houston	Byron Palmer
Madelyn Terry	Barbara Bain
Lucky Sterling	Douglas Kennedy
Paula Wallace	Lori March
Floyd Gordon	King Calder

Mythical Monkeys, 2/27/60

A scared secretary is told to deliver a mysterious package. She is convinced someone may kill her to get the package belonging to her author-boss and seeks Perry Mason's help.

Gladys Doyle	Louise Fletcher
Mauvis Meade	Beverly Garland
Richard Gilman	Lew Gallo
Gregory Dunkirk	Lawrence Dobkin
Dukes Lawton	John Reach
Miss Carlisle	Frances Morris
Mrs. Manley	Joan Banks
Kelton	William Boyett
Casper Pedley	Norman Fell

Singing Skirt, 3/12/60

Betty Roberts, a cigarette girl, works in a gambling joint and asks Perry's help when she sees her boss, George Anclitas, and his cohorts fleece a patron. She is told to keep quiet and is afraid her boss will frame her for the crime.

Betty Roberts .... Joan O'Brien
George Anclitas .... Henry Lascoe
Manning Ennis .... Chris Warfield
Sadie Bradford .... Allison Hayes
Wilton (Slim) Marcus .... H. M. Wynant
Police Captain .... Robert B. Williams
Judge .... Richard Gaines
Autopsy Surgeon .... Michael Fox
William Gowrie .... Fredd Wayne

Bashful Burro, 3/26/60

A land boundary is in dispute and only prospector Amos Catledge can help Perry resolve the matter. When murder results, it seems the prospector's placid donkey, a key witness to the crime, can best find him by wandering through the hills in search of him.

Ken Bascombe .... Hugh Sanders
Amos Catledge .... George Mitchell
Sally Norton .... Sue George
Gerald Norton .... Ray Stricklyn
Roy Dowson .... Charles Bateman
Hazel Bascombe .... Elisabeth Fraser
Crawford Wright .... Ben Wright

Crying Cherub, 4/9/60

A museum curator's assistant and a young artist are charged with stealing a Matisse painting and inserting a clever forgery in its place. The pair, June Sinclair and Dave Lambert, are forced to seek Perry's aid.

June Sinclair .... Mala Powers
Dave Lambert .... Joe Maross
Richard Harkens .... Tom Drake
Amelia Harkens .... Kathryn Givney
Liza Carson Lambert .... Carmen Phillips
Sylvester Robey .... Abraham Sofaer
Thomas Clark .... Thomas McBride
Deputy D.A. Mark Hanson .... David Lewis
Artist .... Elizabeth Harrower

Nimble Nephew, 4/23/60

Wealthy tycoon Adam Thompson knows one of his nephews plans to cheat him out of some valuable land but cannot decide which one is guilty.

Ellen Foster .... Linda Leighton
Adam Thompson .... Will H. Wright

Harry Thompson .... Bert Convy
Elliott Carter .... Joel Lawrence
Frank Jarrett .... Crahan Denton
Lydia Logan .... Myrna Fahey
Victor Logan .... Carl Benton Reid
Realtor .... Ted Stanhope
Deputy D.A. Claude Drumm .... Robert Gist

Madcap Modiste, 4/30/60

During a television interview, a celebrated fashion designer, Flavia of California, has an unrehearsed argument with her husband. It seems he announced the sale of the firm's patterns to an Eastern company, and she denies it. Later her husband is suspected of the murder of his wife by poison.

Hope Sutherland .... Leslie Parrish
Flavia of California (Flavia Pierce) ...... Marie Windsor
Charles Pierce .... John Conte
Henry De Garmo .... David White
George Halliday .... Edward Mallory
Leona Durant .... Dorothy Neuman
Deputy D.A. Stewart Linn .... Les Tremayne
Judge .... Morris Ankrum
Television Narrator .... Truman Bradley

Slandered Submarine, 5/14/60

A sailor is charged with murdering his captain and a nightclub entertainer. His father-in-law, Anthony Beldon, an electronics manufacturer, persuades Perry to take the case.

Commander James Page .... Hugh Marlowe
Robert Chapman .... Jack Ging
Gordon Russell .... Robert H. Harris
Vivian Page .... Ann Robinson
Anthony Beldon .... Robert F. Simon
Cmdr. Jerome Burke .... Russ Conway
Lou Hansford .... Robert Brubaker

Ominous Outcast, 5/21/60

Searching for a philanthropist who gave much money for his support in an orphanage during his youth, Bob Lansing comes to the small California town where the man lives. Trying to learn who his parents are, he finds the townspeople and his benefactor are hostile to his search. Soon he is charged with murder.

Bob Lansing .... Jeremy Slate
J. J. Flaherty .... Robert Emhardt
Vivian Bell .... Margaret Hayes

Vivian Bell	Margaret Hayes
Tom Quincy	Denver Pyle
Jim Blackburn	Walter Burke
Amy Douglas	Irene Tedrow
Jeff Douglas	Claude Stroud
Frederick Bell	Henry Norell

Irate Inventor, 5/28/60

Thelma Frazer knows her husband's share in a rich electronics firm will be forfeited unless he soon returns from his mysterious disappearance of three months. The brilliant inventor finally returns, only to be charged with his wife's murder.

Thelma Frazer	Ce Ce Whitney
Jim Frazer	Tom Coley
Lois Langley	Kasey Rogers
Robert Hayden	Ken Lynch
Calvin Boone	Manning Ross
Arthur Hayden	Douglas Odney
Sergeant Quimby	Barry Cahill
Judge	Kenneth MacDonald
Mrs. Nichols	Gertrude Flynn
Sorrell	Arthur Peterson

Flighty Father, 6/11/60

Two men claim to be teenager Trudy Holbrook's long lost father—after she inherits her mother's million-dollar estate. The confused girl turns to Perry Mason for help.

Trudy Holbrook	Anne Benton
Lawrence King	Francis X. Bushman
Jay Holbrook #1	Hayden Rorke
Jay Holbrook #2	Francis De Sales
David	Henry Beckman
Wally Parker	William Allyn
Don Evanson	Berry Kroeger
Peter Sample	Dan Riss
Judge	Grandon Rhodes
Gus Nickels	Tom Fadden
Autopsy Surgeon	Arthur Hanson
Housekeeper	Betty Farrington
Maid	Gail Bonney

Treacherous Toupee, 9/17/60

Harley Basset abruptly returns after an absence of two years. This fact disturbs Peter Dawson, who has taken over Basset's job as company president, and it also disturbs Basset's wife.

Hartley Basset	Thomas B. Henry
Peter Dawson	Philip Ober
Sybil Basset	Peggy Converse
Arthur Colemar	Nelson Olmsted
Dick Hart	Robert Redford
Ken Woodman	Bert Freed
Wilbur Penwick	Lindsay Workman
Stanley Roderick	Jonathan Hole
Teddi Hart	Cindy Robbins
Lorna Grant	Dee Arlen
Judge	Frank Wilcox

Credulous Quarry, 9/24/60

Richard Hammond thinks his friend Dorrell was involved in a fatal hit-and-run accident in which a girl was killed. The two lawyers become involved in the case, as one was actually involved but the other is accused of the murder, too. To protect Dorrell, Hammond tampers with the accident scene.

Richard Hammond	John Conwell
Everett Dorrell	Russell Arms
Clara Thorpe	Katherine Squire
Marvin Claridge	Vinton Hayworth
Alex Hill	Walter Reed
Barbara Claridge	Nan Peterson
Miss Winslow	Renée Godfrey
Judge	Willis Bouchey

Ill-Fated Faker, 10/1/60

Carl Gorman hires Mason to get rid of a freeloading relative, his nephew. In addition, Gorman's wife is neglecting him, as she has fallen in love with the nephew, Jim Ferris.

Carl Gorman	Howard Petrie
Alice Gorman	June Dayton
Jim Ferris	William Campbell
Betty Wilkens	Sue Randall
Stan Piper	James Anderson
Harold Ames	Tyler McVey
Mrs. Ames	Sarah Selby
Prosecutor	Kenneth Tobey

Singular Double, 10/8/60

After delivering some hot money, Lucy Stevens runs her car into the ocean and then assumes a false identity, that of her nonexistent cousin, Carole Morgan. Then she reports the suicide of Lucy Stevens.

Lucy Stevens/Carole Morgan	Connie Hines
Whitney Locke	Alan Baxter

Hugo Burnette .... Wilton Graff
Marjorie Ralston .... Mary Webster
Catherine Locke .... Andrea King
John Ruskin .... Arch Johnson
Switchboard Girl .... Sue England
Judge .... Morris Ankrum
Autopsy Surgeon .... Michael Fox
Grosvenor Cutter .... Harry Townes

Lavender Lipstick, 10/15/60

The secret formulas belonging to Silas Vance's cosmetic company are stolen. A bank book showing two large deposits as well as the phone number of the head of a rival firm are found in Karen Lewis's desk. The attractive young chemist, long considered a trusted company worker, is suspected of selling these secret formulas to the other firm. Before long, Silas Vance is killed, and she is arrested for the crime.

Karen Lewis .... Patricia Breslin
Max Pompey .... Whit Bissell
Gabriel Rawson .... Walter Coy
Peter Nichols .... John Lupton
Prosecutor Ernest Helming .... Joe Maross
Charles Knudsen .... Dabbs Greer
Silas Vance .... James Bell

Wandering Widow, 10/22/60

Merchant seaman Burt Stokes's belated testimony of six years clears Riley Morgan of the murder charge for which he went to prison. Burt tries to blackmail the victim's widow, Lorraine Kendall, to add to his meager income.

Roger McClaine .... Ralph Clanton
Morgan Riley .... Dean Harens
Lorraine Kendall .... Coleen Gray
Burt Stokes .... Casey Adams
Faye Donner .... Marguerite Chapman
Warren Donner .... Hugh Sanders

Clumsy Clown, 11/5/60

Judd Curtis intends to buy out his partner in a circus, and to finance the deal he blackmails clown Felix Heidemann, who is secretly married to Jerry Franklin's wife, who did not get a divorce before she married Franklin. The clown later is charged with the Curtis murder.

Felix Heidemann .... Douglas Henderson
Lisa Franklin .... Chana Eden
Jerry Franklin .... Robert Clarke
Judd Curtis .... Walter Sande
Tim Durant .... Ken Curtis

Tony Gilbert	Willard Sage
Joyce Gilbert	Margaret Hayes

Provocative Protégé, 11/12/60

Anita Carpenter will collect a lot of insurance money if her concert pianist husband's plunge off a cliff was accidental and not a suicide. The police feel his death was murder, which might mean she would also collect, except that she is charged with the crime.

Anita Carpenter	Virginia Field
Andrew Collis	Robert Lowery
James Gracie	Donald Foster
Donna Loring	Kathie Browne
Alice	Cindy Courtland
David Carpenter	Gregory Morton
Judge	Morris Ankrum
Autopsy Surgeon	Jon Lormer
Eric Sturgis	Charles Cooper
George Worthington	Harry Jackson
Sergeant Binns	Barry Cahill
Deputy D.A. Victor Chamberlin	Robert Karnes

Nine Dolls, 11/19/60

Having no family, nine-year-old Peggy Smith wants to establish her identity. Her desire leads her to a rich California family that pays her tuition at exclusive Westcroft School and regularly sends her dolls. Her search also leads to murder.

Peggy Smith	Laurie Perreau
Miss Lorimer, Headmistress	Eleanor Audley
Linda Osborne	Maggie Mahoney

Loquacious Liar, 12/3/60

As a struggle ensues to control a boat firm, Lester Martin becomes convinced his stepfather, Judson Bailey, wants him killed. When Bailey is killed, Lester is the prime suspect, and Perry has to find a missing picture of Bailey and the hired killer.

Hired Killer	Baynes Barron
Lester Martin	Wynn Pearce
Sam Crane	Regis Toomey
Marge Fuller	Jeanne Baird
Judson Bailey	Bruce Gordon
Lois Rogers	Melora Conway
Emma Bailey	Lurene Tuttle

Note: In this episode, Raymond Burr wore a cast on his chest, shoulder and arm, under a larger sized shirt and jacket.

Red Riding Boots, 12/10/60

Young Rita Conover is murdered on the eve of her marriage to Burt Farwell, a rancher several years her senior. Many people opposed the match, including his daughter, Ann, who is charged with the murder.

Ann Farwell	Ellen Willard
Joe Dixon	Frank Maxwell
Deputy D.A. Sampson	H. M. Wynant
Kathy Jergens	Reba Waters
Miss Pennock	Sara Seegar
Jill Farwell	Linda Leighton
Burt Farwell	John Archer
Rita Conover	Shirley Ballard
Rennie Foster	Corey Allen
Deputy Sheriff	Michael Harris

Larcenous Lady, 12/17/60

The mayor's wife, Mona Henderson, gives secret city plans to a real estate man, Tom Stratton, who will not let her off the hook. This fact bodes ill for the mayor, who is in line for a nice post on the State Crime Commission. When Perry Mason is called in, he must try to untangle political rivalries and extortion.

Mayor Jim Henderson	Arthur Franz
Mona Henderson	Patricia Huston
Tom Stratton	Edward Platt
Susan Connolly	Louise Fletcher
William Carter	King Calder
Frank Sykes	Robert Brown
Julia Webberly	Ellen Drew

Envious Editor, 1/7/61

Don Fletcher turns a respected firm's publications into a scandal sheet, and the editor, Edmond Aitken, asks Perry to stop him.

Don Fletcher	James Coburn
Edmond Aitken	Philip Abbott
Lori Stoner	Barbara Lawrence
Mrs. Welsh	Virginia Carroll
Wendell Harding	Vinton Hayworth
Winslow	Paul Power
Alyce Aitken	Sara Shane
Reporter	Jim Drumm
Reporter	Harry Hollins

Resolute Reformer, 1/14/61

Playboy Peter Caine is told by Debra Bradford he was in a hit-and-run accident while drunk. Fearful of involving his prominent father in his troubles, Peter gives her a check to keep her quiet.

Debra Bradford	Diana Millay
Peter Caine	Douglas Dick
William Harper Caine	John Hoyt
Lawrence Kent	Phillip Terry
Charles Sistrom	Byron Palmer
Roger Quigley	James Westerfield
Supervisor Albert Johnson	Hardie Albright
Councilman William Daniels	John McLiam
Lewis Bergdorf	Dennis Quinn
Ron Arthur	Bert Stevens
Jack Parrish	Tony Hughes
Henry Bartlett	Dean Casey
Grace Witt	Maxine Stuart

Fickle Fortune, 1/21/61

Civil servant Ralph Duncan, appointed by the courts to investigate an estate, finds a fortune in old greenbacks, only to lose them to a thief.

Ralph Duncan	Vaughn Taylor
Mrs. Hollister	Helen Brown
Helen Duncan	Virginia Christine
Lloyd Farrell	Liam Sullivan
Charles Nickels	Robert Casper
Nurse Hamilton	Eve March
Albert Keller	Philip Ober
Gertie	Connie Cezon
Norma Brooks	Cathy O'Donnell
Sergeant Brice	Lee Miller
Patrolman	Berkeley Harris
Autopsy Surgeon	Michael Fox
Waiter	Vince Troy
Judge	Richard Gaines
Clerk	Hal Taggart

Waylaid Wolf, 2/4/61

Playboy Loring Lamont manages to trick his father's attractive secretary into a beach house meeting, where he tries to make love to her. The frightened girl, even though alone, flees in panic from him. When he is killed, she is the prime suspect.

Arlene Ferris	Andra Martin
Madge Elwood	Laurie Mitchell
George Albert	Barry Atwater
Edith Bristol	Rebecca Welles
Colong Kim	Benson Fong
Loring Lamont	Tony Travis

Wintry Wife, 2/18/61

Vindictive Laura Randall, hating her husband, plans to blow up his invention, an underwater sounding device.

Judy Baldwin	Sue England
Judge	Willis Bouchey
Walter Randall	Jerome Thor
Mr. Johnson	Barney Phillips
Laura Randall	June Vincent
Deputy D.A. Victor Chamberlin	Robert Karnes
Bruce Sheridan	Alan Hewitt
Detective	Robert Bice
Detective	Charles Stroud
Phyllis Hudson	Marianne Stewart
Roger Phillips	Fredd Wayne
Amelia Phillips	Jean Howell
John Penner	Paul Barselow
Chemist	Rudolph Salinger
Court Clerk	George E. Stone
Autopsy Surgeon	Michael Fox

Angry Dead Man, 2/25/61

Willard Nesbitt fakes his death by drowning, but his widow asks Perry to collect the insurance she is due.

The man returns to the living and finds his ex-partner, Lloyd Castle, is trying to take all the profits from their joint mining venture. When both Nesbitt and Castle are subsequently killed, Nesbitt's widow is the prime suspect. It was also found that Castle forged checks.

Fanny Werbler	Naomi Stevens
Eve Nesbitt	Gloria Talbott
Willard Nesbitt	Les Tremayne
Lloyd Castle	Edward Binns
Jenny Bartlett	Carol Ohmart
Ben Otis	James Millhollin
Professor Laiken	Frank Ferguson
Bruce Nesbitt	Karl Held

Blind Man's Bluff, 3/11/61

In a jewelry store, treachery from within is involved as one of Charlie Slades' employees, Karl Addison, takes a diamond necklace and then quickly replaces it. The scheme is part of a dress rehearsal of his plan to later burglarize the store. Murder results, and a rich young man, Jim Kincannon, supposedly involved in a jewel fencing operation hires Perry Mason when he is charged with the crime.

Helen Slade	Jean Allison
Karl Addison	John Conte
Witness (Mrs. Cartwright)	Geraldine Wall
Charles Slade	George Macready
Jim Kincannon	Jack Ging
Edgar Whitehead	Berry Kroeger
Adele Bentley	Merry Anders
Judge	Nelson Leigh
Jack Shaw	Sid Clute

Barefaced Witness, 3/18/61

Iris McKay wants to stay away from embezzler Fred Swan, who is being released from prison, as the ex-convict will want the money he stole and asked her to keep for him. He is killed, and she is arrested.

Prosecutor Hale	Paul Fix
Miss Sarah	Josephine Hutchinson
Alfred Needham	Malcolm Atterbury
W. L. Picard	Roy Roberts
Dan Southern	Adam West
Fred Swan	Russ Conway
Iris McKay	Enid James
Marta Wiltern	Eloise Hardt
Judge	Lewis Martin
Beller	Tom Fadden
Policeman	Charles Briggs
Clarence Joy	Don Wilbanks
Secretary	Rosemary Day

Difficult Detour, 3/25/61

Contractor Pete Mallory's road building gang is stalled by an unforeseen event: a court order restraining him from further work due to a faulty survey that had led them onto private property. He confronts the person responsible, shady and fast-talking real estate broker Stuart Benton. Shortly after the meeting is over, Benton is killed and Mallory is arrested.

Chet Stark	Lee Farr
Miriam Ames	Joan Camden
Pete Mallory	Jeff York
Ed Parker	Bert Freed
Stuart Benton	Jason Evers
Sheila Benton	Suzanne Lloyd
Sgt. Ben Landro	Mort Mills
Phil Edwards	Joe di Reda
Ames	Neil Hamilton

Cowardly Lion, 4/8/61

Zoo curator Tony Osgood asks Perry to investigate the theft of a valuable baby gorilla. Zoo dentist Braun implies that Fursten, Tony's good friend, took the animal. The doctor is then found dead in the lion's cage.

Boris Zelbowski	Warren Kemmerling
Hilde Fursten	Carol Rossen
Tony Osgood	Fred Beir
Trudie Braun	Betty Lou Gerson
Frieda Crawson	Phyllis Coates
Dr. Walther Braun	Leslie Bradley
Harry Beacom	O. Z. Whitehead
Second Judge	Mack Williams
First Judge	Bill Quinn
Bookkeeper Keller	Eddie Quillan
Sec. Officer Crawford	Paul Birch
Prosecutor Green	Paul Langton

Torrid Tapestry, 4/22/61

Museum employee Claude Demay went to prison for six years for a fire he did not start. Now free, he plans revenge on the man who framed him, Leonard Voss, a wealthy art collector and gallery owner.

Nathan Claver	Conrad Nagel
Brenda Larkin	Paula Raymond
Claude Demay	Robert H. Harris
Sarah Demay	Lillian Buyeff
Leonard Voss	John Holland
Jim Hazlett	Ray Kellogg
Judge	Kenneth MacDonald
Watchman	Syd Saylor
Lawrence	John Graham
Pawnbroker	Percy Helton

Violent Vest, 4/29/61

Ad man Herman Albright, fed up with his wife and her debts, starts to pursue Grace Halley, a model at the ad agency where he works. The displeased Grace, unhappy over his attentions, asks Perry to break the contract she has with the agency.

Grace Halley	Myrna Fahey
Walter Caffrey	Hayden Rorke
Joy Lebaron	Sonya Wilde
Buddy Frye	Joe Cronin
Herman Albright	Erik Rhodes
Ida Albright	Dorothy Green
Barman	Frank Jenks

Judge	Richard Gaines
Mrs. Diamond	Barbara Pepper
Superintendent	Bill Erwin

Misguided Missile, 5/6/61

The missile shot supervised by Major Jerry Reynolds blows up, and the pressure on him becomes so great that a federal investigator is sent to check on the situation. The investigator, Captain Caldwell, is later killed, and Reynolds is arrested.

Major Jerry Reynolds	Robert Rockwell
Dr. Harrison	Richard Arlen
Dan Morgan	Bruce Bennett
Captain McVey	Med Flory
Helen Rand	Jeanne Bal
Captain Mike Caldwell	Simon Oakland
George Huxley	George Neise
Dr. Randy Bradbury	William Schallert
Sgt. Lewis	Ron Knox

Duplicate Daughter, 5/20/61

Muriel Gilman's father vanishes. Perry investigates his workshop and finds evidence of a fight and thousands of dollars lying inside. The father inexplicably disappeared from the breakfast table while his daughter, Nancy, was in the kitchen.

Hartley Elliott	Don Dubbins
Glamis Barlow	Anne Helm
Carter Gilman	Walter Kinsella
Nancy Gilman	Joyce MacKenzie
Muriel Gilman	Kaye Elhardt
Judge	Willis Bouchey
Glenn McCoy	Dick Whittinghill
Connors	Harlan Warde
Cartman Jasper	Nelson Olmsted
Autopsy Surgeon	Michael Fox
Sheriff	Don Harvey
Carlos Barbara	Dan Seymour
Maurice Fellows	George Selk
Court Clerk	Charles Stroud

Grumbling Grandfather, 5/27/61

J. J. Gideon is displeased by his grandson's dates with secretary Dorine Hopkins, especially since she is married, which angers him even more.

David Gideon	Karl Held
Si Farrell	Phil Arthur
J. J. Gideon	Otto Kruger

Dorine Hopkins	Patricia Barry
Sue Franks	Frances Rafferty
Lawrence Comminger	Gavin MacLeod
Witness	Fifi D'Orsay
Stroller	Dub Taylor
Judge	John Gallaudet
Trial Judge	Kenneth MacDonald
Avery Bellison	Henry Hunter
Police Sergeant	John Close
Waitress	Maura McGiveney
Tony Montgomery	Fred Coby

Guilty Clients, 6/10/61

When aircraft designer Jeff Bronson's experimental ship crashes during a test flight, his ex-wife suspects sabatage and at gunpoint tries to get pilot Bill Ryder to admit it.

Clarence Keller	Ben Wright
Jeff Bronson	Charles Bateman
Lola Bronson	Lisa Gaye
Conception O'Higgins	Faith Domergue
Bill Ryder	Guy Mitchell
Violet Ryder	Barbara Stuart
Courtney Patton	Alan Bunce
Leander Walker	William Mims
Divorce Judge	Grandon Rhodes

Jealous Journalist, 9/2/61

Newspaper publisher Joe Davies's fiancée sides with his business rivals (which means she is trying to sell him out), and then says she will marry someone else, Cousin Ralph Quentin.

Boyd Alison	Theo Marcuse
Hope Quentin	Frieda Inescort
Tilden Stuart	Denver Pyle
Joe Davies	Linden Chiles
Grace Davies	Irene Hervey
Ralph Quentin	Jan Merlin
Kerry Worden	Claire Griswold
Seward Quentin	Parley Baer
Miriam Coffey	Bek Nelson

Impatient Partner, 9/16/61

Paint manufacturer Amory Fallon suspects his partner, Ned Thompson, is behind a mysterious fire and explosion that wreck their plant and has been seeing Mrs. Fallon secretly. Fallon goes to Thompson's apartment and leaves a threatening note. Thompson is killed, and Fallon is held for the murder.

Carlos Silva	Dan Seymour
Frank Wells	Ben Cooper
Vivian Ames	Leslie Parrish
Charles Grant	Chet Stratton
Amory Fallon	Wesley Lau
Edith Fallon	Lucy Prentis
Ned Thompson	Peter Adams
Judge	Barney Biro
Mrs. Murdock	Mary Young
Mrs. Temple	Cheerio Meredith
Bert Nichols	Jack Betts

Missing Melody, 9/30/61

Musician Eddy King is left at the altar when his bride, Polly Courtland, sees an unwelcome guest, George Sherwin, holding an envelope aloft. The girl panics and runs from the church screaming.

Polly Courtland	Jo Morrow
Eddy King	James Drury
Jonny Baker	Constance Towers
George Sherwin	Grant Richards
Enid Markham	Andrea King
Bongo White	Bobby Troup
Jack Grabba	Walter Burke
Midge Courtland	Lorrie Richards
David Gideon	Karl Held

Note: With this episode, Karl Held became a cast regular through the 1961–62 season, as David Gideon, a young law student working in Perry's office.

Malicious Mariner, 10/7/61

First Officer Jerry Griffin keeps a freighter, the Janell Trader, from floundering in heavy seas by jettisoning valuable cargo. Ashore, legal problems arise when the Captain wants him tried for mutiny and the court may hold him responsible for the lost cargo.

Charles Griffin	Edward Binns
Jerry Griffin	Lee Farr
Otto Wenzel	Sean McClory
Arthur Janeel	Roy Roberts
Frank Logan	Casey Adams
Julie Abbott	Penny Edwards
Captain Bancroft	Robert Armstrong
Lieutenant Anderson	Wesley Lau
MacLean	Tudor Owen
Captain Lansing	Robert Carson
Lieutenant Gregg	George Ives
Vogel	Robert Foulk
Judge	Kenneth MacDonald

Autopsy Surgeon .... Pitt Herbert
Sheng .... Victor Sen Yung
Captain Wilson .... Douglas Evans
Note: With this episode Wesley Lau became a cast member as Lieutenant Anderson.

Crying Comedian, 10/14/61

Tom Gilrain intends to return his wife to the sanitorium from which she escaped, but comic Charlie Hatch, an old lover, feels the act is spite and seeks Perry Mason's aid. When Gilrain is killed, he confesses to the killing, even though he is innocent. He is protecting Anne Gilrain, thinking she killed her husband. However, Hatch had said he would do something about the situation prior to the slaying.

Charlie Hatch .... Tommy Noonan
Gunner Grimes .... Jackie Coogan
Anne Gilrain .... Gloria Talbott
Tom Gilrain .... Liam Sullivan
Rowena .... Sue Ane Langdon
Sergeant McVey .... Med Flory
Ed Brigham .... Stacy Harris

Meddling Medium, 10/21/61

Sylvia Walker has made several unsuccessful attempts to contact her dead son, Thomas, through spiritualists. Her nephew, Philip Paisley, plans to use this situation for his financial benefit. When this greedy schemer is killed, Perry prepares an intricate electronic trap to snare the murderer.

Sylvia Walker .... Virginia Field
Philip Paisley .... James Forrest
Elaine Paisley .... Ann Carroll
Michael Craig .... Paul Smith
Bonnie Craig .... Sonya Wilde
Helen Garden .... Mary La Roche
Dr. Arthur Younger .... Kent Smith
Judge .... S. John Launer

Pathetic Patient, 10/28/61

Dr. Wayne Edley sees no way out of a malpractice suit brought by Joe Widlock. The man claims the doctor treated him for bursitis when his hip was broken. When the doctor is charged with murder, the beleaguered physician seeks Perry's help. Perry turns up a set of scheming twins and also learns Widlock may be an ex-convict.

Dr. Wayne Edley .... Skip Homeier
Joe Widlock/Hiram Widlock .... Frank Cady
Mrs. Osborn .... Virginia Gregg
District Attorney Parness .... Richard Eastham

Sgt. Ben Landro	Mort Mills
Roger Gates	Peter Whitney
Janice Edley	Bek Nelson
Leslie Hall	Ed Kemmer
Judge	Charles Irving
Asa Cooperman	Percy Helton
Mr. Morgan (Manager)	Wally Brown
Miss York	Maura McGiveney

Traveling Treasure, 11/4/61

Government agents board a fishing boat on which Perry is vacationing. A routine check uncovers cargo embarassing to skipper Scott Cahill. Found are stolen gold bars and the body of the boat owner, Karl Magovern, Cahill's boss. Perry's deep sea fishing trip is rudely interrupted as he is forced to defend the charter boat captain of gold smuggling and murder.

Scott Cahill	Jeff York
Rita Magovern	Lisa Gaye
Karl Magovern	Arch Johnson
Max Bleiker	H. M. Wynant
Professor Sneider	Vaughn Taylor
Ben Wylie	Ron Kennedy
Leon Ulrich	Jack Searl
Smith	Addison Richards
Jones	Hardie Albright
Charles Bender	Baynes Barron
Sergeant Brice	Lee Miller

Posthumous Painter, 11/11/61

Knowing an artist's death usually increases the value of his work, painter Jack Culross hopes to improve his financial situation by faking suicide. His plan works well, as his work is soon worth a lot more for art dealer Austin Durrant. However, his wife, Edna, is not in on the plan and thinks Durrant is a forger. When her husband is killed she is the prime suspect.

Austin Durrant	Stuart Erwin
Dr. Vincent Kenyon	George Macready
Jack Culross	Britt Lomond
Edna Culross	Lori March
Linda Burnside	Carol Rossen
Clint Miller	Jason Evers
Judge	Nelson Leigh
Sergeant Brice	Lee Miller
Lieutenant Anderson	Wesley Lau
Walter Hutchings	James Griffith
Robert Shelby	John McNamara

Injured Innocent, 11/18/61

Manufacturer Walter Eastman imports from Europe both a car engine to be tested in racing competition and driver Vincent Danielli. Danielli deliberately crashes during a test, wrecking the car. Soon Eastman is charged with the scheming driver's murder, who was also romancing Eastman's wife.

Judge	S. John Launer
Sergeant Brice	Lee Miller
Kirby Evans	John Conte
Dr. Mooney	Frank Maxwell
Walter Eastman	Jess Barker
Kate Eastman	Audrey Dalton
Vincent Danielli	Alejandro Rey
Erin Mooney	Linda Lawson
Autopsy Surgeon	Pitt Herbert
Doctor	Walter Stocker
Secretary	Cindy Ames
Dr. Bell	Raymond Bailey
Ralph Townley	Phil Arthur
Mr. Ellis	Noel Drayton
Lt. Anderson	Wesley Lau

Left-Handed Liar, 11/25/61

Athlete Ward Nichols, working at a health club, wants to get married but faces two obstacles: His boss Bernard Daniels thinks he is a check forger and Veronica Temple believes he is a blackmailer.

Ward Nichols	Ed Nelson
Veronica Temple	Leslie Parrish
Bernard Daniels	Les Tremayne
Casey Daniels	Maggie Pierce
Buzz Farrell	Dabbs Greer
Eugene Houseman	Alan Baxter
Rhonda Houseman	Joan Banks
Kenny	Kyle Cittadin
Judge	Kenneth MacDonald
Dr. Harrison Berry	Richard Derr
Clara Prentice	Amzie Strickland

Brazen Bequest, 12/2/61

Dr. Cromwell, dean of Euclid College, is uptight about a meeting with Robert Haskell regarding the handling of James Vardon's million dollar grant to the school. He must convince the rich man his gift will be handled properly and that the occasion of the gift will be dignified. Then a drunken old woman lurches into the room and talks of scandal in the dean's past.

Dick Wilson .... John Wilder
Maizie Freitag .... Barbara Stuart
Mary Cromwell .... Phyllis Avery
Dr. Marcus Tate .... Alan Hewitt
Charles Cromwell .... Karl Weber
Robert Haskell .... William Allyn
James Vardon .... Will Wright
Sgt. Ben Landro .... Mort Mills
Peter Gibson .... Strother Martin
Deputy District Attorney Horner .... Joseph Julian

Renegade Refugee, 12/9/61

At a weekend spiritual retreat for members of a defense firm, reporter Lawrence Vander is slain and a possible clue is discovered: he was on the trail of an escaped Nazi war criminal. A businessman is charged with the crime, which had been preceded by blackmail.

Father Paul .... Frank Overton
Harlan Merrill .... Dick Foran
Lawrence Vander .... Paul Lambert
Clifton Barlow .... John Sutton
Arthur Hennings .... Ronald Long
Winifred Dunbrack .... Jennifer Howard
Phyllis Merrill .... Donna Atwood
Emery Fillmore .... Denver Pyle
Judge .... John Gallaudet
Lieutenant Anderson .... Wesley Lau
Buck Osborn .... William Boyett
Autopsy Surgeon .... Jon Lormer
Colonel .... Robert Nash

Unwelcome Bride, 12/16/61

When former nightclub singer Sue Ellen Frazer meets her father-in-law, he offers her $50,000 as a wedding gift to divorce his son. She defies the millionaire by rejecting his offer, even though her husband is a parking lot attendant. Her defiance is a one-way ticket to get jail and a murder charge.

Judge .... Willis Bouchey
Walter Frazer .... Torin Thatcher
Sue Ellen Frazer .... Diana Millay
Peter Thorpe .... De Forrest Kelley
Lon Snyder .... Alan Hale
Amanda Thorpe .... Melora Conway
Gregson Frazer .... Bryan Grant
Cary Duncan .... Ben Young
Court Clerk .... George E. Stone
Joe Medeci .... Gerald Mohr

Roving River, 12/30/61

Judy Bryant thinks the boundary on the land she owns changed when a nearby river took a new course, and she needs the support of her derelict, ailing stepfather to back up her claim. The sick man will gladly do her this favor, as long as he receives $10,000 from her.

Judy Bryant	Sarah Marshall
Frank Deane	Harry Carey, Jr.
Matt Lambert	Bruce Bennett
Judge Holmes	Ed Prentiss
Sheriff Ward Vincent	Kelly Thordsen
Prosecutor	Paul Fix
Neil Gilbert	Dirk London
Amos Bryant	Robert Lowery
Ralph Ordway	Sherwood Price
Harvey Farrell	Phil Ober
Judge Libott	Lewis Martin
Chloris Bryant	June Vincent
Seth Tyson	J. Pat O'Malley

Shapely Shadow, 1/6/62

Morley Theilman orders his secretary to put a suitcase packed with money in a railroad station locker. The girl feels he is being blackmailed and takes the money to Perry Mason, asking for his help. When she is charged with the man's murder, Perry finds a shapely shadow is involved in the case.

Cole B. Troy	Robert Rockwell
Carlotta Theilman	Dorothy Green
Janice Wainwright	Elaine Devry
Mrs. Theilman	Barbara Lawrence
Morley Theilman	George Neise
Fred Carlyle	James Callahan
Judge	Willis Bouchey
Meteorologist	Austin Green
Henry Battle	Ray Hemphill
Autopsy Surgeon	John Zaremba
Technician (Moulage Man)	Hal Smith
Newsdealer	William McLean

Captain's Coins, 1/13/62

Shipping line owner Ben Farraday is a crusty old salt who opposes his niece's choice of a fiancé, history teacher Phil Andrews. Later Andrews is charged with Farraday's murder, and in defending him, Perry Mason comes across a rare commemorative coin, which proves to be a vital clue.

Phil Andrews	Jeremy Slate
Purser Evans	Arthur Franz
Evelyn Farraday	Joan Patrick

Nickolas Trevelian .... Jay Novello
Ben Farraday .... Herbert Rudley
Edward Farraday .... Parley Baer
Carter Farraday .... Don Beddoe
Sid Garth .... Henry Beckman
Jane Weeks .... Allison Hayes
Henry Cosgrove .... Lauren Gilbert
Judge .... Morris Ankrum
Photographer .... Eddie Quillan
Charles Noymann .... Tom Palmer
Sailor .... Will J. White
Mrs. Ionescu .... Tafa Lee

Note: With this episode and continuing through the 1964–65 season, Wesley Lau became a cast regular as Lieutenant Anderson. The worsening health of Ray Collins made it necessary to hire Lau. Collins was forced to leave the series entirely due to his illness and eventually died.

Tarnished Trademark, 1/20/62

In a Danish town, Martin Somers buys the business of Danish cabinetmaker Axel Norstaad by making him an offer he can't refuse. However, Somers makes inferior merchandise, which angers Norstaad, who is ashamed his name will appear on the products. He threatens to kill Somers unless the poorly made products are recalled and is arrested for murder.

Axel Norstaad .... Karl Swenson
Lisa Pedersen .... Osa Massen
Martin Somers .... Dennis Patrick
Edie Morrow .... Marie Windsor
Maigret .... Malcolm Atterbury
Latham Reed .... Phillip Terry
Carl Pedersen .... Morgan Woodward
Sam Hadley .... Edward Norris
Floyd Chapman .... Francis De Sales
Foreman .... Ted White
Judge .... S. John Launer

Glamorous Ghost, 2/3/62

Playboy Doug Hepner is murdered and clues at the crime scene lead police to believe a woman killed him. Then his fiancée Eleanor Corbin turns up as an apparent amnesiac and is charged with the murder.

Eleanor Corbin .... Mary Murphy
Ethel Belan .... Jeanne Cooper
Suzanne Granger .... Ziva Rodann
Sadie Hepner .... Merry Anders
Walter Richey .... Douglas Dick
Olga Jordan .... Coleen Gray

Poison Pen-Pal, 2/10/62

Peter Gregson and Carl Holman of Gregson Canneries have worked long to bring about a merger with Super Brands Company. They felt the deal was secret. The news may have been leaked by the letters written by Gregson's daughter to her young pen pal in San Francisco. However the news leaked, it caused the stock to fluctuate widely. When Wilma Gregson is murdered, Peter is charged with involvement with the woman arrested, Karen Ross.

Inspector Wade	Paul Genge
Mrs. Thatcher	Barbara Lawrence
Matt Clark	Harry Jackson
District Attorney	Everett Sloane
Karen Ross	Patricia Breslin
Peter Gregson	Douglas Henderson
Carl Holman	Bert Freed
Lee Gregson	Wright King
Wilma Gregson	Kathryn Givney
Florence Holman	Joan Tompkins
Sandra Gregson	Chrystine Jordan

Mystified Miner, 2/24/62

Secretary Susan Fisher, working overtime one Saturday at the office, is startled when her boss's little boy, Carlton Campbell, rushes into the office with a shoebox filled with a great deal of money. When she is charged with murder, Perry must locate the money, $200,000 of embezzled funds.

Susan Fisher	Kathie Browne
Amelia Corning	Josephine Hutchinson
Alfredo Gomez	Carlos Rivas
Endicott Campbell	Bartlett Robinson
Elizabeth Dow	Sheila Bromley
Carlton Campbell	Patrick Thompson
Judge	John Gallaudet

Crippled Cougar, 3/3/62

Hunters Jamison and Keith shoot a mountain lion but fail to make sure it is dead. Oilman Mike Preston rages at them for negligence, as he had witnessed the event. Later, he learns there is oil on his land. He fires the prospecting crew and puts the place up for sale. This strange behavior causes Mason to suspect the whole scheme, particularly the low prices for which the leases are to be sold.

Mike Preston	Bill Williams
Hugh Jamison	John Howard
Arnold Keith	John Bryant
Lydia Reynolds	Rita Lynn
Sgt. Ben Landro	Mort Mills
Harlow Phipps	Noah Keen

Paula Hamilton	Abigail Shelton
Watchman	Tom Fadden
Elliot Dunbar	Simon Scott
Judge	Willis Bouchey
Grace Keith	Florence Wyatt

Absent Artist, 3/17/62

Cartoonist Gabe Phillips tells his astonished assistant, Pete Manders, he will sell him his successful cartoon feature for $10,000. Phillips says that amount will give him enough money to go away to paint seriously in Majorca, like the controversial artist Otto Gervaert. Later when Otto is killed, Manders is arrested for killing the artist. Perry finds the man was leading a double life.

Daphne Whilom	ZaSu Pitts
Pete Manders	Wynn Pearce
Charles (Monty) Montrose	Richard Erdman
Gabe Phillips	Mark Roberts
Otto Gervaert	Mark Roberts
Leslie Lawrence	Pamela Curran
District Attorney Harry Clark	Jay Barney
Alexander Glovatski	Victor Buono
Fiona Cregan	Arline Sax
Myer	Carl Don
Sgt. Arnold Buck	Lane Bradford
Newburgh	Barney Phillips
Judge	Bill Zuckert

Melancholy Marksman, 3/24/62

Ted Chase suspects his scheming, unfaithful wife is seeing another man but does not know the man, Len Dykes, who owns a gun shop. Later he is arrested when the woman is slain.

Ted Chase	Paul Richards
Sylvia Dykes	Jeff Donnell
Len Dykes	William Schallert
Irene Chase	Mari Blanchard
Ballistics Expert	John Harmon
Ellen Chase	Ann Rutherford
Medical Examiner	Jon Lormer
Tony Benson	Peter Baldwin
Betty Chase	Betsy Hale
Charles Vale	Edward Ashley
Anne Chase	Shari Lee Bernath
Cecil	Jesse White
Mabel Richmond	Cindy Robbins
Judge	S. John Launer
Watchman	Lester Dorr

Angry Astronaut, 4/7/62

When space pilot Mitch Heller is washed out of his moon project job by General Addison Brand, he becomes a civilian astronaut. Brand retires and becomes head of the firm where Heller works.

General Addison Brand	James Coburn
Mitch Heller	Robert Bray
Dr. Linda Carey	Jeanne Bal
Bonnie Winslow	Patricia Donahue
Eddie Lewis	Steve Brodie
Terry Faye	Paula Raymond
Matthew Owen	John Marley

Borrowed Baby, 4/14/62

Perry Mason and Della Street return to the office one evening to clean up some work and find a baby on his desk. Perry's search for the baby's parents leads to murder.

Jarvis Baker	Hugh Marlowe
Florence Baker	Maria Palmer
Ginny Talbot	Kaye Elhardt
Lester Menke	Corey Allen
Dr. Paul Hogathy	Gregory Morton
Holly Cosgrove	Nellie Burt

Counterfeit Crank, 4/28/62

Since wealthy August Dalgran is in a mental institution, his business partners decide to double-cross him. He finds out about the scheme and flees from the sanitarium. He is later charged with killing his nephew, who he felt had betrayed him.

August Dalgran	Otto Kruger
Martha Blair	Jeanette Nolan
Kenneth Dalgran	Don Dubbins
Sandra Dalgran	Connie Hines
Jay Fenton	John Larkin
Chuck Blair	Burt Reynolds
Superior Court Judge	S. John Launer
Don Morley	Michael King
Dr. Jackman	William Woodson
Bertram Telford	Paul Langton
Misdemeanor Court Judge	Charles Irving

Note: Burt Reynolds became a famous film and television star not long after playing bit parts like this one.

Ancient Romeo, 5/5/62

A dueling scene from Shakespeare's *Romeo and Juliet* becomes too realistic when actor Franz Lachman is killed before a spellbound and marveling audience. Steve Brock shoots Paris (Lachman) with a supposedly blank cartridge, which proves to be real. The acting troupe has been plagued by jealousy and financial woes.

Steve Brock	Rex Reason
Phil Scharf	Harry Von Zell
Claire Adams	Patricia Huston
Ellen Carson	Antoinette Bower
Franz Lachman	Jeff Morrow
Margit Bruner	K. T. Stevens
Kevin MacRae	Kendrick Huxham
Carl Bruner	Robert Cornthwaite
Shipping Agent	Stafford Repp
Amos Martin	Donald Curtis
Helen Finney	Rosemary Day
Judge	Willis Bouchey

Promoter's Pillbox, 5/19/62

Herbert Simms, an aspiring television writer, asks Perry to help him sue producer Charlie Corby for plagiarizing one of his ideas.

Miriam Waters	Geraldine Brooks
Nelly Lawton	Dianne Foster
Herbert Simms	Linden Chiles
Charlie Corby	John Lasell
Mike Flint	George Matthews
Davis Crane	Ben Cooper
Judge	John Gallaudet
Autopsy Surgeon	Michael Fox
Jerome Stokes	Edmon Ryan
Markett	Dan Seymour
Witness (Mrs. Simms)	Geraldine Wall

Lonely Eloper, 5/26/62

Although nearly 21, immature heiress Merle Telford is very much under the thumb of her domineering Aunt Olivia, but she manages a few romantic moments with Danny Pierce and now plans to elope. When Aunt Olivia, who opposed the marriage, is slain, Merle is arrested for the crime.

Merle Telford	Jana Taylor
Danny Pierce	Jack Ging
Julian Kirk	John Dall
Gina Gilbert	Joan Staley
Olivia Langley	Jorja Curtright
Howard Langley	Paul Tripp

Judge	Kenneth MacDonald
Dr. Wales	John Zaremba
Corbett	Billy Halop

Bogus Books, 9/27/62

Bookstore owner Joseph Kraft fakes first editions of valuable books and starts to get rich.

Professor Carlos Muntz	John Abbott
Joseph Kraft	Maurice Manson
George Pickson	Woodrow Parfrey
Ellen Carter	Phyllis Love
Pete Norland	Adam West
Pearl Chute	Allison Hayes
Gene Torg	H. M. Wynant
Kenneth Carter	Joby Baker

Capricious Corpse, 10/4/62

Carleton Gage, a philanthropist, supports a children's foundation but finds that his two beneficiaries, his nephew George and his longtime employee Ernest Demming, want to close the facility when they gain control of his estate. Before he can draw up a new will changing his beneficiaries, he lapses into a coma. Later the case is complicated by a samurai figure and a missing corpse.

Dr. Guy Omstead	John Howard
Carleton Gage	Everett Glass
George Gage	Jacques Aubuchon
Nicholas Blake	Lee Farr
Olive Omstead	Lori March
Ernest Demming	John Morley
Claudia Demming	Jean Engstrom
Joanne Proctor	Jan Shepard
Judge	Willis Bouchey
Timmy	Dennis Rush
Nurse Evelyn King	Evelyn Ward

Playboy Pugilist, 10/11/62

Trainer Jim West has young Davey Carroll, a promising fighter, under contract. Sportsman Tod Richards wants to acquire him by fair or foul means. When Richards is slain, Perry uncovers a highly coordinated blackmail racket as well.

Davey Carroll	Gary Lockwood
Jimmy West	Robert Armstrong
Tod Richards	Mark Roberts
Lori Richards	Dianne Foster
Jo Sands	Dolores Michaels

Keith Lombard .... Anthony Caruso
George Hale .... Joseph Sirola

Double Entry Mind, 10/18/62

Clem Sandover, a shy bookkeeper, is meticulously devoted to his work, as he has embezzled $200,000 so far. He becomes mad enough to kill when his long-term plans are ruined by a wily secretary.

Clem Sandover .... Stuart Erwin
Frank Sellers .... Karl Weber
Enos Watterton .... Jack Betts
Steve Banks .... Paul Tripp
Beth Sandover .... Virginia Christine
Sally .... Joan Staley
Lita Krail .... Kathleen Hughes
Potkin .... Richard Reeves
Judge .... Grandon Rhodes

Hateful Hero, 10/25/62

Policeman Otto Norden is shot during a robbery of an industrial plant and his rookie partner, Jim Anderson, flees from the crime. Even worse, plant executive Dwight Wilson says he saw the cop leave the plant when the robbery was taking place. The rookie cop is dismissed from the force on this trumped-up charge and gets into more trouble trying to clear himself.

Erna Norden .... Jeanette Nolan
Otto Norden .... William Boyett
Carrie Wilson .... Mabel Albertson
Arthur Morrell .... Edmon Ryan
Jerel Leland .... Leonard Stone
James Anderson .... Dick Davalos
Dwight Wilson .... William Phipps

Dodging Domino, 11/1/62

Mona White sues Broadway producer Alex Chase for stealing a song from her husband. It also seems Chase has a musical and wants the woman for his leading lady. When she hears the score, she is convinced he stole it from her husband, Damion, and sues him for plagiarism.

Alex Chase .... Jeff Morrow
Freda Chase .... Janet Ward
Mona Winthrope White .... Ellen McRae
Damion White .... David Hedison
Rudy Mahlsted .... Lloyd Corrigan
Jerry Janda .... Robert H. Harris
Leonard Buckman .... Eddie Firestone
Phil Schuyler .... James Forrest

Unsuitable Uncle, 11/8/62

Seaman Dickie Durham visits his rich brother, Russell, after 20 years and asks for money to buy a pub in Australia. This supposedly poor seaman is killed and a will with $300,000 of bequests is found.

Dickie Durham	Liam Sullivan
Harry Fothergill	Sean McClory
Russell Durham	Ford Rainey
Paula Durham	Barbara Parkins
Frank Warden	Howard Smith
Gil Simpson	George Kane
Crystal Durham	Anna Lee
Judge	Charles Irving

Stand-In Sister, 11/15/62

After appearing at a Senate hearing, convict Stefan Jahnchek tries to escape. After Perry Mason becomes involved with the case, he finds a $100,000 trust fund is involved as he defends two brothers—a mobster and a rich businessman— charged with murder.

Stefan "Big Steve" Jahnchek	Peter Whitney
Karl Corby	Ralph Clanton
John Gregory	R. G. Armstrong
Captain Nick Paolo	Peter Mamakos
Helen Gregory	Susan Seaforth
David Bickel	Parley Baer
Franz Moray	Steven Geray
Mrs. Margaret Stone	Meg Wyllie
Judge	S. John Launer

Weary Watchdog, 11/29/62

Alton Brent has complete trust in his employee Ed Franklin. His socialite wife, Janet, a friend of Della's, knows better, since the man is blackmailing her. Janet sees Perry about the matter but is then arrested for Franklin's murder.

Carlyle Chang	Keye Luke
Judge	Willis Bouchey
Janet Brent	Mala Powers
Alton Brent	Wesley Addy
Zaneta Holmes	Doris Dowling
Edward Franklin	John Dall
Commodore Holmes	Robert Carson
Trixie Tong	Judy Dan
Dean Chang	James Hong
James Wong	Philip Ahn
Asst. D.A. Jack Alvin	Kenneth Tobey

Lurid Letter, 12/6/62

In a small town, a high school English teacher, Jane Wardman, is asked to resign by the local board of education after an anonymous letter charges her with making romantic advances toward her male students outside of class. Her problems mount when she is charged with murder.

Jane Wardman	Mona Freeman
Booby Slater	Tom Lowell
Judge Ed Daley	Edgar Buchanan
Everett Rixby	Robert Rockwell
Cornelia Slater	Ann Doran
Pat Mangan	John Durren
Doris Wilson	Kaye Elhardt
Gus Weller	Chris Alcaide
Terry Wardman	Mark Murray
Dr. Steve Grant	Noah Keen
Sheriff Watson	Kelly Thordsen

Fickle Filly, 12/13/62

Jennifer Wakely's love for Brad Shelby is not returned. Shelby gets the racehorse she prizes highly and marries another woman. When the fortune hunter is slain, the jilted Jennifer is charged with his murder.

Jennifer Wakely	Joan Freeman
Brad Shelby	Bob McQuain
Roberta Harper	Lisabeth Hush
George Tabor	Jim Davis
Sergeant Landro	Mort Mills
Emmett Pearson	Bartlett Robinson
Madelon Shelby	Jennifer Howard
Judge	Frederic Worlock

Note: Jim Davis became famous on the "Dallas" television show as head of the Ewing family. Bartlett Robinson had played Perry Mason on radio.

Polka Dot Pony, 12/20/62

Twenty years before, Angela Fernaldi's ex-husband left their baby girl on an orphanage doorstep. Now the woman is rich, and two young girls claim to be her missing daughter.

Angela Fernaldi	Virginia Field
Burt Renshaw	Jesse White
Richard Champion	Burt Metcalfe
Jim Grove	Ben Cooper
Judge	Morris Ankrum
Maureen Thomas	Melinda Plowman
Maureen Franklin	Eileen Janssen

Shoplifter's Shoe, 1/3/63

Perry Mason hears that Sarah Breel has been accused of shoplifting, but he gets her released from the charge because of his knowledge of legal rights and procedures. The woman's niece, Virginia, comes to Perry again when she feels her aunt has stolen some valuable diamonds this time.

Virginia Trent	Margaret O'Brien
Sarah Breel	Lurene Tuttle
Ione Bedford	Melora Conway
Sergeant Gifford	Richard Coogan
Bill Golding	Arthur Batanides
Austin Cullens	Blair Davies
Pete Chennery	Leonard Nimoy
Judge	Charles Irving

Note: Nimoy became famous as Dr. Spock in "Star Trek."

Bluffing Blast, 1/10/63

In the small town of Ladena, Linda Blake claims she is the daughter of the late Addison Blake, a rich local citizen. If her claim is valid, she will be wealthy, but Floyd Grant tells the district attorney she is a fraud.

Floyd Grant	Bill Williams
Linda Blake	Antoinette Bower
Clay Elliot	Peter Breck
Judge	Bill Zuckert
Deputy D.A. Nelson Taylor	Frank Overton
Donella Lambert	Mary La Roche
Charles Lambert	Robert Knapp
Sheriff Orville Ramsey	Frank Ferguson

Note: Bill Williams (Barbara Hale's husband) substituted for Raymond Burr, who had had major surgery and was recuperating.

Prankish Professor, 1/17/63

English Professor Ronald Hewes stages a practice shooting in his classroom. Later he finds real bullets in the gun, except for one blank that, luckily, had been fired during the demonstration. His estranged wife is on trial for his murder when it is discovered he made money writing a lurid novel under a pen name.

Dr. Curtis Metcalfe	Kent Smith
Ollie Benson	Jack Searl
Sally Sheldon	Joyce Van Patten
Judge	John Gallaudet
Esther Metcalfe	Constance Towers
Laura Hewes	Patricia Breslin
Professor Ronald Hewes	Barry Atwater
Barbara Rice	Karyn Kupcinet
Ned Bertell	Don Dubbins

Sergeant Brice .... Lee Miller
Mrs. Williamson .... Barbara Pepper

Note: Kent Smith substituted for Raymond Burr, who was recuperating from major surgery.

Constant Doyle, 1/31/63

Young Cal Leonard is arrested for breaking into a factory and beating up the night watchman. Since his lawyer is dead, the lawyer's widow, Constance Doyle, also an attorney, decides to help him. They cannot agree on things, and she decides not to take his case. However, the factory owner, Lawrence Otis, visits her and is so eager to drop the charges that she decides to take Cal's case after all.

Constance Doyle .... Bette Davis
Fred McCormick .... Neil Hamilton
Cal Leonard .... Michael Parks
Letty Arthur .... Peggy Ann Garner
Lawrence Otis .... Les Tremayne
Miss Givney .... Frances Reid

Note: Bette Davis substituted for Raymond Burr, who was recovering from major surgery and was seen in a brief scene in a hospital room.

Libelous Locket, 2/7/63

Ed Lindley is visited by a law student of his, Janice Norland, who says she is the killer of a dancer teacher. However, at the murder scene they cannot find the body of the man.

Professor Edward Lindley .... Michael Rennie
Janice Norland .... Patricia Manning
Maureen Norland .... Patrice Wymore
Raul Perez .... Carlos Romero
Vivian Cosgrove .... Ruta Lee
Darwin Norland .... John Hoyt
Sidney Hawes .... Harry Von Zell

Note: Michael Rennie subbed for Raymond Burr.

Two-Faced Turn-A-Bout, 2/14/63

A foreign interior minister makes a $500,000 deal to sell secret plans to columnist Elihu Laban. During this transaction the minister dies, and Laban is arrested for his death.

Bruce Jason .... Hugh O'Brian
Elihu Laban .... Abraham Sofaer
Alyssa Laban .... Lisa Gaye
Garrett Richards .... Trevor Bardette

Note: Hugh O'Brian was Raymond Burr's substitute in this episode.

Surplus Suitor, 2/28/63

Industrialist John Wilburn gets an anonymous phone call from a blackmailer saying he knows that Wilburn has secret money in a Swiss bank and that he never pays taxes on it.

Sherman Hatfield	Walter Pidgeon
Hollis Wilburn	Joyce Bulifant
John Wilburn	Carl Benton Reid
Martin Potter	James Best
Mrs. Abernathy	Nellie Burt
Sergeant Boyle	Stefan Gierasch
Alf	Marc Cavell
Jean Crewe	Andrea King
Vernon Elliot	Linden Chiles
Gage McKinney	Hayden Rorke
Alex Gaussner	John Siegfried

Note: Walter Pidgeon substituted for Raymond Burr.

Golden Oranges, 3/7/63

Amos Keller, an orange grower, spoils a nice, juicy real estate deal for Gerald Thornton. Thornton takes Keller to court, charging his dog attacked and bit him. When Thornton is later murdered, Perry defends the young man charged with the crime. He has to depend on the testimony of a surprise witness—the dog.

Amos Keller	Arthur Hunnicutt
Gerald Thornton	Arch Johnson
Sandra Keller	Natalie Trundy
Janis Carr	Erin O'Brian
James Wheeler	Allen Case
Grace Doyle	Mary Munday
Edward Doyle	Lee Van Cleef
John Grimsby	Hugh Sanders
Courtney Osgood	Henry Norell
Judge Stanley	Charles Irving
Judge Gray	Nolan Leary

Note: Raymond Burr resumed his role as Perry Mason following his long recuperation from major surgery.

Lawful Lazarus, 3/14/63

Trevor Harris, legally dead, appears at the bedside of his dying wife. He will not accept her wish to make her uncle guardian of their children's millions.

Trevor Harris	David McLean
Nora Kasner	Maria Palmer
Edgar Thorne	Phil Bourneuf
Jill Garson	Irene Hervey
Clarence Henry	Max Showalter

Velvet Claws, 3/21/63

Politician Harrison Burke and his girlfriend, Eva, are photographed as they leave a gambling club. He fears for his political future and she for her marriage.

Eva	Patricia Barry
Harrison Burke	James Philbrook
Carl Griffin	Wynn Pearce
Mrs. Vickers	Virginia Gregg
Norma	Anna Lisa

Lover's Leap, 4/4/63

Roy and Valerie Comstock are getting divorced, but for unusual reasons: it is an elaborate scheme to swindle his business partner, Peter Brent. Peter is later charged with murder.

Valerie Comstock	Julie Adams
Roy Comstock	John Conte
Peter Brent	Carleton Carpenter
Willie	Richard Jaeckel
Gloria Winters	Maura McGiveney
F.J. Weatherby	Marvin Miller
Judge	John Gallaudet
Medical Examiner	John Zaremba

Elusive Element, 4/11/63

Austin Lloyd fails to frame his wife and his business partner, Dwight Garrett, for embezzlement, but later they are charged with his murder.

Bonnie Lloyd	Gloria Talbott
Austin Lloyd	Gerald Mohr
Dwight Garrett	Douglas Henderson
Roscoe Pearce	George Macready
Ned Chase	Douglas Dick
Judge	S. John Launer

Greek Goddess, 4/18/63

Sculptor John Kenyon falls in love with a model, a lovely Greek girl named Theba, and her mother opposes the union.

John Kenyon	John Larkin
Theba	Marianna Hill
Dan O'Malley	John Anderson
Cleo Grammas	Faith Domergue
George Spangler	George Kennedy
Ken Judson	Robert Harland
Roger Correll	Russell Arms

Charles Welsh .... Tol Avery
Judge .... Willis Bouchey

Note: John Larkin had also played Perry Mason on radio.

Skeleton's Closet, 5/2/63

Author Richard Harris is sued for invasion of privacy by the people of a small town, whom Perry is assisting in their suit. They are not impressed by the fact that the novel is a best-seller.

Dave Weaver .... Keith Andes
Margaret Layton .... Peggy McCay
Harry Collins .... Frank Aletter
Richard Harris .... Michael Pate
Albert McCann .... David Lewis
Jack Tabor .... Dabbs Greer

Potted Planter, 5/9/63

Frances Walden goes to great lengths to break up her brother's marriage to Andrea Walden, even paying her nephew, Roy Mooney, to have an affair with Andrea.

Andrea Walden .... Diane Brewster
Frances Walden .... Constance Ford
District Attorney Hale .... Paul Fix
Martin Walden .... Robert Bray
Roy Mooney .... Mark Goddard
Nelson Tarr .... Joe Maross
Melinda Tarr .... Davey Davison
David Pinter .... William Allyn
Chris Hearn .... Harry Lauter

Witless Witness, 5/16/63

Judge Daniel Raymond, running for lieutenant governor, is accused by Martin Weston of conspiring to defraud the government years before. When Martin is found poisoned, the judge is accused of the crime and calls Perry Mason to help him.

Judge Daniel Raymond .... Robert Middleton
Martin Weston .... Vaughn Taylor
Victor Kendall .... David White
Gus Sawyer .... Jackie Coogan
James Wall .... Lee Bergere
Quinn Torrey .... Steve Brodie
Marian Lamont .... Florida Friebus
Madge Eberly .... Rita Lynn

Nebulous Nephew, 9/26/63

Con artist John Brooks tells Sophia and Minerva Stone he is the long-lost heir to their fortune. Both sisters believe him and accept John as their kin.

Sophia Stone	Beulah Bondi
Nineveh Stone	Meg Wyllie
John Brooks	Ron Starr
Irene Stone	Kate Manx
Ernest Stone	Hugh Marlowe
Sister Theresa	Irene Tedrow
Wayne Jameson	Mark Roberts
Caleb Stone	Ivan Dixon
Judge	Kenneth MacDonald
Leonard	Arthur Space

Deadly Verdict, 10/3/63

Perry Mason finally loses a case when Janice Barton holds back information that would clear her. When the jury delivers the verdict, Hamilton Burger knows he has finally won a case against Perry. But did he? Paul Drake and Perry begin a new investigation to prove Janice is innocent.

Janice Barton	Julie Adams
Emily Green	Joan Tompkins
Letitia Simmons	Erin O'Brien Moore
Paulette Nevin	Jan Shepard
Christopher Barton	Stephen Franklin
Dr. Nevin	Lee Bergere
Violet Barton Ames	Hollis Irving
Arthur Jacks	Mike Mazurki
Judge Ryder	S. John Launer

Shifty Shoe-Box, 10/10/63

John Flickinger robs the trucking firm where his sister works. When his young nephew finds the gun used in the robbery, the crime seems to be a family affair.

Sylvia Thompson	Constance Ford
John Flickinger	Benny Baker
Miles Thompson	Billy Mumy
Frank Honer	Denver Pyle
Bill Sheridan	Joseph Sirola
Joe Downing	Ray Teal

Drowsy Mosquito, 10/17/63

Someone in Gold Gulch is selling worthless gold mines and the activity eventually leads to murder. The accused is an old prospector named Sandy Bowen, and Perry agrees to defend him.

Sandy Bowen	Arthur Hunnicutt
Jason Sparks	Archie Moore
Banning Grant	Russell Collins
Lillian Bradisson	Kathleen Crowley
James Bradisson	Robert Knapp
Deputy Coroner Chute	Clinton Sundberg
Gerald Sommers	Strother Martin
George Moffgat	Woodrow Parfrey
Deputy Sheriff Connors	Robert J. Wilke

Decadent Dean, 10/24/63

Someone is blackmailing Aaron Stuart, dean of an exclusive school. He risks having both his and the school's reputation ruined if he does not comply. When Stuart's assistant (the blackmailer) is murdered, he confesses to the crime.

Dr. Aaron Stuart	Milton Selzer
Marian Stuart	Joan Tetzel
Harvey Forrest	Lloyd Corrigan
Tobin Wade	H. M. Wynant
Jenkins	Eddie Firestone
Sheriff Ward Vincent	Kelly Thordsen
Chuck Emmett	Paul Lukather
John Marshall Baxter	Blair Davies
Mr. Ryan	Lauren Gilbert
Janet Gwynne	Stanja Lowe

Reluctant Model, 10/31/63

After millionaire Otto Olney buys a valuable Gauguin masterpiece, art dealer Colin S. Durant starts a rumor it is a forgery. When a suspected artist-forger is killed, Perry agrees to defend the dead man's pretty model.

Otto Olney	John Larkin
Colin S. Durant	John Dall
Grace Olney	Joanna Moore
Goring Gilbert	Robert Brown
Leslie Rankin	Margaret Hayes
Maxine Lindsay	Erin O'Donnell
Judge	Charles Irving

Bigamous Spouse, 11/14/63

Door-to-door saleswoman Gwynn Elston finds that her best friend's husband is a bigamist. Gwynn tells Nell Grimes about her husband, but Nell refuses to believe it. Felton Grimes dies, and Hamilton Burger gets an indictment against Gwynn.

Gwynn Elston	Pippa Scott
Felton Grimes	Mike Conrad

Nell Grimes	Jacqueline Loughery
Carl Jasper	Alan Melvin
George Belding Baxter	Patrick McVey
Corley Ketchum	Karl Swenson
Judge	Charles Irving

Floating Stones, 11/21/63

Juli Eng goes to Hong Kong to claim the diamonds she inherited from her grandfather, only to find out they are lost. Perry defends Juli against a charge of murder when a suspectd smuggler is killed.

Juli Eng	Irene Tsu
Tudor Sherwin	James Forrest
Gilbert Tyrell	Victor Maddern
Lorraine	Joyce Jameson
Ralph Iverson	Jerry Oddo
Agatha Culpepper	Gertrude Flynn
District Attorney	Walter Brooke
Wendel	Ken Lynch

Festive Felon, 11/28/63

Rich Bebe Brent has little time to live and leaves one million dollars to her nurse, Hetty Randall, which surprises her relatives. Hetty's young niece Madeline is involved in the fight and finds she really needs Perry's help when Lieutenant Anderson arrests her for the murder of one of the would-be heirs.

Max Randall	Jon Hall
Madeline Randall	Sherry Jackson
Carla Eden	Kathie Browne
Eloise Brent	Elisabeth Fraser
Hetty Randall	Anne Seymour
Justin Grover	John Howard
Lawton Brent	Jeff Morrow
Reed Brent	Ray Stricklyn
Chester Brent	Gilbert Green
Bebe Brent	Anne Barton

Note: Jon Hall came out of a five year retirement to accept this role.

Devious Delinquent, 12/5/63

A teenage heir to a large fortune starts associating with a young hoodlum and his family almost is blackmailed. Blackmail turns to murder, and Tim finds himself in jail.

Timothy Balfour, Sr.	Otto Kruger
Tim Balfour, Jr.	John Washbrook
Miss Adler	Frances Rafferty

Edith Summers	Virginia Christine
Harold Minter	Barton MacLane
Luke Balfour	David Lewis
Chick Montana	David Winters

Bouncing Boomerang, 12/12/63

Despite his wife's protests, Grover Johnson will not sell his land, until a rich Texan makes him a very tempting offer. Grover does not know his wife, Eula, is really involved in a swindle leading to a murder—Eula's.

Nelson Barclift	Alan Hale, Jr.
Willard Hupp	Parley Baer
Grover Johnson	Rod Cameron
Eula Johnson	Diana Millay
Walter Jefferies	Paul Picerni
Les Gilpin	Berkeley Harris
Sidney Welpo	Wright King

Badgered Brother, 12/19/63

Martin Baylor objects when his half-brother, Todd, inherits equal ownership of the family business, a chain of department stores. The rivalry is intense and results in a literally murderous situation, with Todd as the corpse.

Todd Baylor	Robert Harland
Martin Baylor	Peter Walker
Joseph Rinaldi	Gregory Morton
Jane Alder	Patrice Wymore
Carla Rinaldi	Nancy Kovack
Nicolai Wright	Patricia Blair

Wednesday Woman, 1/2/64

An insurance investigator is still interested in the Jokarta diamond, though he no longer works for the firm that paid off when it was stolen. Phillip Stewart served time for the theft but claims he never stole the gem.

Jack Mallory	Michael Pate
Phillip Stewart	Phillip Pine
Katherine Stewart	Phyllis Hill
Joyce Hadley	Lisa Gaye
Lester Ormesby	Douglas Dick
Helen Reid	Marie Windsor
Thomas Webber	John Hoyt

Accosted Accountant, 1/9/64

Ed Lewis and his father-in-law accuse each other of stealing from the family firm. Lewis goes to Perry Mason for advice when someone kills his father-in-law.

Sylvia Cord	Lynn Bari
Edward Lewis	Richard Anderson
B. K. Doran	Murray Matheson
Leslie Ross	Dee Hartford
Gertrude Lewis	Gail Kobe
Arthur Sutton	Leonard Stone
Judge Penner	John Gallaudet

Capering Camera, 1/16/64

A photographer is shot while model Judith Blair points a prop gun at him. She says she did not pull the trigger. Judith's sister is being blackmailed, and Miss Blair is caught in the middle.

Judith Blair	Margo Moore
Irene Grey	Elaine Stewart
Katherine Ames	Paula Raymond
Penny Ames	Karyn Kupcinet
Harper Green	Byron Palmer
Norman Ames	Mark Dempsey
Karl Kadar	Kurt Kreuger
Judge	Grandon Rhodes

Ice-Cold Hands, 1/23/64

Rod Banks is charged with embezzling funds to bet on the horses. Nancy Banks tries to help him; she refuses to believe he would risk everything to gamble on the ponies. Her faith in him backfires when she is implicated in a murder.

Marvin Fremont	Arch Johnson
Rodney Banks	Dick Davalos
Nancy Banks	Joyce Bulifant
Lorraine Lawton	Lisabeth Hush
Larsen Halstead	Dabbs Greer
Inez Fremont	Phyllis Coates
Burdett	Paul Bryar
Judge	Willis Bouchey

Bountiful Beauty, 2/6/64

Stephanie Carew claims a sensational best-seller is based on her life and is grounds for a libel suit. Deborah Dearborn, the author, claims her novel is pure fiction. The legal battle is curtailed when one of Perry's clients is murdered.

Mrs. Mitchell	Jean Carson
Stephanie Carew	Sandra Warner
John Carew	Ryan O'Neal

Deborah Dearborn	Zeme North
Rubin Cason	Douglas Fowley
Gideon Long	John van Dreelen
Chet Worth	Maxwell Reed
Medical Examiner	John Zaremba
Judge	Sydney Smith

Nervous Neighbor, 2/13/64

After finding Charles Fuller's mother, Paul Drake discovers she is an amnesia victim and does not know she is wanted for the murder of her husband. She is going by the name of Mary Browne. Perry clears her but winds up defending Charles Fuller when he is accused of embezzlement and murder.

Charles Fuller	Richard Rust
Mary Browne	Jeanne Cooper
Vera Hargrove	Katherine Squire
Henry Clement	Paul Winchell
Alice Bradley	Sheila Bromley

Fifty Millionth Frenchman, 2/20/64

Phillipe Bertain is in love with Ninette Rovel, a married woman. She asks him for money to pay off her husband. After the transaction, Armand Rovel is murdered, and police arrest Phillipe as the prime suspect.

Phillipe Bertain	David McCallum
Ninette Rovel	Roxane Berard
Armand Rovel	Jacques Bergerac
Carole Ogilvie	Janet Lake
Ron Litten	Jackie Coogan
Linda Sutton	Coleen Gray
Peter Hayes	Don Collier
Ray Ogilvie	Arthur Franz

Frightened Fisherman, 2/27/64

After his lab develops an important antibiotic, Randolph James finds his wife is threatening to sell her controlling stock to a competitor. Furious, Randolph vows to stop Natalie but his plans did not include murder. When she is killed, he becomes the prime suspect.

Randolph James	Lee Farr
Natalie James	Marian Collier
Helen Bradshaw	Mala Powers
Mrs. Pennyworth	Connie Gilchrist
Marion Devlin	Richard Devon
Hudson Bradshaw	Bartlett Robinson
Hans Lang	Emile Genest

Gretchen Lang .... Ilze Taurins
Andy Witcoe .... Bill Smith
Note: Bartlett Robinson also played Perry Mason on radio.

Arrogant Arsonist, 3/5/64

A retired fire chief, Carey York, asks Perry Mason to file a libel suit against a reporter that publicly charged him with burning his own warehouse to collect the insurance.

Carey York .... Tom Tully
Tommy Towne .... Frank Aletter
Ross Walker .... Jeff York
Dorian York .... Wynn Pearce
Sylvia Gwynne .... Elaine Devry
Farrell .... Russell Thorson
Otto Joseph .... Tenen Holtz
Captain Hillman .... Byron Morrow
Gertie .... Connie Cezon
Elaine Joseph .... Holly McIntire

Garrulous Go-Between, 3/12/64

Clairvoyant Madame Zillia foretells a death in the life of Amy Scott. The prophecy comes true when her landlord is killed.

Amy Scott .... Sue Randall
Madame Zillia .... Lori March
Howard Kern .... Anthony Eisley
Victor Bundy .... Jacques Aubuchon
Joyce Carlton .... Merry Anders
Tommy Stiller .... John Napier
Dora .... Lillian Buyeff
Judge .... Nelson Leigh
Court Clerk .... Charles Stroud

Woeful Widower, 3/26/64

Housekeeper Nellie Conway fears her employer, Newton Bain, will murder his invalid wife. Nellie asks Perry Mason for help.

Newton Bain .... Harry Townes
James Douglas .... Jerry Van Dyke
Nellie Conway .... Joan Lovejoy
Gertie .... Connie Cezon
Mary Douglas .... Nancy Gates
Carole Moray .... Joyce Meadows
Georgiana Douglas .... Ann Carroll
Prosecutor .... Allen Joseph

Sergeant Steve Toland .... Frank Gerstle
Elizabeth Bain .... Shirley Mitchell

Simple Simon, 4/2/64

A young stranger tells actress Ramona Carver he thinks he's her son. Ramona does not know what to believe and seeks Perry's advice.

Ramona Carver .... Virginia Field
Red Doyle .... Don Barry
John Sylvester Fossette .... Victor Buono
Guy Penrose .... Tom Conway
Douglas McKenzie .... Douglas Lambert
Scott Everett .... James Stacy
District Attorney .... Jay Barney
Ogden Kramer .... Sherwood Keith

Illicit Illusion, 4/9/64

A terrifying series of events convinces Rosanne Ambrose she is losing her mind. Fearing she is having a nervous breakdown, Rosanne goes to her doctor. Perry suspects someone is trying to make it appear she is mentally ill. Before Mason can act, Rosanne is in jail for murder.

Rosanne Ambrose .... Mona Freeman
Vera Janel .... Jena Engstrom
Dr. Jesse Young .... Keith Andes
Kirk Cameron .... Berry Kroeger
Hubert Ambrose .... Ron Randell
Winifred Wileen .... Norma Varden
Leslie Eden .... Rebecca Welles
Fillmore Garrett .... Oliver McGowan

Antic Angel, 4/16/64

Alcoholic William Sherwood starts drinking again when he thinks he sees his wife, who supposedly died five years ago in an air crash. It is true she is alive, but someone murders her, and Lieutenant Anderson arrests William for the murder.

William Sherwood .... Peter Breck
Sidney Falconer .... George Tobias
Bartender .... Billy Halop
Vince Kabat .... Michael Ansara
Lynn Bowman .... Janet Dey
Harry Niles .... Richard Erdman

Careless Kidnapper, 4/30/64

Young David Pelham has some delightful pals. One of them sends a note to his father, telling him David has been kidnapped. Someone gained possession of Dr. Gregory Pelham's list of alcoholic patients and threatens to reveal the names to the press. Dr. Pelham goes to Perry for help when he refuses to be intimidated in the deadly game.

Dr. Gregory Pelham	Peter Hobbs
David Pelham	Thomas Lowell
Susan Pelham	Marilyn Erskine
Mary Manning	Regina Gleason
John Lathrop	Burt Metcalfe
Sande Lukins	Mimsy Farmer
Michael Da Vinci	Mark Slade
Joe Velvet	Ron Kennedy
Capt. Horatio Jones	Tudor Owen

Drifting Dropout, 5/7/64

Successful junk dealer Mort Lynch gives young drifter Barry Davis a job, which he quits after they have a heated argument. The businessman has political aspirations in his small town, but someone murders him, and Barry is arrested.

Barry Davis	Carl Reindel
Dell Harper	Malcolm Atterbury
Mort Lynch	Ted de Corsia
Annalee Fisher	Cynthia Pepper
Grove Dillingham	Neil Hamilton
Sanford Harper	Vaughn Taylor

Tandem Target, 5/14/64

Folk singer Con Bolton is suspected of having taken a shot at rich Sumner Hodge, who told him to stop seeing his daughter.

Sumner Hodge	Philip Ober
Adrian Hodge	Philip Ober
Mona Hodge	Ann Rutherford
Con Bolton	Paul Carr
Jack Talley	Lonny Chapman
Irma Hodge	Natalie Trundy
Miss Young	Pat Priest
Leo Lazaroff	Dan Seymour
Noonan	Vince Barnett
Cooper	Tom Fadden

Ugly Duckling, 5/21/64

Alice Trilling was never attractive until portrait painter Anthony Usher took a sudden interest in her. Uncle Harry doesn't approve of the romance and insists Alice end the affair. When Uncle Harry is killed, Alice is arrested.

Alice Trilling .... Anne Whitfield
Natalie Graham .... Constance Towers
Anthony Usher .... Adam La Zarre
Talbot Sparr .... Max Showalter
Harry Trilling .... Ford Rainey
Albert Charity .... Reginald Gardiner

Missing Button, 9/24/64

Five-year-old Button Blake has a four million dollar trust fund and two estranged parents. Dirk Blake tries to prove his wife, Janice, is an unfit mother. Dirk is arrested on a murder charge when someone kills a blackmailer trying to smear Janice.

Janice Blake .... Julie Adams
Dirk Blake .... Ed Nelson
Button Blake .... Claire Wilcox
Vince Rome .... Anthony Eisley
Naomi Sutherland .... Lyse D'Anjou
Judge Norris .... Otto Kruger
Lois Gray .... Dee Hartford

Paper Bullets, 10/1/64

Susan Foster has been dating the stepson of her brother Jason's opponent in the upcoming state senate election. Jason's wife, Margaret, thinks the romance is a ploy to get information in order to discredit her husband. Lieutenant Tragg arrests Margaret when the suitor is murdered.

Jason Foster .... Richard Anderson
Susan Foster .... Lynn Loring
Margaret Foster .... Jan Shepard
Harry Mardig .... Patrick McVey
Randolph Cartwell .... Ford Rainey
David Cartwell .... Stewart Moss
Alma Rice .... Melora Conway
Edgerton Cartwell .... Arthur Space

Scandalous Sculptor, 10/8/64

Scandal threatens the respectable publishing house run by Everett Stanton. His brother-in-law, a sculptor, has been carrying on with a beautiful model while married to Everett's sister, Mona. The model demands $10,000 to keep quiet about the affair but is murdered, and Lieutenant Tragg thinks Mona did it.

Everett Stanton	Stuart Erwin
Ivy Stanton	Nydia Westman
Mona Stanton Harvey	June Lockhart
Hannibal Harvey	Sean McClory
Rex Ainsley	Simon Scott
Bonnie	Sue Ane Langdon
Dickens	Dan Tobin
Nonno Volente	Carlos Romero
Judge	Willis Bouchey
Secretary	Ellen Atterbury

Sleepy Slayer, 10/15/64

Ailing Abner Gordon informs his niece Rachel she will be disinherited and face legal action if she fails to replace money she has diverted from his funds.

Rachel Gordon	Phyllis Hill
Dr. Lambert	Hugh Marlowe
Phyllis Clover	Gigi Perreau
Bruce Jay	John Napier
Abner Gordon	Richard Hale
Tracey Walcott	Robert Brown
Harlan Farrell	J. Edward McKinley
Medical Examiner	William Woodson
Charles Norman	Karl Swenson
Sadie Norman	Joan Tompkins
Judge	Morris Ankrum

Betrayed Bride, 10/22/64

Nellie Meachem's husband died while they were touring Europe. Members of her family are waiting at the airport to greet her and are startled when she gets off the plane with a new husband young enough to be her son. The family believe the Frenchman has an ulterior motive. Perry Mason gets involved for some legal advice and soon is deep into a murder case.

Nellie Meachem	Jeanette Nolan
Todd Meachem	John Larkin
Elaine Meachem	Dianne Foster
Jimmy Meachem	Guy Stockwell
Pierre Du Bois	Michael Forrest
Marie Claudel	Annie Farge
Roger Brody	Jacques Aubuchon
Victor Billings	Neil Hamilton
Monsieur	Paul Dubov
Judge	Grandon Rhodes

Nautical Knot, 10/29/64

Retired Harvey Scott resumes control of the family mining firm after nephew Rick is injured in a mine accident. Rick is well now but urges nurse Joanna Monford to keep him in Mexico, away from Pamela Blair. Harvey fostered a belief that Rick had run off because he wanted Pamela for himself. Someone wants Harvey dead, and Lieutenant Anderson arrests Pamela for the murder.

Harvey Scott	Tom Tully
Joanna Monford	Anne Whitfield
Rick Scott	Henry Brandt
Pamela Blair	Lisa Gaye
Ben Scott	Mark Roberts
Laurence Barlow	Whit Bissell
Elayne Scott	Barbara Bain
Emmalou Schneider	Arline Judge

Bullied Bowler, 11/5/64

Attorney Joe Kelly subs for Perry, who is out of the country temporarily. The Duchess, a small California town's most influential citizen, has good reason for having the bowling alley of son-in-law Bill Jarvis closed down. Joe Kelly starts a countersuit by Bill and Alan Jarvis. Courtroom fencing turns to murder, with the Duchess's infant grandson playing a key role in the mystery.

Joe Kelly	Mike Connors
Bonnie Mae Wilmet (Duchess)	Anne Seymour
Rose Carol	Jeff Donnell
Dr. Max Taylor	Milton Selzer
Marla Carol	Patricia Morrow
Bill Jarvis	Robert Harland
Alan Jarvis	Paul Lukather
Jack Baker	Charles Gray

Note: Raymond Burr had infected teeth problems, so Mike Connors substituted for him until his jaw healed.

A Place Called Midnight, 11/12/64

Perry is in Europe on business and becomes involved in international intrigue. He travels to Switzerland to meet U.S. Army Lt. Frederic Ralston. Perry finds more than intrigue when he uncovers an international con game leading to the death of one of Frederic's superior officers.

Lt. Frederic Ralston	Fred Vincent
Alan Durfee	Gerald Mohr
Colonel Owens	Harry Townes
Frank Appleton	Robert Emhardt
Greta Koning	Susanne Cramer
Hurt	Werner Klemperer

Also with Jim Davis and Eddie Firestone.

Tragic Trophy, 11/19/64

Returning home from a trip, movie director Anthony Fry introduces fiancée Kathy Anders to the press, then hurries to a parked car, where another woman waits. The fiancée asks Paul Drake to find out who the woman is.

Anthony Fry	Richard Carlson
Kathy Anders	Mimsy Farmer
Coley Barnes	George Brenlin
Howard Stark	John Fiedler
J. J. Pennington	Paul Stewart
Lydia Lawrence	Patricia Huston
Joanne Pennington	Constance Towers
Judge	Kenneth MacDonald
Medical Examiner	Reed Hadley
Janitor	Alvin Childress
Reporter	Alex Bookston
Reporter	Walter Mathews

Reckless Rockhound, 11/26/64

Reba Burgess, widow of a mining company executive, has a shoebox full of uncut diamonds in her bank safety deposit box. A small-time embezzler and forger claims he is entitled to half of everything she owns, including the gems. He is killed, and Perry gets involved in the case when the stranger produces a document, supposedly signed by Reba's late husband, backing up his claim.

Reba Burgess	Audrey Totter
Malone	Bruce Bennett
Polek	Ted de Corsia
Bascom	Jeff Corey
Reel Pete	Elisha Cook, Jr.
Kinder	Douglas Lambert
Kelly	Ben Johnson

Latent Lover, 12/3/64

Eric Pollard, a respectable investment broker with a fine future, behaves peculiarly by accusing his wife of having an affair. He has dizzy spells at the office and commandeers a taxi to rob a bank. Perry has an idea his wife is behind all this, especially when Sibyll is murdered and the police arrest Eric.

Eric Pollard	Lloyd Bochner
Roy Galen	Jason Evers
Dr. Richard Jenkins	John Matthews
Sibyll Pollard	Marion Moses
Dean Franklin	John Lasell
Harlan Talbot	Gilbert Green
Judge Robert Adler	Douglass Dumbrille
Leo Mann	Emory Parnell
Aimee Wynne	Charlotte Fletcher

Wooden Nickels, 12/10/64

Minerva Doubleday hires Paul Drake to act as a courier in the sale of one of her uncle's rarest coins, a confederate half-dollar worth $50,000. Paul runs up against a crooked coin dealer and murder, and Perry comes to his aid.

Minerva Doubleday	Phyllis Love
Homer Doubleday	Will Kuluva
Museum Curator	Sherwood Keith
Judge	Grandon Rhoades
Howard Hopkins	Murray Matheson
Vivian Norman	Nancy Berg
Kelso (panhandler)	Walter Burke
Rexford Wyler	Berry Kroeger
George Parsons	Hunt Powers

Blonde Bonanza, 12/17/64

Della's friend Dianne Adler signs a curious contract: She receives $200 per week to gain weight for a modeling assignment. Both women think the job is strange and ask Perry to investigate.

Dianne Adler	Mary Ann Mobley
George Winlock	Bruce Gordon
Harrison Boring	Paul Gilbert
Marvin Palmer	Jonathan Lippe
Dillard	Michael Constantine
Mrs. Winlock	Ruth Warrick
Montrose Foster	Vaughn Taylor
Judge	John Gallaudet

Ruinous Road, 12/31/64

Pierce Construction Company's latest project is already overestimated. Chief engineer Joe Marshall tells Pierce there is a good chance someone in the firm is tampering with the budget and trying to bankrupt the company by sabotaging its jobs.

Quincy Davis	Grant Williams
Adam Conrad	Allen Case
Joe Marshall	Bert Freed
Marguerite Keith	Meg Wyllie
Ed Pierce	Les Tremayne
Archer Osmond	Barton MacLane
Hilary Gary	Joan Blackman
Harley Leonard	John Howard

Frustrated Folk Singer, 1/7/65

Young Amy Jo Jennings is more concerned with a show business career than with the financial empire she inherited. Her contract with a Hollywood agent seems to be a result of amazing luck. Amy learns she has been tricked when she signed the contract and asks Perry's advice on how to break the contract. However, the agent is unceremoniously murdered.

Jazbo Williams	Gary Crosby
Amy Jo Jennings	Bonnie Jones
Harry Bronson	Robert H. Harris
Lester Crawford	Mark Goddard
Evelyn Bronson	Gale Robbins
Lionel Albright	Richard Garland
Natalie Graham	Lee Merriwether
Al Siebring	Leonard Stone
Chris Thompson	John Considine

Thermal Thief, 1/14/65

Lawyer Ken Kramer subs for Perry, and Lona Upton asks him to get a friend out of jail. She was picked up by the police after stealing a $50,000 necklace. Kramer finds a murder trial brewing when the female jewel thief is murdered.

Ken Kramer	Barry Sullivan
Amy Reid	Bettye Ackerman
Lona Upton	Kathie Browne
Roland Canfield	Richard Eastham
Jeff Mills	Burt Metcalfe
Pete Kamboly	Robert Strauss
Fay Gilmer	Joyce Van Patten
Barman	Dick Whittinghill
Desk Sergeant	Harlan Warde
Judge	S. John Launer
Dion	John Hart

Note: Barry Sullivan was an ailing Raymond Burr's substitute.

Golden Venom, 1/21/65

Widow Lucille Forrest hires Perry to override a strange proviso in her late husband's will. She has always believed her son did not die accidentally, but the will is preventing her from reopening the investigation—she will be disinherited if she does. She asks Perry to find a legal loophole in the document. Meanwhile, she finds the man she believes was responsible for her son's death, but before she can bring the man to justice someone kills him, and now she is on trial for murder.

Lucille Forrest	Frances Reid
Tony Claus	Noah Beery, Jr.
Walter Coffee	Frank Ferguson
Mirna Lawrence	Carole Wells

Ralph Day	Arthur Malet
Sergeant Ben Landis	Mort Mills

Telltale Tap, 2/4/65

Clyde Darrell's company is short $200,000, but he signs all the checks. Clyde is the victim of an elaborate frame and scheme to bilk the company out of millions of dollars. Clyde's supposedly loyal secretary is murdered, and Clyde is arrested for it.

Clyde Darrell	Linden Chiles
Vera Wynne	Jeanne Bal
Archer Bryant	Roland Winters
Nancy Bryant	Indus Arthur
Ian Jarvis	Parley Baer
Elliot Forrest	William Allyn
Glen Holman	H. M. Wynant
Karl Lewis	Seamon Glass
Judge	S. John Launer
Bartender	Lester Dorr

Feather Cloak, 2/11/65

Perry Mason goes to Hawaii with Paul Drake and Della Street to investigate some land dealings for a hotel chain. Included in the case are a drifting beach bum and a wealthy Hawaiian planter.

Professor Gustave Heller	David Opatoshu
Anona Gilbert	Wende Wagner
Lieutenant Kia	Jon Hall
Auntie Hilo	Miriam Goldina
Jarvis Logan	John van Dreelen
Doctor	Victor Sen Yung
Douglas Kelland	Michael Dante
Dolly Jameson	Joyce Jameson
Attorney Roberts	Tom Palmer
District Attorney Alvarez	James Frawley
Choy	Keye Luke
Jon Kakai	Tony Scott
Judge Kee	Arthur Wong

Lover's Gamble, 2/18/65

Art student Betty Kaster's job as secretary to lecturer Philip Stark is no lark. She is convinced her boss will kill his bedridden wife. When she takes her theory to Perry, he finds himself involved with Stark's murder.

Estelle Mabury	Elizabeth Perry
Dr. Philip Stark	Donald Murphy
Betty Kaster	Margaret Bly

Jill Fenwick	Joan O'Brien
Frances Stark	June Dayton
Freddy Fell	Harold Peary
Link	Orville Sherman
Henry Thomas	Roy Roberts
Truck Driver	Hal Baylor
Marta Glenhorn	Minerva Urecal
Sarah Thomas	Linda Leighton
Beauty Operator	Barbara Perry
Judge	Grandon Rhodes
Newsboy	Robert Hernandez

Fatal Fetish, 3/4/65

Hamilton Burger is upset when his young assistant becomes infatuated with a lady who has a bad reputation. Not only that, she turns out to be a blackmailer and her target is Burger.

Mignon Germaine	Fay Wray
Neil Howard	Richard Devon
Kent Ordway	Alan Hewitt
Carina Wileen	Karen Steele
Ruth Duncan	Lynn Bari
Larry Germaine	Gary Collins
Brady Duncan	Douglas Kennedy
Agnes Fanchon	Erin Leigh
Jack Randall	James Griffith
Nurse	Breena Howard
Judge	John Gallaudet
Secretary	Roni Adler
Choreographer	Wilda Taylor
Kenneth	Bill Keene
Emcee	John Francis

Sad Sicilian, 3/11/65

Enrico Bacio, the tyrannical head of a transplanted Sicilian family, learns a man named Pedro has come to call. He fears a century-old vendetta will be renewed, with him as the target. However, Enrico is mistaken—Pedro does not want to kill him, but someone else does.

Serafina	Margo
Enrico Bacio	Anthony Caruso
Massimo Bacio	Rudy Salari
Paulo Porro	Fabrizio Mioni
Father Reggiani	Paul Comi
Elizabeth Bacio	Linda Marsh
Giangiacomo	Nico Minardos
Dodson	Dabbs Greer
Café Owner	Jack LaRue

Murderous Mermaid, 3/18/65

Aspiring movie actress Reggie Lansfield agrees to stand in for an aging film star's publicity stunt—swimming the hazardous Catalina Channel off Southern California. Perry Mason gets involved in the death of a one-time movie swimming star caught in fraud and embezzlement.

Victoria Dawn	Patrice Wymore
Reggie Lansfield	Jean Hale
Charlie Shaw	Bill Williams
Douglas Hamilton	Jess Barker
Ben Lucas	Richard Erdman
Dr. George Devlin	Lee Bergere
Lillian Keely	Nan Leslie

Careless Kitten, 3/25/65

Even the police are sure Matilda Shore's husband, missing for ten years, must be presumed dead. Matilda disagrees and refuses to probate her husband's will. Behind this lie another murder case and a dead blackmailer, plus a Siamese kitten who is the clue to another murder.

Matilda Shore	Louise Latham
Gerald Shore	Lloyd Corrigan
Helen Kendall	Julie Sommars
Thomas Link	Allan Melvin
Doctor	Francis De Sales
Frank Templar	Alan Reed, Jr.
Cosmo	Hedley Mattingly
Sergeant Brice	Lee Miller
Hotel Clerk	Percy Helton
Veterinarian	Raymond Guth

Deadly Debt, 4/1/65

Detective Danny Talbert blames his brother, Chris, for their father's death from a heart attack at the train station. Danny knows his brother is in trouble again and their father made the trip to the station on his way to bail Chris out of jail. Danny learns that a syndicate head is behind Chris problems. Then the crime leader is murdered.

Chris Talbert	Chris Robinson
Danny Talbert	Robert Quarry
Charles Judd	Max Showalter
Louie Parker	Joe De Santis
Stella Radom	Allison Hayes
Kitty Delaney	Joan Huntington
Mrs. Talbert	Sheila Bromley
Steve Radom	Gregory Morton
Sergeant Brice	Lee Miller

Gambling Lady, 4/8/65

Perry is helping Peter Warren in his divorce case with his wife, Myrna. An investigator arrives asking Peter to identify the lady in a picture taken at a Nevada gambling casino. Perry gets involved in a plot to embezzle money from a group of casino owners and the murder of a crooked gambler.

Peter Warren	Peter Breck
Tony Cerro	Jesse White
Myrna Warren	Myrna Fahey
Irene Prentice	Ruta Lee
Jerome Bentley	Benny Baker
Jacob Leonard	Kevin Hagen
Ned Beaumont	John Rayner
Croupier	Dan Seymour
Judge	Kenneth MacDonald

Duplicate Case, 4/22/65

When salesman Herbie Cornwall, a spectacular failure, throws his sample case down in disgust, he is astonished to see a bundle of bills in large denominations fall out of the case. Herbie had the misfortune of stumbling on an embezzlement and the murder of a cheating wife who tried to steal money from her boss.

Herbie Cornwall	Martin West
Burt Blair	Don Dubbins
Charlie Parks	Steve Ihnat
Minnie Cornwall	Susan Bay
A. K. Dudley	David Lewis
Ernest Hill	Herbert Voland
Bartender	Dave Willock
Judge	Douglass Dumbrille
Miss Dahlbert	Audrey Larkin

Grinning Gorilla, 4/29/65

Della buys the personal papers of a dead woman at a public auction and soon is offered a thousand dollars for the seemingly worthless correspondence. Perry meets an amateur anthropolgist doomed to die. The coroner's inquest rules that the scientist was killed by a gorilla, but Perry is not so sure.

Josephine Kempton	Lurene Tuttle
Nathan Fallon	Victor Buono
Benjamin Addicks	Harvey Stephens
Helen Cadmus	Charlene Holt
F. A. Snell	Robert Colbert
Mortimer Hershey	Gavin MacLeod
Sydney Hardwick	Bartlett Robinson
Attendant	True Boardman
Estate Guard	Jim Boles
Deputy	Bob Foulk
Jefferson	Tom Farrell

Wrongful Writ, 5/6/65

Young attorney Ward Toyama agrees to use his influence with his Dad's export firm to aid a secret agent who wants to ship a mysterious cargo to the Far East. Ward unwittingly becomes involved in a shipment of arms to the guerillas going to the Indochina area. The secret agent is murdered, and the district attorney arrests Ward.

Ward Toyama	James Shigeta
Harry Grant	Philip Abbott
Captain Otto Varnum	Peter Whitney
Esther Norden	Katherine Squire
Frank Jones	Douglas Henderson
Sally Choshi	Nobu McCarthy
Smitty	Bobby Troup
Judge Simpson	Bill Zuckert
Ursula Quigley	Francine York
Judge	Douglas Evans

Mischievous Doll, 5/13/65

Perry is puzzled when an excited and confused girl named Dorrie Ambler bursts into his office asking to be identified.

Dorrie Ambler	Mary Mitchel
Minerva Minden	Mary Mitchel
Jasper	Ben Cooper
Rita Jasper	Allyson Ames
Del Compton	Paul Lambert
Henrietta Hull	Marge Redmond
Joe Billings	Phil Arthur
Airport Clerk	Byron Foulger

Laughing Lady, 9/12/65

Carla Chaney is charged with the murder of Gerald Havens, a hack journalist. He is killed with a knife bearing her fingerprints. She tells Perry she saw the real killer on a television program.

Leona Devore	Constance Towers
Carla Chaney	Jean Hale
Peter Stange	Bernard Fox
Dr. Durwood Tobey	John Abbott
Cho Sin	Allison Hayes
Roan Daniel	John Dall
Lenny Linden	Mickey Manners
Terrence Clay	Dan Tobin
Judge	John Gallaudet
Superintendent	Shirley O'Hara

Matron .... Irene Anders
Lt. Steve Drumm .... Richard Anderson

Note: This was Richard Anderson's first appearance as Lt. Steve Drumm, who replaced Lt. Anderson (Wesley Lau).

Fatal Fortune, 9/19/65

Career woman Pat Kean is worried by her boss's marriage proposals. An astrologer has told her she will soon be a widow if she weds him, wearing white followed by black. Pat marries him and the prediction comes true when her new husband is murdered and Pat is arrested by Lt. Steve Drumm.

Patricia L. Kean .... Julie Adams
Max Armstead .... Jesse White
Gordon Evans .... Lee Philips
Dr. Fisher .... Ford Rainey
Terrence Clay .... Dan Tobin
Beth Fuller .... Nan Martin
Daniel Buckley .... Dean Harens
Marius Stone .... James Lanphier
Landlady .... Norà Marlowe
Gypsy .... Belle Mitchell
Desk Clerk .... Alex Bookston
Judge .... Grandon Rhodes

Note: Dan Tobin became a member of the regular cast.

Candy Queen, 9/26/65

The secretary of candy manufacturer Claire Armstrong finds poison in the firm's product after she eats some. She learns a gambler has gotten hold of the formula for her candy and wants money to keep him from turning it over to Claire's competitors.

Claire Armstrong .... Nancy Gates
Ed Purvis .... Robert Rockwell
Mark Chester .... John Napier
Wanda Buren .... Patricia Smith
Harry Arnold .... John Archer
Carol Olin .... Nina Shipman
Tony Mario .... H. M. Wynant
Terrence Clay .... Dan Tobin
Intern .... Walter Mathews
Judge .... Kenneth MacDonald
Landlady .... Kitty Kelly
Hatcheck Girl .... Bebe Kelly

Cheating Chancellor, 10/3/65

After learning his exam questions have been copied, Dr. Stuart Logan accuses his class of cheating. The same charge is leveled at him by his assistant, who got no credit for a book he helped the professor write. When the assistant is killed, Dr. Logan puts in a call to his former student Perry Mason for help.

Medical Examiner	Joseph Mell
Mrs. Hyatt	Linda Leighton
Guard	Dirk Evans
Bob Hyatt	Peter Helm
James Hyatt	Peter Hobbs
Van Fowler	James Noah
Dr. Stuart Logan	G. B. Atwater
Myra Finlay	Adrianne Ellis
Joe Price	Michael Walker
Evelyn Wilcox	Lee Merriwether
District Attorney	Jay Barney
Shirley Logan	Louise Latham
Judge	Stacy Keach, Sr.

Impetuous Imp, 10/10/65

Perry helps a young lady swimmer and then is tagged as her accomplice in a $50,000 jewel robbery. There is more to this case besides larceny: a wealthy woman is murdered, and her husband is suspected of the crime.

Henry Simmons	Stuart Erwin
Diana Carter	Bonnie Jones
Helga Dolwig	Hanna Landy
Bill Vincent	Don Dubbins
Henning Dolwig	Jeff Cooper
Mike Carson	Frank Marth
Addison Powell	Richard Webb
Judge Brawley	Byron Morrow
Harvey Blake	James McCallion
Dr. Lund	Michael Fox
Terrence Clay	Dan Tobin
Judge	Ed Prentiss

Note: This episode was based on Erle Stanley Gardner's book *The Case of the Negligent Nymph.*

Carefree Coronary, 10/17/65

Perry Mason is hired by a small insurance company facing bankruptcy because of a suspiciously high number of claims made by heart attack victims.

Arthur Wendell	Robert Emhardt
Reve Watson	Bruce Bennett
Dennison Groody	Whit Bissell
Jerry Ormond	Benny Baker
Doreen Wilde	Tracy Morgan
Wallis Lamphier	David Lewis
Dr. Chauncy Hartland	Lawrence Montaigne

Dr. Paul Caudere .... Joseph Sirola
Marilyn David .... Shirley Mitchell
Jack David .... Hal Baylor
Terrence Clay .... Dan Tobin
Dr. Williard Shelby .... William Woodson
Nappy Tyler .... Dan Seymour

Hasty Honeymoon, 10/24/65

Lucas Tolliver has Perry draft a will leaving all his wife owns to him—before they are married. His new wife is soon murdered, and Lieutenant Drumm has the will as a motive for the killing.

Lucas Tolliver .... Noah Beery, Jr.
Alice Munford .... K. T. Stevens
Guy Munford .... Hugh Marlowe
Millicent Barton .... Cathy Downs
Roy Hutchinson .... Strother Martin
Carl Snell .... Robert Colbert
Terrence Clay .... Dan Tobin
Larry Dunlap .... Richard Evans

12th Wildcat, 10/31/65

The train bringing the Wildcat football team to Los Angeles also contains the dead husband of team owner Ellen Payne, the chief suspect in his death. Perry believes she is being framed and that the case against her by Hamilton Burger is just too pat.

Ellen Payne .... Mona Freeman
Burt Payne .... Bill Williams
Andy Grant .... Regis Toomey
Jud Warner .... John Conte
Unk Hazekian .... Karl Swenson
Casey Banks .... Robert Quarry
Harvey Skeen .... Roy Roberts
Assistant Coach .... Lindon Crow
Judge .... Willis Bouchey
Ski .... Mel Profit

Note: Members of the Los Angeles Rams pro football team played given small roles: Don Chuy, Roman Gabriel, Lamar Lundy, Marlin McKeever, and Bill Munson.

Wrathful Wraith, 11/7/65

Louise Selff, found innocent of the death of her husband, who vanished mysteriously, tells Perry the killer must be found. Then her husband returns and is really killed later. Hamilton Burger, even though he couldn't convict her the first time, now arrests her again.

Louise Selff	Marion Moses
Rosemary Welch	Jeanne Bal
Ted Harberson	Douglas Dick
Ralph Balfour	Gene Lyons
Ed Allison	Robert Easton
Glenn Arcott	Lee Farr
Willa St. Sutton	Winifred Coffin

Runaway Racer, 11/14/65

Angered because he cannot get out of his driving contract, race car driver Pete Griston roars onto the track in another car, which loses power abruptly and causes an accident that seriously injures his best friend. Pete finds the car had been tampered with and suspects his partner. Before he can prove it, the man is killed and Pete is on trial.

Pete Griston	Henry Brandt
Pappy Ryan	Michael Constantine
Marge Leonard	Jan Shepard
Harvey Rettig	Anthony Caruso
Oliver Stone	Richard Eastham
Marty Webb	Robert H. Harris
Dan Platte	Gavin MacLeod
Mitch	Paul Winfield
Joe	Seamon Glass
Drunk	Jim Cross

Silent Six, 11/21/65

On his way to warn Joe Oliver to stay away from his sister, police sergeant Dave Wolfe hears her scream for help. When he gets to her apartment, she is dead, and he is arrested for the murder of Joe Oliver.

Reporter	Walter Matthews
Sgt. Dave Wolfe	Skip Homeier
Linda Blakely	Dianne Foster
Ron Peters	David Macklin
Hamp Fisher	Hampton Fancher
Flo Oliver	Virginia Gregg
Monk Coleman	Peter Baron
Susan Wolfe	Chris Noel
Judge Carter	Kenneth MacDonald
Craig Jefferson	Cyril Delevanti
Herb Jackson	Tyler MacDuff
Sergeant Brice	Lee Miller
Arch	John Heath

Fugitive Fraulein, 11/28/65

Perry Mason, Della Street, and Paul Drake travel to West Berlin to defend a woman who is accused of murdering an East German agent. The communists had kidnapped Gerta Ritter in an effort to get her father, physicist Hans Ritter, to defect. In order to defend his client, Perry must go behind the Iron Curtain.

Professor Hans Ritter	Wolfe Barzell
Gerta Ritter	Susanne Cramer
Emma Ritter	Jeanette Nolan
Border Guard	Horst Ebersberg
Wolfgang Stromm	Gregory Morton
Samuel Carleton	Kevin Hagen
Elke	Eileen Baral
Judge Magistrate	Barbara Morrison
Waitress	Marta Schroeder
Franz Hoffer	Ronald Long
Matron	Lilyan Chauvin

Baffling Bug, 12/12/65

Dr. Malcolm Stratton suspects a rival firm has pirated his new desalinization process. When murder strikes Tryon Industries, Perry gets involved with industrial espionage.

Dr. Todd Meade	Grant Williams
Rhoda Coleridge	Dee Hartford
Dr. Malcolm Stratton	Gilbert Green
Lowell Rupert	Ben Cooper
Dr. Nina Revelli	Alizia Gur
Dr. MaseoTachikawa	Teru Shimada
Horace Lehigh	Bryan O'Byrne
Judge	S. John Launer
Bess	Mary Treen

Golden Girls, 12/19/65

Victor Montalvo is one of two partners in a successful girlie magazine and a chain of nightclubs. One night he picks up a pretty hitchhiker and finds himself involved in blackmail. Someone kills his partner, and he is charged with murder.

Victor Montalvo	Philip Bourneuf
Debbie Conrad	Angela Dorian
Rick Durbin	Bruce Glover
Corinne Richland	Jean Engstrom
Beverly Garnett	Paula Stewart
Irving Florian	Mark Roberts
Terrence Clay	Dan Tobin
Sergeant Brice	Lee Miller
Judge	John Gallaudet
Stacey Garnett	George Neise

Bogus Buccaneers, 1/9/66

Things look bad for accused murderer Tony Polk. He has a criminal record, and a witness saw him fight with the victim. What's more, he owns the murder weapon. Mason's job is to break down the eyewitness on the stand in court.

Tony Polk	Steve Harris
Martin Eldridge	Rhodes Reason
Beth Polk	Mary Mitchel
Ann Eldridge	Patricia Cutts
Harlan Kean	Leonard Stone
Mrs. Webb	Meg Wyllie
Clayton Douglas	John Milford
Mike Woods	Richard Jaeckel
Abe Heyman	Michael Fox
Grace Knapp	Kathleen Crowley
Sergeant Brice	Lee Miller
Judge	Willis Bouchey
Receptionist	Patricia Joyce

Midnight Howler, 1/16/66

Perry is listening to a late night talk show when he hears the station owner's conversation stopped by the sound of gunfire.

Dan Thorne	Lee Patterson
Holly Andrews	Myrna Fahey
Barney Austin	Dan Travanty
Gordon Sellers	Alan Baxter
Abel Jackson	Ian Wolfe
Clara Michaels	Cathleen Cordell
Judge	Grandon Rhodes
Sergeant Brice	Lee Miller
Court Clerk	Charles Stroud
Medical Examiner	Pitt Herbert
Control Room Man	Marc Desmond

Vanishing Victim, 1/23/66

Miriam Fielding hires Perry Mason to investigate her husband's financial holdings. She knows he is hiding money from her. What begins as a routine case turns into a bizarre one. Perry is faced with the crash of Stacey Fielding's private plane, his double life, and a missing drug supply. This episode was based on Erle Stanley Gardner's *The Case of the Fugitive Nurse.*

Jud Bennett	Richard Erdman
Miriam Fielding	Jeanne Cooper
Reed Kavanaugh	Russell Arms

Laraine Keely .... Lisa Gaye
Stacey Fielding .... George Wallace
Judge Telford .... S. John Launer
Terrence Clay .... Dan Tobin
Ruth Kavanaugh .... Carol Brewster
FAA Investigator .... John Matthews
Al Dolby .... John Goddard
McGill .... Glen Vernon
Process Server .... Tom Vize
Operations Clerk .... Carl Prickett

Golfer's Gambit, 1/30/66

Pro golfer Chick Farley finds ways to add to his income by blackmailing a golf club official and threatening to blame his assistant for a three thousand dollar deficit in the pro shop. Farley overextends himself, however. Soon after his biggest tour victory, he is killed. Lieutenant Drumm arrests Farley's young assistant, Danny Bright, for the crime.

Danny Bright .... Carl Reindel
Edward "Pat" Patterson .... Bartlett Robinson
Chick Farley .... Dennis Patrick
Dina Brandt .... Nancy Kovack
Erwin Brandt .... Harry Townes
Alma Farley .... Phyllis Hill
Jim Harrell .... Alan Reed, Jr.
Bill Vincent .... Don Dubbins
Rosalie .... Regina Gleason

Sausalito Sunrise, 2/13/66

Perry's clients, art gallery owner Francis Clune and his pretty secretary, are accused of the murder of a private detective who was on the trail of an art hijacking ring. Before he can defend the pair, they are accused of a second murder.

Olaf Deering .... Peter Mamakos
Terrence Clay .... Dan Tobin
Francis Clune .... Don Murphy
Bert Kannon .... Allan Melvin
Estelle Paige .... Elisabeth Fraser
Sgt. Deke Bradley .... Mark Tapscott
Bobbi Dane .... Francine York
Campbell Boyd .... Richard Angarola
Bud .... Paul Genge
Counterman .... William Erwin
Mac .... Steve Conte
Nurse .... Bebe Kelly
Judge .... Kenneth MacDonald
Floyd Walters .... Stanley Clements

Scarlet Scandal, 2/20/66

Tempers are high in a small town when the wife of the leading citizen is murdered by a blackmailer. Everyone feels musician Donald Hobart did it.

Donald Hobart	Will Hutchins
Moose Dalton	Gene Evans
Cynthia Perkins	Luana Patten
Richard Bayler	Lloyd Gough
Elaine Bayler	Mala Powers
Ed Kesko	Richard Devon
Aaron Chambers	Clint Sundberg
Howard Bayler	Dee Pollock
Natasha	Connie Gilchrist
Woodmire	Blair Davies
Judge Seymour	M. William Keane
Mark	Carl Prickett

Twice Told Twist, 2/27/66

In a modern version of *Oliver Twist*, police are convinced 18-year-old Lennie Beale belongs to a car stripping gang that stole accessories from Perry's car. However, Perry decides not to press charges.

Ben Huggins	Victor Buono
Lennie Beale	Kevin O'Neal
Bill Sikes	Scott Graham
Robin Spring	Lisa Seagram
Donna Reales	Lisa Pera
Jody Laird	Marc Rambeau
Tick Gleason	Nicolas Surovy
Terrence Clay	Dan Tobin
Sue	Beverly Hills
Sgt. Roddin	Harlan Warde
Deputy District Attorney	Will J. White
Tom Loman	Judson Pratt
Policeman	Coby Denton
Welfare Worker	Helen Kleeb

Note: This episode was the only one of the nine year series to be made in color, as requested by president of CBS William S. Paley. Until the 1980s and 1990s, it was never part of the rerun package.

Avenging Angel, 3/13/66

Rich Cameron Burgess hires Perry to obtain Clete Hawley's services in developing a young rock and roll singer into a star. Hawley will not talk to Burgess, so the impresario gets Perry to sign him up. However, Burgess wishes to remain anonymous. During a recording session, Burgess is shot and killed. The young singer then becomes Perry's client.

Clete Hawley	Richard Carlson
Sherry Lawler	Sandy Descher
Dotty Merrill	Sue Ane Langdon
Henrietta McLeod	Lurene Tuttle
Cameron Burgess	Paul Stewart
Sandy Chester	Martin Horsey
Riff Lawler	Chick Chandler
June Burgess	Patricia Owens
Technician	Mike McGiveney
Policeman	John McKee
Judge	Douglas Evans

Tsarina's Tiara, 3/20/66

Madame Sonya Gallinova, believing she was given phony jewels as payment for a debt, asks Perry to press charges. Then she changes her mind upon learning they are real and worth a million dollars! Back of all this is an international jewel thief who outstays his welcome and is murdered. Perry decides to defend the South American jeweler charged with the crime.

Sonya Gallinova	Virginia Field
Gerald Van Ness	Kendall Clark
Joachim De Vry	Wesley Addy
Vyacheslav Gerznov	Leonid Kinskey
Pauline Thorsen	Vivienne Segal
Lisabeth	Janet Degore
Ricardo Arena	Carlos Romero
Assistant	Barbara Perry
Dinaldo	Dante Orgolini
Sergeant Brice	Lee Miller
Judge	Kenneth MacDonald
Nils Dorow	Fred Krone
Rolf Thorsen	Phillip Terry

Fanciful Frail, 3/27/66

Ethel Andrews's wedding day turns sour when the groom fails to show up. Her boss is missing $50,000 in securities, with her signature on the selling transfer authorization. Perry gets involved with two young women who switch identities: Ethel, who is accused of the theft, and another who is trying to escape a hired killer.

Ethel Andrews	Pippa Scott
Frank Carruthers	Arch Johnson
Martha Erskine	Coleen Gray
Park Milgrave	Barry Kelley
Bruce Strickland	Hunt Powers
Althea Milgrave	Joan Huntington
Tierney	John Raynere

Peggy Sutton .... Abigail Shelton
Reverend Alford .... Henry Hunter
Waiter .... Tim Blake
Judge .... S. John Launer

Unwelcome Well, 4/3/66

Oil tycoon Jerome Klee's testing crews are drilling on Jason Rohan's farm. Jason is spending money he does not have in the hopes he will become rich. Also being fooled is geologist Allan Winford. Later, after the scam is discovered by all parties, Klee is killed and Winford arrested.

Jerome Klee .... Wendell Corey
Jason Rohan .... Paul Brinegar
Allan Winford .... James Best
Mirabel Corum .... Marilyn Erskine
Harry Lannon .... Les Tremayne
Prince Ben Ali Bhudeem .... Edmund Hashim
Monique .... Danielle De Metz
Minna Rohan .... Gloria Talbott

Dead Ringer, 4/17/66

Perry is charged with trying to buy off a witness in a hearing over a one million dollar patent dispute. Meanwhile, a cockney merchant seaman bears a remarkable resemblance to Perry Mason and hatches a plot to blackmail the famous lawyer. The double, a man named Grimes, tries to buy off one of the witnesses, thus making it appear as if Perry had stooped to bribery.

Grimes .... Raymond Burr
Sandra Dunkel .... Arlene Martel
Dan Swanson .... Stewart Moss
Barbara Kramer .... Indus Arthur
William March .... Henry Beckman
Otis Swanson .... Oliver McGowan
Jess Parkinson .... Maurice Manson
Franklin Bates .... Tom Palmer
Minister .... Chet Stratton
Trial Judge .... Grandon Rhodes
Bouncer .... Roland La Starza
Makeup Man .... Anthony Jochim

Misguided Model, 4/24/66

Former boxer Duke Maronek tells Perry he killed a man in self-defense. He was trying to wreck Sharon Carmody's modeling career. He won't let Perry give this information to the police—even though another man has been charged with the crime—and makes it difficult for Mason to meet his responsibilities toward his clients.

Sharon Carmody .... Mary Ann Mobley
Dennis "Duke" Maronek .... Paul Lukather
Rudy Blair .... Anthony Eisley
Fern Bronwyn .... Rita Lynn
Madame Rosa Bruening .... Isabel Randolph
Jake Stearns .... James Griffith
Deputy District Attorney Vincent .... Don Dubbins
DeWitt .... Armand Alazamora
Judge .... Harry Holcombe

Positive Negative, 5/1/66

Roger Brandon may be forced to reject the chance to head his town's anticrime commission. If he takes the post, his wife will be viciously smeared. The retired general has never backed away from a fight and does not intend to do so now. He charges forward and seems to be outflanked when the local syndicate head is murdered and General Brandon is framed for it.

General Roger Brandon .... Brian Donlevy
Laura Brandon .... Bettye Ackerman
Frank Cummings .... Parley Baer
Bill Cotton .... Dabbs Greer
Stan Overton .... Simon Scott
Emory .... Ted de Corsia
Warren Cotton .... Anthony Hayes
Judge .... John Gallaudet
Photographer .... Jim Drum

Crafty Kidnapper, 5/15/66

Scandal columnist Dan Shine is dead drunk when he gets into Jerry Staley's car to go home. When they get there, he is really dead, and Gloria Shine accuses Jerry of the murder. He is powerless to prove his innocence, since all the potential witnesses who can back up his story refuse to testify.

Dan Shine .... John Lasell
Greg Stanley .... Douglas Henderson
Gloria Shine .... Cloris Leachman
Alex Tanner .... Gary Collins
Patricia Tanner .... Anne Whitfield
Norma Fenn .... Pat Priest
Sergeant Brice .... Lee Miller
Lola Stanley .... Mary Foskett
Leon Vandenberg .... William Bramley
Bruno Grant .... John Holland

Final Fadeout, 5/22/66

Television star Barry Conrad refuses to sign a contract with producer Jackson Sidemark. He plans to star in and own a series of his own. Murder results during a filmed gunfight when someone substitutes real bullets for the blanks and kills Conrad. Jackson Sidemark is charged with his murder.

Barry Conrad .... James Stacy
Leif Early .... Dick Clark
Erna Landry .... Marlyn Mason
Jackson Sidemark .... Denver Pyle
Winifred Glover .... Estelle Winwood
Andy Rubin .... Gerald Mohr
Pete Desmond .... Jackie Coogan
First Judge .... Kenneth MacDonald
Second Judge .... Erle Stanley Gardner
Sergeant Brice .... Lee Miller

Note: This was the last episode of the nine year series and everyone, including producer Gail Patrick Jackson, the crew, and even Erle Stanley Gardner, was given lines.

The episodes went into syndication immediately and have been seen in almost every country in the world and dubbed in many languages. Thirty-five years later, they are still being shown.

As far as can be determined William Hopper (Paul Drake) appeared in all 271 episodes. Barbara Hale was in all but four or five.

William Talman (Hamilton Burger) was in all episodes except those made during a period in 1960 when he was arrested on a morals charge and suspended by CBS. By December 1960 he was reinstated with a new and better contract at the insistence of Raymond Burr and the crew when it was proven he was innocent of the charge.

Shooting Schedule of "The Case of the Dead Ringer," 4/17/66

Coproducers: Arthur Marks and Art Seid
Director: Arthur Marks
Assistant Director: Gordon Webb

Perry Mason and Grimes played by Raymond Burr.

First Day Shooting Schedule

Set & Scene	Pages of Dialogue	Misc. Props	Cast Character
Exterior (N) Waterfront Street & Car (N) Scene 4-5-6	2 2/8	Atmosphere Car Spec. Eff. Fog	Dan Swanson Otis Swanson March
Scenes 2-3 (N) same exterior	1	Atmos. Fog	Grimes, Bouncer, Mexican worker
Interior (N) Herman's Blue Lagoon Scenes 7 thru 10	2 3/8	Atmos.	Grimes, Bouncer, Dan Swanson, Otis Swanson Makeup Man

Set & Scene	Pages of Dialogue	Misc. Props	Cast Character
Interior (D) Herman's Blue Lagoon Scene 101	5/8		Drake, Grimes, Bouncer
Interior (N) Hotel Room Scenes 11, 12	1 3/8		Grimes, Otis Swanson Makeup man
Interior (N) Scenes 52 thru 57	1 2/8		Grimes, Dan Swanson, Makeup Man

End of First Day's Shooting

Exterior (D) Waterfront Scenes 60, 62, 63	4/8	Atmos. Taxi	March
Exterior (D) Waterfront (Process) Scenes 63, 65	1/8		Drake
Exterior (D) Ship's Railing (Process) Scene 45	2/8		Grimes (Burr)
Exterior (N) Swanson Front Door Scene 74	1/8		Drake
Exterior (N) Swanson Front Door Scene 78	1/8		Grimes (Burr)
Exterior (N) Swanson Drive & Car Scenes 71, 72, 73	3/8	Car	Drake
Interior (N) Swanson Study and Window Scenes 76, 77, 79 thru 84	1 4/8	Light Chg. Spec. Eff. Fireplace	Drake, Grimes, Otis Swanson, Barbara
Interior (N) Swanson Study Scenes 52 thru 59	3 6/8		Dan Swanson, March, Otis Swanson
Interior (N) Swanson House Scenes 48 thru 51	2 2/8	Atmos.	Dan Swanson, Otis Swanson, Barbara
Interior (N) Swanson House Scene 75	1/8		Drake

End of Second Day

Set & Scene	Pages of Dialogue	Misc. Props	Cast Character
Interior (D) Courtroom (2nd) (Split Screen) Scenes 102 thru 114	10 3/8	Atmos.	Perry Mason, Drake, Burger, Drumm, Grimes, Dan Swanson, March, Sandra, Barbara, 2nd Judge, Parkinson
Interior (D) Courtroom (2nd) Scenes 85 thru 98	8 5/8	Atmos.	Mason, Della, Burger, Drumm, Dan Swanson, March, Sandra, Barbara, 2nd Judge, Parkinson

End of Third Day

Set & Scene	Pages of Dialogue	Misc. Props	Cast Character
Interior (D) Courtroom (2nd) Scenes 102 thru 114 85 thru 98 (to complete)		Atmos.	Mason, Della, Drake, Burger, Drumm, March, Dan Swanson, Sandra, Barbara, Parkinson
Interior (N) Hotel Room Scenes 16, 17, 18	2 2/8		Grimes Made Up like Perry Mason, Dan Swanson, Otis Swanson, Makeup Man
Exterior (N) Street & Entrance to Hotel Scenes 21, 22, 32	3/8	Atmos.	Grimes Made Up like Perry Mason (Ray Burr)
Interior (N) Hotel Lobby Scenes 23 thru 31	2	Atmos.	Grimes Made Up like Mason, Dan Swanson, Sandra Hartley, Minister, Asst. Mgr.

End of Fourth Day

Set & Scene	Pages of Dialogue	Misc. Props	Cast Character
Interior (D) Court Corridor Phone Booth Scenes 99, 100	3/8	Atmos.	Perry Mason
Interior (D) 1st Courtroom	5 4/8	Atmos.	Mason, Della, Dan Swanson,

Set & Scene	Pages of Dialogue	Misc. Props	Cast Character
(With Jury Box DeLongpre End Open) Scenes 33 thru 38			March, Otis Swanson, Sandra Hadley, Bates, Barbara, 1st Judge, Parkinson, Minister

End of Fifth Day

Set & Scene	Pages of Dialogue	Misc. Props	Cast Character
Interior (N) Clay's Grill (Tag) Scenes 115, 116, 117	1 4/8	Atmos.	Mason, Drake, Burger, Drumm, Terrence Clay
Interior (D) Mason's Office Scenes 39 thru 44	3 4/8		Mason, Della, Drake, Barbara, Parkinson
Interior (N) Mason's Office Scenes 66, 67	1 5/8		Mason, Della, Drake
Interior (N) Della's Office Scenes 68, 69, 70	3		Mason, Della, Drake, Barbara
Interior (N) Della's Office Scenes 19, 20	4/8		Della

End of Sixth Day

"The Return of Perry Mason"

Episode	Ratings	Shares	The Case of the	Rank	Date Shown
1	27.2	39	Perry Mason Returns	1	12/1/85
2	23.3	42	Notorious Nun	3	5/25/86
3	23.6	37	Shooting Star	7	11/9/86
4	21.3	33	Lost Love	10	2/23/87
5	20.5	35	Sinister Spirit	3	5/24/87
6	18.1	29	Murdered Madam	17	10/4/87
7	16.6	26	Scandalous Scoundrel	22	11/15/87
8	17.4	26	Avenging Ace	16	2/28/88
9	22.6	35	Lady in the Lake	1	5/15/88
10	19.9	30	Lethal Lesson	15	2/12/89
11	17.4	26	Musical Murder	16	4/9/89
12	16.5	26	All-Star Assassin	17	11/19/89
13	16.0	24	Poisoned Pen	21	1/21/90
14	17.0	27	Desperate Deception	13	3/11/90
15	16.5	27	Silenced Singer	8	5/20/90
16	14.7	24	Defiant Daughter	24	9/30/90

Episode	Ratings	Shares	The Case of the	Rank	Date Shown
17	14.0	21	Ruthless Reporter	24	1/6/91
18	14.0	22	Maligned Mobster	34	2/11/91
19	12.8	22	Glass Coffin	22	5/14/91
20	14.6	23	Fatal Fashion	26	9/24/91
21	12.9	20	Fatal Framing	42	3/1/92
22	14.7	23	Reckless Romeo	19	5/5/92
23	12.1	21	Heartbroken Bride	19	10/30/92
24	13.3	22	Skin Deep Scandal	30	2/19/93
25	13.1	24	Tell-Tale Talk Show Host	19	5/21/93
26	13.4	19	Defense Rests Tribute to Raymond Burr Followed by Rerun of Number 25	52	10/22/93
26	19.3	29	Killer Kiss Raymond Burr filmed this last episode before he died September 12, 1993	5	11/29/93

Reruns

Episode	Rating	Share	The Case of the	Rank	Date
1	15.1	27	Perry Mason Returns	9	7/19/87
2	16.8	29	Notorious Nun	4	6/26/88
3	14.6	26	Shooting Star	12	8/14/88
4	10.2	17	Sinister Spirit	53	11/18/88
5	16.7	30	Murdered Madam	5	6/18/89
6	14.6	26	Lost Love	7	8/6/89
7	14.0	23	Scandalous Scoundrel	17	9/11/89
8	14.6	24	Lady in the Lake	16	4/22/90
9	11.9	22	Avenging Ace	14	7/1/90
10	12.6	22	Musical Murder	31	11/21/90
11	11.4	21	Lethal Lesson	19	7/14/91
12	11.1	19	All Star Assassin	12	8/11/91
13	10.3	20	Desperate Deception	30	5/22/92
14			Murdered Madam		8/18/92
15			Sinister Spirit		8/19/92
16			Lost Love		8/20/92
17			Musical Murder		8/21/92
18			Notorious Nun		10/13/92
19			Avenging Ace		10/14/92
20	11.5	20	Silenced Singer	47	11/6/92
21	10.2	19	Ruthless Reporter	61	11/20/92
22	9.7	17	Fatal Framing	53	12/4/92
23	10.1	17	Maligned Mobster	53	12/11/92
24	14.2	18	Defiant Daughter	43	1/15/93
25	11.5	20	Fatal Fashion		1/22/93
26			Reckless Romeo		2/5/93
27	9.8	18	Heartbroken Bride	43	4/23/93

Episode Ratings	Shares		The Case of the	Rank	Date Shown
28			Poisoned Pen (Channel 4)		4/30/93
29			Lady in the Lake (Channel 9)		4/30/93
30	8.7	15	Defiant Daughter	62	12/3/93

All two-hour Perry Masons were repeated many times on various channels and cable Turner Broadcast System throughout 1993. Some ratings were not printed in various rating lists.

The New Adventures of Perry Mason

60 minutes for CBS from September 16, 1973, until January 27, 1974.

Cast

Perry Mason .... Monte Markham
Della Street .... Sharon Acker
Hamilton Burger .... Harry Guardino
Paul Drake .... Albert Stratton
Lt. Arthur Tragg .... Dane Clark
Gertie Lade .... Brett Somers
Music: Earle Hagen, Lionel Newman

The Raymond Burr version was still being shown in the syndicated reruns throughout the United States and other countries. Hence the short run of the newer version. In the public's mind, perhaps the only Perry Mason was and is Raymond Burr.

Appendix E: Speech by Raymond Burr to the Los Angeles World Affairs Council

July 26, 1965

Ladies and gentlemen, good afternoon. In appearing before you today, I am fulfilling a mission that began for me twenty months ago, when I left on my first trip to South Vietnam. I have just completed my fourth. My mission will be fulfilled today because I will have the opportunity of giving you, gathered together at this luncheon, at least a partial summing-up of those trips.

Unless I can bring to you some of the tension that grips Southeast Asia today, describe the sense of urgency and dedication that motivates our people—and the South Vietnamese, for whom all this is about—a great part of my small effort has been in vain. There exists today a gap on our understanding of that war, in our appreciation of what is at stake . . . but above all in our understanding of the need for our support of the struggle there.

Why do we have a lack of understanding? Probably because of the great complexity of the situation in Vietnam.

Probably because the volumes upon volumes of the printed word it would take to explain these complexities and probably because of the many myths and fables that have sprung up concerning South Vietnam.

I want to talk about some of the things I saw for myself over there, and how they fail to correspond, to tally with what you have heard. For I hear these fables, too. And for whatever reasons they were created, and by whatever elements in our society, fables they remain.

Fable No. 1 says that the people of South Vietnam lack the will to resist, that without us they would quit. Ladies and gentlemen, the people of South Vietnam have been resisting oppression for more than twenty years.

Think of it: a population of fifteen million, woefully underdeveloped, saddled with the burden of warfare for nearly a generation. It goes without saying that these people have become weary, but it should be equally clear that they do not lack a will to resist. The President himself and our Secretary of State have both stated that the casualties suffered by the South Vietnamese are proportionately higher than we have ever borne in our history as a nation.

Fable No. 2 has it that if left to themselves, the South Vietnamese people would

291

choose Communism, or at least neutrality. The point is, the communists would never let us find out, because since 1954, they have been conducting massive and growing aggression from the North, precisely to prevent the South Vietnamese people from deciding their own fates.

However, I would like to report one significant development to you. For the first time there is currently a considerable stream of refugees fleeing from terror in Viet Cong controlled areas, and seeking sanctuary in the relative security provided by the armed forces of the South Vietnamese government.

We found this new condition to exist in many areas across the country. In fact it is providing a major problem in resettlement as the government forces try to supply housing, food and employment for the refugees. I must add that this is one problem that is heartily welcomed by all of our friendly forces in the country. Another significant development finds that in spite of terror aimed at their families, desertions are now taking place in the ranks of the Viet Cong itself.

Fable No. 3 states that the Americans, both civilian and military, who serve in Vietnam today have no clear understanding of their mission. May I say that in meetings with more than twenty-seven thousand Americans there, from private soldiers to the Ambassador himself, I found a deeper grasp of America's role in Southeast Asia among these people than among most Americans at home.

Fable No. 4 is the cruelest of all. It holds that it is the Viet Cong who are really concerned about the people of South Vietnam, and that America is interested only in propping up an unpopular and corrupt regime that cares nothing about the people of that stricken land.

This fable is the most blatant and the most cruel because the tragic consequences of the "concern" of the Viet Cong are so evident in the villages of Vietnam: women with arms severed because their husbands were provincial officials: schools burned, teachers executed, hospitals looted—not by the Saigon regime, but by the so-called compassionate Viet Cong.

In direct contrast are the widespread evidences of American assistance, of the seemingly infinite capacity of Americans to lend a hand.

In the village of Plei Mrong, where we visited six American Special Forces advisors commanded by Captain Heffner of Chicago, a talented and brilliant black officer, we saw how American ingenuity had wrought a revolution in sanitation. By building a rudimentary dam across a local stream and diverting the water through twelve pipes set across the top of the dam, Captain Heffner in a personal project had introduced these villagers to their first shower baths. A few weeks before that, he had brought the first bar of soap into the village.

As surely as I am standing here, that dam and those twelve showers and the human progress they represent would be gone in a few minutes if the Viet Cong were to occupy that village.

So would any school building, hospital or village official that were there because of American help.

The fact is, the Viet Cong and their North Vietnamese and Chinese masters represent the forces of darkness in Southeast Asia today. It is *they* who would return South Vietnam to the old days of filth, disease and ignorance. Make no mistake about it: the Viet Cong are not agrarian reformers, or reformers in any sense of the word.

Let me give you one set of figures to illustrate this point. In 1964, the Viet Cong killed 436 hamlet chiefs in South Vietnam. More than 1,000 were kidnapped, and more than 1,350 civilians were murdered in terrorist acts. At least 8,400 civilians were kidnapped by the Viet Cong. These wanton acts were not random. Deliberately, the terrorists chose the most skilled and respected members of these villages to murder and abduct: the teachers, the medical workers, administrators and village leaders.

Contrast this with the effect of America's presence in South Vietnam over the last ten years. (I should add here that the Viet Cong stand not just against the United States in this campaign of destruction and terror.

(To date, 34 different nations of the free world have contributed to raising the level of education, medical care and diet of the South Vietnamese people. One example is Guatemala, which this year sent 15,000 doses of typhoid serum.)

Now let us dramatize this effort. I should like to create for you a fictional South Vietnam village and 500 people live in this village, which is guarded from Viet Cong attack by a company of Vietnamese soldiers advised by four U.S. Special Forces officers.

Ten years ago, the village required every bit of the rice grown in the neighborhood to feed its own people. Indeed, there were periods when the villagers went hungry. There was no school in the village, and only one person could read or write any language. The nearest hospital was 50 miles away, but more important there was no doctor or nurse in the entire village. At least once a year the village experienced an epidemic of some kind which killed at least ten children. The only protein in the diet of any villager was an occasional morsel of fish, usually rotten. The only government these people knew was a village council, ruled by the local strongman, who existed on what he could steal and coerce from the villagers. The business of government ended with the welfare of the council itself.

Today, that village has progressed in every respect except one: the degree of its security from oppression. Today, rice production is doubled, thanks to the development and introduction of improved seed, more fertilizer, better insect and disease control and improved agricultural techniques. The village now has a one-room schoolhouse in which every child between the ages of five and eight is given at least some education.

Today, the U.S. Special Forces team fills first aid and basic medical requirements on a full-time basis, while instituting sanitation and malaria control programs that have virtually eliminated epidemics. Nearly 20,000 rats have been slain and their breeding places destroyed. A fully democratic program of self-government, with technical advice and assistance from U.S. and South Vietnamese experts, now guides village affairs.

Let us look for a moment at that one area of regression in our mythical village: the decline in the villagers' security from attack and harassment.

Last year, in two separate attacks, two village chiefs were slain, their decapitated bodies left as a lesson for other potential chiefs. Two teachers kidnapped, a medical assistant trained by the Special Forces team had an arm severed and 36 young men were kidnapped to serve in the Viet Cong. Only a magnificent courage and will to resist terror has kept this village from slipping back into the mire of poverty, pestilence and perversity.

Every load of rice, every piece of agricultural equipment, or clothing . . . anything of value is subject to expropriation by the Viet Cong.

Medical supplies are no exception, and shipments of drugs must be as closely guarded as shipments of arms, since these are priority items for the insatiable Viet Cong. Moreover, in many instances the villagers are paying not one but two sets of taxes—one to their own government and one to the Viet Cong—and of the two, the Viet Cong's demands are heavier.

We have made such progress in South Vietnam. We have helped institute programs and policies there which, if left to develop and reach fruition, may yet save the next generation of South Vietnamese from the awful blight that has stripped that region for decades.

But those programs and policies are seriously jeopardized today. The Viet Cong and their masters from the North simply cannot afford to let them succeed. I do not contend that it is the aim of the Communist aggressors to permanently reduce South Vietnam to peonage and despair, *but it is the calculated policy of those forces to scourge that land of all traces of progress wrought with the help of the Allies, of which the Americans are a major contributor.* On the ashes of the hospitals and schools we helped to build, the Communists hope to erect their own totalitarian structure.

If I had to sum up my impressions of Vietnam today in a single word, I would choose the word "need." No one who has not seen the conditions in Vietnam can possibly appreciate the depth and range of human want in that tragic corner of the world.

Not all of the need belongs to the Vietnamese. Our people, the military and civilian government personnel, and equally important those not connected with the government, have needs that are just as real. I'm talking about the Americans who are working in Vietnam today for such agencies as CARE, for MEDICO, for Protestant and Catholic Charities, for the Foster Parents Plan and others.

They labor in a hundred different ways—a hundred human and civilized ways—to raise the level of life there, even as they share that life with the Vietnamese people.

What they are trying to accomplish there extends over a whole range of human need. Such down to earth items as soap, or bolts of cotton cloth or toweling—all of these are moving out into the hinterlands of Vietnam, thanks to their efforts. Many of the people they serve have never seen a bar of soap, and their only baths have been drenchings from rain.

Today they are learning their first, rudimentary rules of sanitation, with the result that disease and infection are being brought under control there for the first time in human history.

One of the war's most tragic by-products is the orphaned or abandoned child. Thanks to the efforts of the different orphanages and to groups such as the Foster Parents Plan, many Vietnamese children are being saved from death or abandonment through "adoption" by American donors. For 15 dollars a month, these people undertake the care of such a youngster, permitting him to remain with his own family. Frequently these gifts are the difference between life and death.

Another problem in Vietnam today is integration. For centuries, the Vietnamese have held the mountain people, called the Montagnards, in a sort of second class citizenship. Because Montagnard villages are remote and frequently are the prey of Viet Cong terrorists, Montagnard children must come into the lowland areas for schooling. While schoolrooms and teachers may be available, housing is not. For $2,000, a 72-bed dormitory may be built through CARE and the U.S. Operations Mission for these children in the lowland villages, opening for them the golden opportunity to learn.

While these needs in Vietnam are ever-present and great, there are organizations right here in our own community who have already started a steady stream of badly needed supplies to Vietnam. The Hollywood Women's Press Club is organizing itself as an aid unit to obtain soap and cloth and is working to interest all other press groups throughout the nation to join in.

And the Direct Relief Foundation is doing magnificent work in obtaining medical supplies and shipping them to Vietnam with the help of U.S. Navy ships and planes. Santa Barbara has been the "Marshalling yard" for this operation.

Direct Relief has shipped 60,000 pounds of drugs and medicines in the past several months valued at over half a million dollars.

The last need I will mention is closer to home. And it is a more subtle one. I speak of the need of our own people, the Americans who serve in Vietnam as part of the military, civilian or volunteer effort, for homefront support. That support takes many forms. It may consist merely of the knowledge that someone back here is speaking *for them*. For there is a need for a voice—indeed many voices—which will rise in support of our effort there, which will say "NAY" to the detractors and critics of our assistance in Vietnam.

Morale is important. And among our people it cannot be destroyed easily, but perhaps it can be damaged more easily, in a distant, small-scale battlefront. Not enough attention is paid, in my opinion, to the problem of morale among troops in obscure outposts everywhere. With America's role as a guardian of freedom, and our commitment of men around the world, we must think in terms of smaller units for entertainment tours. In Vietnam, for example, the average village outpost had not more than a dozen American troops on station, advising Vietnamese army units.

Such outposts call for something other than the massive camp shows that featured much of the entertainment brought to our troops in World War II. What it requires is individual visits of an hour or so duration by entertainers who can not only "entertain" as such, but who can talk ... and listen—who can just plain pay a visit. This not only means people from the stage, television, motion pictures and radio, but also leading personalities in the field of sports.

In my years of travel around the world, I have seen many thousands of Americans living in other countries. But I have never been more deeply impressed than by the Americans in Vietnam today.

Americans working among the people of that region, sharing their hardships and perils. Of these Americans we can be damned proud. They are not, as the critics were once wont to say, Americans telling the Vietnamese they must live like us. What they *are* doing is showing the Vietnamese the best we have to offer and letting them decide for themselves.

Not the least of what we need to offer is our willingness to help.

But we also need time. Perhaps this is the most precious commodity at our disposal, and the one the Viet Cong can least tolerate. With time, they fear we can succeed. Without it, they know we cannot. There, perhaps, is what our commitment there is all about. You may build the most effective, most viable society in the world, but unless you protect it through its infancy and adolescence, you cannot expect it to grow and mature ... or even to survive.

For that reason, it is important, I think, that we safeguard the meager advances we have helped to make there. We must, if you like, throw a shield before the free nations of Southeast Asia ... not just South Vietnam, but Thailand and Burma, the Malaysian States, indeed India itself ... until either no shield is needed or until these people are able to forge one for themselves.

What of the nature of the shield that stands there today? No one to my knowledge has criticized it on any basis but quantity. The quality of our own fighting men, and those of the South Vietnamese government, is excellent. But the enemy is hidden and he is skilled.

Above a certain level of command the Viet Cong soldier represents an intelligent, resourceful fighting man.

Still, cracks are beginning to show. Desertions among the Viet Cong troops are on the rise. There is an increasing resistance to Viet Cong terror at the village level, where they now realize that collaboration does not mean security. And, in recent engagements—notably at Ba Gia, at Song Be and Quang Ngai—overwhelming forces of Viet Cong failed to dislodge Vietnamese and American defenders in spite of severe and prolonged attack. The ratio of Viet Cong to Vietnamese losses is swinging our way, slowly but perceptibly.

From a personal standpoint I should like to say a few words about the Americans I personally met on my last trip, from our top enlisted men to our top generals in 147 installations . . . men of the Army, the Marines, the Air Force, the Navy, and last but not least, a magnificent group of civilians.

I would like to avoid such overworked terms as brave, dedicated and hardworking in describing these, our people, but I cannot. And words of exceptional praise must go to them all—all those in South Vietnam today, who work under the most backward and frustrating conditions.

They work under threat of daily Viet Cong attack, using only their own wits, their fighting skill and the goodwill they build among the people to protect them.

Do these men deserve our support? Of course they do. I did not come here to discuss the pros and cons of our being in South Vietnam . . . for the fact is . . . *WE ARE THERE!* Thousands of our men are at this moment in the field in that embattled republic, putting their lives on the line for me . . . for you, and for the cause of freedom! Until such time as it is right and proper for us to withdraw, our men there deserve our full and unswerving support. I for one do not intend to deny them this right, for I have sat with them in their bunkers and slit trenches; visited them in their hilltop defense positions surrounded by jungle and observed their dedication and gallantry in the villages and hamlets. Yes . . . *We are there . . . I am with them and I hope that you are with them too!*

Thank you.

Bibliography

Books

Alexander, Diane. *Playhouse, Pasadena Playhouse*. Los Angeles, CA: Dorleac MacLeish, 1984.

Bergan, Ronald. *United Artists Story*. New York: Crown Publishing, 1986.

Blum, Daniel. *A Pictorial History of the Talkies*. New York: G. P. Putnam's Sons, 1958.

_____. *Screen World, 1953*. Vol. 4. New York: Greenberg Publishing, 1953.

British Columbia: Earliest Times to Present. Vols. 3 and 4.

Brooks, Tim and Earle Marsh. *The Complete Directory to Primetime Network TV Shows 1946–1979*. New York: Ballantine Books, 1979.

Brough, James and Hedda Hopper. *The Truth and Nothing But*. New York: Pyramid, 1963.

Buxton, Frank and Bill Owen. *The Big Broadcast, 1920–1950*. New York: Viking Press, 1972.

Campbell, Robert. *The Golden Years of Broadcasting: 50 Years of Radio and TV on NBC*. New York: Charles Scribner and Sons, 1976.

Castleman, Harry and Walter J. Padrazik. *Watching TV*. New York: McGraw-Hill, 1982.

Chilton. *A Pictorial History of TV*. New York: Bonanza Book Publishing, 1959.

Dunning, John. *Tune In Yesterday, 1926–1976*. Englewood Cliffs, NJ: Prentice-Hall, 1976.

Eames, James Douglas. *Paramount Story*. New York: Crown Publishing, 1985.

Eells, George. *Robert Mitchum*. New York: Franklin Watts, 1984.

Fireman, Judy, ed. *TV Book: Photo History of TV*. New York: Workman Publishing Co., 1977.

Fitzgerald, Michael G. *Universal Studios*. New Rochelle, New York: Arlington House, 1977.

Forbes Cameron Publicity. Underground (stage play). Manchester, England.

Greenfield, Jeff. *Television: The First 50 Years*. New York: Harry N. Abrams, 1977.

Harris, Jay S. *"TV Guide": The First 25 Years*. New York: Simon and Schuster, 1978.

Hirschhorn, Clive. *The Warner Brothers Story*. New York: Crown Publishing, 1979.

Howard, Ronald. *In Search of My Father*. New York: St. Martin's Press, 1981.

Hughes, Dorothy B. *The Case of the Real Perry Mason: A Biography of Erle Stanley Gardner*. New York: William Morrow and Co., 1978.

Jewell, Richard B. and Vernon Harbin. *The RKO Story*. London: Octopus Books, 1982.

Kaplan, Mike, ed. *Variety's Who's Who in Show Business*. New York: Garland Publishing, 1983.

Larkin, Rochelle. *Hail Columbia*. New Rochelle, New York: Arlington House, 1975.

Lee, Raymond and B. C. Van Hecke. *Gangsters and Hoodlums: The Underworld in the Cinema*. New York: Castle Books, 1971.

McDonald, Margaret Lillooet. "History of the Burr Family, New Westminster, 1859–1871." University of British Columbia, 1947.

Marill, Alvin H. *Movies Made for TV, 1964–1986*. New York: Zoetrope, 1987.

Meyers, Richard. *The TV Detectives*. La Jolla, California: A. S. Barnes, 1981.

Norback, Craig T. and Peter G. Norback. *"TV Guide" Almanac Source Book*. New York: Ballantine Books, 1980.

Parish, James Robert. *Actors' Television Credits, 1950–1972*. Metuchen, NJ: Scarecrow Press, 1973.

————. *Hollywood Character Actors*. New Rochelle, NY: Arlington House, 1978.

————. *The Tough Guys*. New Rochelle, NY: Arlington House, 1976.

———— and Ronald L. Bowers. *The MGM Stock Company*. New Rochelle, NY: Arlington House, 1975.

———— and Gregory Mank. *The MGM Golden Years, 1928–1959*. New Rochelle, NY: Arlington House, 1981.

———— and Michael R. Pitts. *The Great Gangster Pictures*. Metuchen, NJ: Scarecrow Press, 1976.

Parish, Paul Michael and James Robert Parish. *The Emmy Awards: A Pictorial History*. New York: Crown Publishing, 1971.

Penzler, Otto. *Private Lives of Private Eyes*. New York: Grosset & Dunlap, 1977.

————, Chris Steinbrunner, Marvin Lachman, Charles Shibuk, and Francis M. Nevins, Jr., compilers. *Detectionary*. McGeorge School of Law Library.

Shulman, Arthur and Roger Youman. *How Sweet It Was*. New York: Bonanza Books, 1966.

Stacy, Jan and Ryder Syvertsen. *The Great Book of Movie Villains*. Chicago, IL: Contemporary Books, 1984.

Taylor, John Russell. *Life and Works of Alfred Hitchcock*. Boston, MA: Faber and Faber, 1978.

Terrace, Vincent. *The Complete Encyclopedia of Television Programs, 1947–1976*. Cranbury, NJ: A. S. Barnes, 1976.

————. *Radio's Golden Years, 1930–1960*. La Jolla, CA: A. S. Barnes, 1981.

Thomas, Tony and Aubrey Solomon. *Films of 20th Century–Fox*. Secaucus, NJ: Citadel Press, 1979.

Tomkies, Mike. *Robert Mitchum: It Sure Beats Working*. Chicago, IL: Henry Regney Co., 1972.

Weaver, John T. *Forty Years of Screen Credits, 1929–1969*. Vol. 1. Metuchen, NJ: Scarecrow Press, 1970.

Who's Who in America. 1962.

Wilk, Max. *Golden Age of Television*. New York: Delacorte Press, 1976.

Libraries

Academy of Motion Picture Arts and Sciences, Beverly Hills, California
British Film Institute, London
City of Sydney, Australia

Cranston, Rhode Island
Denver, Colorado
Free Library of Philadelphia, Theater Collection, Philadelphia, Pennsylvania
Huntington Library, San Marino, California
Irving House Historic Centre, New Westminster, British Columbia
Kitchener, Ontario, Canada
Library of Congress, Washington, D.C.
Lincoln Center Theater Collection, New York, New York
London, England
Metropolitan Toronto Library Board, Toronto, Canada
New Orleans, Louisiana
New Westminster, British Columbia, Canada
New Westminster Historic Centre and Museum, Archie W. Miller, Curator
Pasadena, Research Section, Pasadena, California
Pawtucket, Rhode Island
Provincial Archives, Victoria, British Columbia, Canada
Public Archives of Canada, Ottawa
Public Library of Queensland, Brisbane, Australia
Sacramento City, County Library, Sacramento, California
UCLA Film and Television Archives, Los Angeles, California
Vancouver, British Columbia, Canada
Variety Arts Theater Library, Los Angeles, California
Variety Entertainers Guild of America, Los Angeles
State Library of Victoria, Melbourne, Australia
Oral Histories of Maude Prickett Cooper, Peggy Ebright, and Leonore Shanewise

Newspapers

Associated Newspaper Group, Ltd., London
Auckland Star, New Zealand
Boston Globe
Chicago Daily News and *Sun Times*
Chicago Tribune
Cleveland Plain Dealer
The Columbian, New Westminster, British Columbia
Daily Chronicle, Centralia, Washington
Daily Colonial, New Westminster, British Columbia
Daily News, Los Angeles
Daily Telegraph, Melbourne, Australia
Denver Post
The Dominion, Wellington, New Zealand
Edmonton Journal, Edmonton, Canada
The Evening Post, Wellington, New Zealand
Family Scene TV Times of Britain
The Globe, West Palm Beach, Florida
Herald Tribune News Service
Highlander Publications, City of Industry, California
Hollywood Reporter
Information Please Almanac, 1987
London Daily Mail, London Daily Mirror, London Evening News

London Express News and Feature Service
Los Angeles News Bureau
Mirror-Australian Telegraph Publications, Sydney, Australia
Mirror Group Newspapers, Ltd., London
Montreal Daily Star
New York Daily News
New Zealand Herald
Newark Star Ledger
People Magazine
Phoenix Republic and Gazette
Picturegoer National Weekly, London
Politiken, Kobenhavn, Denmark
Rocky Mountain News, Denver
Sacramento Bee and Sacramento Union
San Francisco Chronicle and Examiner
San Jose News and Mercury, San Jose, California
Seattle Times
The Star, Tarrytown, New York
Times Picayune Publishing Corp., New Orleans
USA Today
Vancouver Magazine, Vancouver, B.C.
Washington Post
Waterloo-Kitchener Chronicle, Kitchener, Canada

Universities

British Columbia Department of History, Vancouver, British Columbia
California Research Library Section, Los Angeles
Denver Department of Mass Communications
Michigan at Ann Arbor
Stanford Department of Special Collections

Index